Numerical Machine Learning

Authored by

Zhiyuan Wang

DigiPen Institute of Technology Singapore
Singapore

National University of Singapore
Singapore

Sayed Ameenuddin Irfan

DigiPen Institute of Technology Singapore
Singapore

Christopher Teoh

DigiPen Institute of Technology Singapore
Singapore

&

Priyanka Hriday Bhoyar

DigiPen Institute of Technology Singapore
Singapore

Numerical Machine Learning

Authors: Zhiyuan Wang, Sayed Ameenuddin Irfan, Christopher Teoh & Priyanka Hriday Bhoyar

ISBN (Online): 978-981-5136-98-2

ISBN (Print): 978-981-5136-99-9

ISBN (Paperback): 978-981-5165-00-5

need for a court order if at any point you breach any terms of this License Agreement. In no event will any delay or failure by Bentham Science Publishers in enforcing your compliance with this License Agreement constitute a waiver of any of its rights.

3. You acknowledge that you have read this License Agreement, and agree to be bound by its terms and conditions. To the extent that any other terms and conditions presented on any website of Bentham Science Publishers conflict with, or are inconsistent with, the terms and conditions set out in this License Agreement, you acknowledge that the terms and conditions set out in this License Agreement shall prevail.

Bentham Science Publishers Pte. Ltd.
80 Robinson Road #02-00
Singapore 068898
Singapore
Email: subscriptions@benthamscience.net

BENTHAM SCIENCE

CONTENTS

PREFACE

In recent years, machine learning has become increasingly popular and pervasive, with applications ranging from self-driving cars and facial recognition to personalized website recommendations and stock market forecasting. The increased availability of data and advancements in computer power have made it possible to apply machine learning algorithms to a vast array of problems with impressive outcomes. Machine learning is currently utilized in a variety of areas, including banking, healthcare, marketing, and manufacturing, and it is anticipated that it will continue to play a significant role in the development of new technologies in the future. Consequently, machine learning has emerged as an essential subject of study for people interested in data science, artificial intelligence, and related fields. As machine learning continues to evolve and expand its reach, researchers and practitioners are constantly developing new techniques and algorithms to address specific challenges or improve upon existing methods. In this ever-changing landscape, it is crucial for those working in the field to stay up-to-date with the latest advancements and trends. This includes not only mastering the fundamental concepts and algorithms, but also understanding how to adapt and apply them in novel ways to solve real-world problems. By embracing the interdisciplinary nature of machine learning, and collaborating with experts from diverse fields, we can accelerate the development of innovative solutions that have the potential to transform industries, enhance the quality of life, and create a more sustainable future for all.

From our experiences of teaching machine learning using various textbooks, we have noticed that there tends to be a strong emphasis on abstract mathematics when discussing the theories of machine learning algorithms. On the other hand, in the application of machine learning, it usually straightaway goes to import off-the-shelf libraries such as scikit-learn, TensorFlow, Keras, and PyTorch. The disconnect between abstract mathematical theories and practical application creates a gap in understanding. This book bridges the gap using numerical examples with small datasets and simple Python codes to provide a complete walkthrough of the underlying mathematical steps of machine learning algorithms. By working through concrete examples step by step, readers/students can develop a well-rounded understanding of these algorithms, gain a more in-depth knowledge of how mathematics relates to the implementation and performance of the algorithms, and be better equipped to apply them to practical problems.

Beginning with an introduction to machine learning in Chapter 1, the remaining chapters of the book cover seven commonly used machine learning algorithms and techniques, including both supervised and unsupervised learning, as well as both linear and nonlinear models. The book requires some prerequisite knowledge of basic probability and statistics, linear algebra, calculus, and Python programming. The book is intended for university students studying machine learning and is used as our primary teaching material for the "Introduction to Machine Learning" module at DigiPen Institute of Technology Singapore.

In conclusion, we would like to acknowledge Mr. Tan Chek Ming (Managing Director), Prof. Prasanna Ghali (Provost), Ms. Caroline Tan (Deputy Director), Ms. Angela Tay (Senior Manager), and all at DigiPen Institute of Technology Singapore, for their consistent support and help. We also wish to thank a number of our students (including Nelson Ng, Rhonda McGladdery, Farhan Fadzil, Lim Li Jia, Musa Ahmad Dahlan, Jeremy Yap, and Seah Jue Chen) for their diligence in spotting several typographical errors during their course of studies. Also, it has been a delight working with Bentham's professional editorial and production staff. We particularly thank Noor Ul Ain Khan, Humaira Hashmi, and Obaid Sadiq for their consistent, timely, and kind support throughout the development of this book. Furthermore, we extend our heartfelt appreciation to our families (including Xiaoyue Cui, Muyuan Wang, Safura Tazeen, Khasim BI, Shirleen Chow, Adler Teoh, Hriday Bhoyar, Swati Kolkhede, and all) for their unwavering encouragement throughout the creation of this book. We dedicate this book to them. The first author, Zhiyuan Wang, would also like to convey special thanks and appreciation to his Ph.D. advisors, Prof. Zhe Wu, Prof. Xiaonan Wang, and Prof. Gade Pandu Rangaiah from the National University of Singapore. Although they were not involved in this book, Zhiyuan deeply cherishes their sincere and invaluable guidance in his Ph.D. journey, which has helped him become a better researcher and educator.

Despite our best efforts to ensure the accuracy of the content within this book, errors may inadvertently persist. If you come across any inaccuracies or omissions, we kindly request that you bring them to our attention by emailing us at wangzhiyuan@u.nus.edu. We are committed to rectifying such oversights in future editions and will post corrections on our shared folder in Google Drive: https://drive.google.com/drive/folders/1FqJvo4ZPazNbEH_GlHFoodqvegnQmHcn?usp=share_link

Zhiyuan Wang
DigiPen Institute of Technology Singapore
Singapore
National University of Singapore
Singapore

Sayed Ameenuddin Irfan
DigiPen Institute of Technology Singapore
Singapore

Christopher Teoh
DigiPen Institute of Technology Singapore
Singapore

&

Priyanka Hriday Bhoyar
DigiPen Institute of Technology Singapore
Singapore

## CHAPTER 1

Introduction to Machine Learning

Abstract: Machine learning, a rapidly growing subfield of computer science, has had a significant impact on many industries and our lives. This chapter discusses the brief history of machine learning, its widespread adoption as a de facto feature, and fundamental concepts such as supervised and unsupervised learning, regression and classification, and underfitting and overfitting. We also emphasize the importance of understanding machine learning through numerical examples, which can bridge the gap between abstract mathematical theories and practical applications of machine learning algorithms. By developing a strong foundation in machine learning, readers/students can harness its potential to address challenges and opportunities across diverse sectors.

Keywords: Numerical Examples, Machine Learning History, Supervised Learning, Unsupervised Learning, Regression, Classification, Underfitting, Overfitting

1.1. BRIEF HISTORY OF MACHINE LEARNING

Machine learning is a subfield of computer science that involves the creation of algorithms that can learn from data and make predictions. It has a long and rich history [1], with roots dating back to the 1950s when the field of artificial intelligence was founded. This field focused on developing machines that could perform tasks that typically require human-like intelligence, such as recognizing patterns, learning from experience, and making decisions. The first machine learning algorithms were developed in the 1960s, including decision tree and nearest neighbor algorithms. The 1980s saw the rapid growth of the field with the development of algorithms such as artificial neural network and support vector machine. These algorithms were applied to a wide range of applications in the 1990s, including natural language processing, computer vision, and speech recognition. In the 2000s, the field continued to evolve with the development of new algorithms, such as gradient boosting, and the increasing use of machine learning in industries such as finance and healthcare. The 2010s saw the widespread adoption of machine learning, aided by the advent of big data and the development of powerful graphics processing units (GPU) that could be used to train large and complex machine learning models. The subfield of deep learning [2], which typically involves the use of multi-layered neural networks, became particularly popular and found application across a diverse range of domains. Today, machine learning is a rapidly growing field that is currently being applied in various sectors.

Zhiyuan Wang, Sayed Ameenuddin Irfan, Christopher Teoh & Priyanka Hriday Bhoyar

It has the potential to revolutionize many industries and has already had a significant societal impact.

1.2. MACHINE LEARNING AS A DE FACTO FEATURE

Machine learning is expected to be a transformative technology over the next two decades due to several factors. One key factor is the increasing availability of data, which is expected to continue to grow significantly in the coming years. As machine learning algorithms are particularly well suited for analyzing and making sense of large amounts of data, this will create new opportunities for their application in a variety of fields, including but not limited to healthcare, finance, transportation, education, manufacturing, and beyond. In these and other areas, machine learning has been adopted to automate some tasks that are currently performed by humans, freeing up humans to focus on more creative and high-level work [3].

In addition to automation, machine learning algorithms can be used to improve decision-making by analyzing large amounts of data and making predictions or recommendations based on that data. This can be particularly useful in fields such as finance, where machine learning can be used to identify patterns and trends that can inform investment decisions, or in healthcare, where machine learning can be used to predict patient outcomes and identify potential health risks, or in semiconductor manufacturing, where machine learning can be employed to detect defects and analyze their causes in real-time. By providing valuable insights and recommendations based on data analysis, machine learning has the potential to enhance the efficiency and effectiveness of decision-making in a wide range of fields.

Another key benefit of machine learning is its ability to enhance personalization by tailoring products and services to individual preferences and behaviors. For example, machine learning can be used to recommend products or content to users based on their past behavior, or to tailor advertising to specific audiences. By providing personalized experiences, machine learning has the potential to improve customer satisfaction and engagement.

Overall, machine learning is expected to have a significant impact in a wide range of fields over the next two decades, influencing many aspects of our lives. Its ability to automate tasks, improve decision-making, and enhance personalization make it a technology with the potential to revolutionize industries and change the way we live and work.

1.3. SUPERVISED AND UNSUPERVISED

Supervised and unsupervised learning are two prominent types of algorithms in machine learning [4]. In supervised learning, a model is trained using labeled data, which includes the correct output for each instance in the training set. The model generates predictions based on this labeled data, enabling it to make accurate predictions for new, previously unseen examples. Some common supervised learning tasks include regression, which aims to predict a continuous value, and classification, which focuses on predicting a categorical label. Conversely, unsupervised learning involves training a model with unlabeled data, meaning the correct output is not provided. In this case, the model must independently identify patterns and relationships within the data. Examples of unsupervised learning tasks encompass clustering, where the objective is to group similar examples, and dimensionality reduction, where the goal is to decrease the number of features in the data while preserving as much relevant information as possible.

1.4. REGRESSION AND CLASSIFICATION

In machine learning, regression and classification are two types of supervised learning, in which a model is trained on labeled data to make predictions about new, unseen examples. In regression, the model is used to predict a continuous value, such as a price or probability. For example, a regression model might be used to predict the price of a house based on features such as its size, number of bedrooms, and location. On the other hand, classification involves predicting a categorical value, such as a class label. For example, a classification model might be used to predict whether an email is spam or not, or to recognize the type of object in an image.

Both regression and classification are widely used in many fields and have a broad range of applications. In addition to the examples mentioned earlier, regression can be applied in finance to predict stock prices, in healthcare to predict patient outcomes, in meteorology to predict weather patterns, and in electric vehicle industry to predict charging demand [5]. Classification, on the other hand, is used in a wide range of applications, such as natural language processing, where it is used to classify text into different categories, and fraud detection, where it is used to classify transactions as legitimate or fraudulent. Despite their differences, regression and classification share many similarities and are both essential tools in the field of machine learning. By understanding both, we can select the most appropriate method for a specific problem and achieve more accurate predictions.

1.5. UNDERFITTING AND OVERFITTING

While training machine learning models, it is common to encounter issues such as underfitting and overfitting [6]. Underfitting occurs when a model is too simple to accurately capture the underlying patterns in the data, leading to poor performance on both the training data and new, unseen examples. On the other hand, overfitting occurs when a model is too complex and tries to fit the noise or random fluctuations in the training data rather than generalizing the underlying patterns, resulting in a good performance on the training data but poor performance on new, unseen examples. To avoid these issues, it is important to find the right balance between model complexity and the amount of training data available. This can often be achieved through techniques such as cross-validation and regularization.

1.6. THE IMPORTANCE OF UNDERSTANDING MACHINE LEARNING THROUGH NUMERICAL EXAMPLE

From our experiences teaching machine learning using various textbooks, we have noticed that there tends to be a strong emphasis on abstract mathematics when discussing the theories of machine learning algorithms. On the other hand, in the application of machine learning, it usually straightaway goes to import off-the-shelf libraries such as scikit-learn, TensorFlow, Keras, and PyTorch. The disconnect between abstract mathematical theories and practical application creates a gap in understanding. This book bridges the gap using numerical examples with small datasets and simple Python codes to provide a complete walkthrough of the underlying mathematical steps of machine learning algorithms. There are several benefits to understanding machine learning through numerical examples. For one, it allows readers to see how the algorithms work in practice, which can help readers better understand the concepts and ideas behind them. Additionally, working through numerical examples can help readers develop intuition about how the algorithms behave under different circumstances and how input parameters can affect the output. This can be especially useful for developing problem-solving skills, as machine learning often involves finding the best solution to a problem given a dataset. By working through numerical examples, readers can learn to approach different types of problems in a systematic way. Furthermore, seeing how machine learning algorithms behave on actual data can help readers identify common pitfalls and avoid them in their works. Overall, working through numerical examples can be an effective way to learn about machine learning and develop the necessary skills and knowledge to apply it. By following a step-by-step process through numerical examples, readers/students can gain a tangible understanding of the algorithms, see how the mathematics relates to their implementation and performance, and be better equipped to apply them to practical problems.

CONCLUSION

In conclusion, machine learning is a rapidly evolving field with a rich history and an expanding range of applications across various industries. As a transformative technology, it has the potential to revolutionize numerous aspects of our lives. This book bridges the gap between abstract mathematical theories and the practical application of machine learning through easy-to-understand numerical examples and simple Python codes. This approach helps readers develop a more tangible understanding of machine learning algorithms, develop intuition about their behavior, and improve problem-solving skills. By working through numerical examples, readers/students can learn to approach various types of problems systematically and be better equipped to apply these algorithms to real-world challenges.

As machine learning continues to advance and become even more pervasive in the coming years, it is crucial for practitioners, researchers, and students to develop a strong foundation in the fundamental concepts and techniques of the field. By acquiring this knowledge and building upon it, they will be better positioned to contribute to the ongoing growth and development of machine learning and to harness its transformative potential to address a wide range of challenges and opportunities in various sectors.

REFERENCES

[1] A.L. Fradkov, "Early history of machine learning", *IFAC-PapersOnLine,* vol. 53, no. 2, pp. 1385-1390, 2020.
      http://dx.doi.org/10.1016/j.ifacol.2020.12.1888
[2] I. Goodfellow, Y. Bengio, and A. Courville, *Deep Learning.* MIT Press: London, England, 2016.
[3] J.P. Mueller, and L. Massaron, *Machine Learning for Dummies.,* 2nd ed John Wiley & Sons: Nashville, TN, 2021.
[4] A.C. Mueller, and S. Guido, *Introduction to machine learning with python: A guide for data scientists.* O'Reilly Media: Sebastopol, CA, 2016.
[5] M. Park, Z. Wang, L. Li, and X. Wang, "Multi-objective building energy system optimization considering EV infrastructure," *Appl. Energy*, vol. 332, p. 120504, 2023.
[6] S. Raschka, *Python Machine Learning*. Birmingham, England: Packt Publishing, 2015.

## CHAPTER 2

Linear Regression

Abstract: In this chapter, we delve into linear regression, a fundamental machine learning algorithm for predicting numerical values. While maintaining a concise overview of the mathematical theories, we prioritize an accessible approach by focusing on a concrete numerical example with a small dataset for predicting house sale prices. Through a step-by-step walkthrough, we illustrate the inner workings of linear regression and demonstrate its practical implementation. Additionally, we offer sample codes and a comparison with the linear regression model from scikit-learn to reinforce understanding. Upon completing this chapter, readers will gain a comprehensive understanding of linear regression's inner workings and its relationship to algorithm implementation and performance, and be better prepared to apply it to real-world projects.

Keywords: Linear Regression, Numerical Example, Small Dataset, Housing Price Prediction, Scikit-Learn

2.1. INTRODUCTION TO LINEAR REGRESSION

Linear regression is a supervised machine learning algorithm that aims to determine the best-fit linear line between a dependent variable and one or more independent variables. It typically carries out regression tasks. It is one of the easiest, most well-understood, and most popular algorithms in many machine learning applications [1, 2]. It can be employed to predict the values of continuous numerical variables such as salary, sales revenue, dividend yield, greenhouse gas emission, and house price, to name a few.

Despite its simplicity, linear regression remains a powerful tool in the field of machine learning, providing a strong foundation for understanding the underlying input-output relationships between variables. It serves as an excellent starting point for beginners in the field, offering a straightforward and interpretable approach to modeling. Moreover, linear regression can act as a benchmark for evaluating the performance of more complex algorithms, allowing practitioners to gauge the effectiveness of their chosen models. While linear regression may not always be the most advanced or accurate method for every situation, its ease of use, interpretability, and versatility continue to make it a valuable asset in a variety of real-world applications and industries.

There are several fundamental assumptions associated with linear regression [3, 4]. Firstly, it is assumed that the dependent variable is linearly correlated to the

Zhiyuan Wang, Sayed Ameenuddin Irfan, Christopher Teoh & Priyanka Hriday Bhoyar

independent variable(s). Secondly, when there is more than one independent variable, no correlation should exist between the independent variables (*i.e.,* no multicollinearity). Thirdly, the errors between the true values and predicted values by the linear regression model should approximately conform to a normal distribution, with most having errors close to 0. Fourthly, the spread of the errors (*i.e.,* the variance of the errors) ought to be constant along the values of the dependent variable. This is technically known as homoscedasticity, which can be checked by creating a scatterplot of errors versus the dependent variable.

2.2. MATHEMATICS OF LINEAR REGRESSION

The mathematics of linear regression starts from a simple linear equation, shown in Equation (2.1) and (Fig. **2.1**), where there is only one independent variable X and one dependent variable Y.

$$Y = b + wX \qquad\qquad (2.1)$$

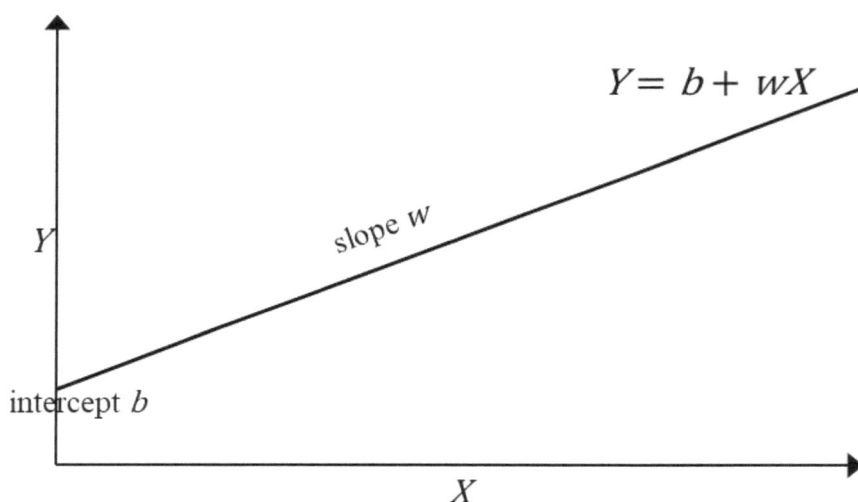

Fig. (2.1). Plot of simple linear equation $Y = b + wX$.

Variable X has an associated coefficient w, which is often used interchangeably with the terms: *weight*, *slope*, or *gradient*. In the context of machine learning, it is most often referred to as weight.

Likewise, b represents the intercept with Y-axis and is often known as *bias* in machine learning. The independent variable X is commonly called *input*, which is used interchangeably with the following terms: *input feature, attribute, characteristic, field,* and *column.* The dependent variable Y is commonly referred to as *output, target, class,* and *label.*

In reality, more often than not, we will have more than one independent variable, and Equation (2.1) would have to be updated to a general term Equation (2.2) to cater for this.

$$Y = b + \sum_{j=1}^{n} w_j X_j \qquad (2.2)$$

Here,

Y is the dependent variable
b is the bias
n is the number of input features
w_j is the weight of the jth feature
X_j is input value of the jth feature

The goal of linear regression is to find the best-fit linear equation model that maps the relationship between input X and output Y, in the form of Equation (2.2) with the optimal weights and bias, which produces the least error (synonymously known as loss in machine learning) between the known true output Y values and predicted output Y values by the model.

Fig. (2.2). Illustration of notations using an exemplary training dataset.

Let us use lowercase x_i to denote the feature values of the ith sample (out of the total m rows of samples from the training dataset), then x_{ij} will be the value of the jth feature (out of the total n input features) at the ith sample, as shown in Fig.

(2.2). Lowercase y_i is used to represent the known output value (*i.e.,* true output value) of the ith sample, and $\hat{y}_i$ is used to denote the corresponding predicted output value by the linear equation model. Equation (2.2) is then updated to Equation (2.3).

$$\hat{y}_i = b + \sum_{j=1}^{n} w_j x_{ij} \tag{2.3}$$

Here,

$$i \in [1, m]$$

m is the number of training samples
x_{ij} is the value of the jth feature at the ith sample

b is the bias
n is the number of input features
w_j is the weight of the jth feature
$\hat{y}_i$ is the predicted value for the ith sample

The Mean Squared Error (MSE) function (Equation 2.4) is commonly employed to quantify the mean loss (L) of the predicted output value against the true output value. In Layman's term, it is an indication of how well the model's prediction is.

$$\begin{cases} L_i = (y_i - \hat{y}_i)^2 \\ MSE = L = \dfrac{1}{m} \sum_{i=1}^{m} L_i \end{cases} \tag{2.4}$$

Here,

L is the mean loss
m is the number of training samples
y_i is the true value for the ith sample
$\hat{y}_i$ is the predicted value for the ith sample

Next, the Gradient Descent optimization algorithm is used to find the optimal bias and weights by iteratively tweaking their values a tiny bit at a time in the direction of reducing the loss.

In order to carry out the optimization, we first need to find the partial derivative of the mean loss (L) with respect to the bias and weights, namely, $\frac{\partial L}{\partial b}$ and $\frac{\partial L}{\partial w_j}$, denoting the contribution to the mean loss by the bias and each of the weights. This can be done by applying the chain rule, shown in Equations (2.5) to (2.9).

$$\frac{\partial L_i}{\partial \hat{y}_i} = 2(y_i - \hat{y}_i)(-1) \tag{2.5}$$

$$\frac{\partial \hat{y}_i}{\partial b} = 1 \tag{2.6}$$

$$\therefore \frac{\partial L}{\partial b} = \frac{1}{m}\sum_{i=1}^{m}\frac{\partial L_i}{\partial b} = \frac{1}{m}\sum_{i=1}^{m}\left(\frac{\partial L_i}{\partial \hat{y}_i} \cdot \frac{\partial \hat{y}_i}{\partial b}\right)$$

$$= \frac{1}{m}\sum_{i=1}^{m}(2(y_i - \hat{y}_i)(-1) \cdot 1)$$

$$= \frac{\sum_{i=1}^{m}2(y_i - \hat{y}_i)(-1)}{m} \tag{2.7}$$

$$\frac{\partial \hat{y}_i}{\partial w_j} = x_{ij} \tag{2.8}$$

$$\therefore \frac{\partial L}{\partial w_j} = \frac{1}{m}\sum_{i=1}^{m}\frac{\partial L_i}{\partial w_j} = \frac{1}{m}\sum_{i=1}^{m}\left(\frac{\partial L_i}{\partial \hat{y}_i} \cdot \frac{\partial \hat{y}_i}{\partial w_j}\right)$$

$$= \frac{1}{m}\sum_{i=1}^{m}\left(2(y_i - \hat{y}_i)(-1) \cdot (x_{ij})\right)$$

$$= \frac{\sum_{i=1}^{m}2(y_i - \hat{y}_i)(-1)(x_{ij})}{m} \tag{2.9}$$

Here, $j \in [1, n]$ and n is the number of features.

Subsequently, gradient descent is used to update the bias, b (Equation 2.10) and the weights, w (Equation 2.11).

$$b_{\text{new}} = b_{\text{old}} - \frac{\partial L}{\partial b} \cdot \alpha \tag{2.10}$$

$$w_{j\ new} = w_{j\ old} - \frac{\partial L}{\partial w_j} \cdot \alpha \tag{2.11}$$

Here, α is the learning rate (typically a small value, *e.g.*, 0.1, 0.01, 0.001).

It is worth noting that the mathematical notations and Python codes in this chapter are somewhat similar to those in Chapters 3 and 4 of this book [5, 6]. However, the focuses of Chapters 3 and 4 are on regularization and logistic regression, respectively, whereas the focus of this chapter is on linear regression.

2.3. NUMERICAL EXAMPLE OF LINEAR REGRESSION

Suppose we have a small training dataset (presented in Table **2.1**) with only 3 samples (*i.e.*, $m = 3$), which pertains to the sale price of houses in millions of dollars (abbreviated as **sale_price_million**) based on 2 input features (*i.e.*, $n = 2$), namely, the size of a house in square feet (abbreviated as **size_sqft**) and the total number of bedrooms in a house (abbreviated as **num_bedrooms**). In other words, for this example, X is size_sqft and num_bedrooms, and Y is sale_price_million. Our task is to build a best-fit linear regression model that maps the X and Y.

Table 2.1. The small dataset for linear regression.

size_sqft	num_bedrooms	sale_price_million
1600	5	2.28
1200	4	1.5
740	2	0.88

Next, normalize the feature values (*i.e.*, the values of size_sqft and num_bedrooms columns) to bring them to a common scale between 0 and 1, using Max-min normalization, as shown in Equation (2.12). Without normalization, some feature(s) might dominate the machine learning process.

$$normalized\ x_{ij} = \frac{x_{ij} - min_{k\in[1,m]}x_{kj}}{max_{k\in[1,m]}x_{kj} - min_{k\in[1,m]}x_{kj}} \tag{2.12}$$

The maximum and minimum of size_sqft are 1600 and 740, respectively. Likewise, the maximum and minimum of num_bedrooms are 5 and 2, respectively. The output values (*i.e.,* sale_price_million) are left as they are, without any normalization. The small dataset after Max-min normalization on the features is presented in Table **2.2**.

Table 2.2. The small dataset after Max-min normalization for linear regression.

size_sqft	num_bedrooms	sale_price_million
1	1	2.28
0.5349	0.6667	1.5
0	0	0.88

Now, let us start the machine learning process to build a linear regression model.

Initialize the bias:

$$b = 0$$

Initialize the weight for feature size_sqft:

$$w_1 = 0$$

Initialize the weight for feature num_bedrooms:

$$w_2 = 0$$

Set the learning rate:

$$\alpha = 0.01$$

Note that for simplicity of writing and expression, all the following x_{ij} refers to the *normalized* x_{ij} by default, unless otherwise stated.

2.3.1. Start the First Iteration of Learning

Take the input values of the first training sample and calculate the predicted $\hat{y}_1$:

$$\hat{y}_1 = b + \sum_{j=1}^{n} w_j x_{1j} = b + w_1 x_{11} + w_2 x_{12} = 0 + 0 \times 1 + 0 \times 1 = 0$$

Take the input values of the second training sample and calculate the predicted $\hat{y}_2$:

$$\hat{y}_2 = b + \sum_{j=1}^{n} w_j x_{2j} = b + w_1 x_{21} + w_2 x_{22} = 0 + 0 \times 0.5349 + 0 \times 0.6667 = 0$$

Take the input values of the third training sample and calculate the predicted $\hat{y}_3$:

$$\hat{y}_3 = b + \sum_{j=1}^{n} w_j x_{3j} = b + w_1 x_{31} + w_2 x_{32} = 0 + 0 \times 0 + 0 \times 0 = 0$$

Calculate the value of $\frac{\partial L}{\partial b}$:

$$\frac{\partial L}{\partial b} = \frac{\sum_{i=1}^{m} 2(y_i - \hat{y}_i)(-1)}{m}$$

$$= \frac{2 \times (2.28 - 0) \times (-1) + 2 \times (1.5 - 0) \times (-1) + 2 \times (0.88 - 0) \times (-1)}{3}$$

$$= -3.1067$$

Calculate the value of $\frac{\partial L}{\partial w_1}$:

$$\frac{\partial L}{\partial w_1} = \frac{\sum_{i=1}^{m} 2(y_i - \hat{y}_i)(-1)(x_{i1})}{m}$$

$$= \frac{2 \times (2.28 - 0) \times (-1) \times 1 + 2 \times (1.5 - 0) \times (-1) \times 0.5349 + 2 \times (0.88 - 0) \times (-1) \times 0}{3}$$

$$= -2.0549$$

Calculate the value of $\frac{\partial L}{\partial w_2}$:

$$\frac{\partial L}{\partial w_2} = \frac{\sum_{i=1}^{m} 2(y_i - \hat{y}_i)(-1)(x_{i2})}{m}$$

$$= \frac{2 \times (2.28 - 0) \times (-1) \times 1 + 2 \times (1.5 - 0) \times (-1) \times 0.6667 + 2 \times (0.88 - 0) \times (-1) \times 0}{3}$$

$$= -2.1867$$

Update the b value:

$$b_{new} = b_{old} - \frac{\partial L}{\partial b} \cdot \alpha = 0 - (-3.1067) \times 0.01 = 0.03107$$

Update the w_1 value:

$$w_{1\ new} = w_{1\ old} - \frac{\partial L}{\partial w_1} \cdot \alpha = 0 - (-2.0548) \times 0.01 = 0.02055$$

Update the w_2 value:

$$w_{2\ new} = w_{2\ old} - \frac{\partial L}{\partial w_2} \cdot \alpha = 0 - (-2.1867) \times 0.01 = 0.02187$$

2.3.2. End the First Iteration of Learning

Now after the very first iteration of learning, there is a set of newly updated bias and weights, *i.e.*, $b = 0.03107$, $w_1 = 0.02055$ and $w_2 = 0.02187$. With these, the latest mean loss (*i.e.*, MSE) can be calculated as follows:

$$MSE = L = \frac{\sum_{i=1}^{m}(y_i - \hat{y}_i)^2}{m}$$

$$= \frac{[2.28 - (0.03107 + 0.02055 \times 1 + 0.02187 \times 1)]^2}{3}$$

$$+ \frac{[1.5 - (0.03107 + 0.02055 \times 0.5349 + 0.02187 \times 0.6667)]^2}{3}$$

$$+ \frac{[0.88 - (0.03107 + 0.02055 \times 0 + 0.02187 \times 0)]^2}{3} = 2.5576$$

So, the latest MSE after the first iteration of learning is 2.5576. Next, let us continue with the second iteration with the updated bias and weights determined above.

2.3.3. Start the Second Iteration of Learning

Take the input values of the first training sample and calculate the predicted $\hat{y}_1$:

$$\hat{y}_1 = b + \sum_{j=1}^{n} w_j x_{1j} = b + w_1 x_{11} + w_2 x_{12}$$

$$= 0.03107 + 0.02055 \times 1 + 0.02187 \times 1 = 0.07349$$

Take the input values of the second training sample and calculate the predicted $\hat{y}_2$:

$$\hat{y}_2 = b + \sum_{j=1}^{n} w_j x_{2j} = b + w_1 x_{21} + w_2 x_{22}$$

$$= 0.03107 + 0.02055 \times 0.5349 + 0.02187 \times 0.6667 = 0.05664$$

Take the input values of the third training sample and calculate the predicted $\hat{y}_3$:

$$\hat{y}_3 = b + \sum_{j=1}^{n} w_j x_{3j} = b + w_1 x_{31} + w_2 x_{32}$$

$$= 0.03107 + 0.02055 \times 0 + 0.02187 \times 0 = 0.03107$$

Calculate the value of $\frac{\partial L}{\partial b}$:

$$\frac{\partial L}{\partial b} = \frac{\sum_{i=1}^{m} 2(y_i - \hat{y}_i)(-1)}{m}$$

$$= (2 \times (2.28 - 0.07349) \times (-1) + 2 \times (1.5 - 0.05664) \times (-1) + 2 \times (0.88 - 0.03107) \times (-1))/3$$

$$= -2.9992$$

Calculate the value of $\frac{\partial L}{\partial w_1}$:

$$\frac{\partial L}{\partial w_1} = \frac{\sum_{i=1}^{m} 2(y_i - \hat{y}_i)(-1)(x_{i1})}{m}$$

$$= \frac{2 \times (2.28 - 0.07349) \times (-1) \times 1}{3} + \frac{2 \times (1.5 - 0.05664) \times (-1) \times 0.5349}{3}$$

$$+ \frac{2 \times (0.88 - 0.03107) \times (-1) \times 0}{3}$$

$$= -1.9857$$

Calculate the value of $\frac{\partial L}{\partial w_2}$:

$$\frac{\partial L}{\partial w_2} = \frac{\sum_{i=1}^m 2(y_i - \hat{y}_i)(-1)(x_{i2})}{m}$$
$$= \frac{2 \times (2.28 - 0.07349) \times (-1) \times 1}{3} + \frac{2 \times (1.5 - 0.05664) \times (-1) \times 0.6667}{3}$$
$$+ \frac{2 \times (0.88 - 0.03107) \times (-1) \times 0}{3}$$
$$= -2.1125$$

Update the b value:

$$b_{\text{new}} = b_{\text{old}} - \frac{\partial L}{\partial b} \cdot \alpha = 0.03107 - (-2.9992) \times 0.01 = 0.06106$$

Update the w_1 value:

$$w_{1 \text{ new}} = w_{1 \text{ old}} - \frac{\partial L}{\partial w_1} \cdot \alpha = 0.02055 - (-1.9857) \times 0.01 = 0.04041$$

Update the w_2 value:

$$w_{2 \text{ new}} = w_{2 \text{ old}} - \frac{\partial L}{\partial w_2} \cdot \alpha = 0.02187 - (-2.1125) \times 0.01 = 0.04299$$

2.3.4. End the Second Iteration of Learning

At the end of the second iteration of learning, we get a set of newly updated bias and weights, *i.e.,* $b = 0.06106$, $w_1 = 0.04041$ and $w_2 = 0.04299$. With these, the latest mean loss (*i.e.,* MSE) can be calculated as follows:

$$MSE = L = \frac{\sum_{i=1}^m (y_i - \hat{y}_i)^2}{m}$$

$$= \frac{[2.28 - (0.06106 + 0.04041 \times 1 + 0.04299 \times 1)]^2}{3}$$
$$+ \frac{[1.5 - (0.06106 + 0.04041 \times 0.5349 + 0.04299 \times 0.6667)]^2}{3}$$
$$+ \frac{[0.88 - (0.06106 + 0.04041 \times 0 + 0.04299 \times 0)]^2}{3} = 2.3865$$

Compared with the previous MSE = 2.5576 after the first iteration, it is noticed that the MSE is now reduced to 2.3865, indicating that the performance of the linear regression model has been improving!

Further, the same learning process is set to repeat a total of 500,000 times to keep updating the bias and weights until the mean loss between the true and predicted output values stabilizes and reaches its minimum; only then are the optimal bias and weights said to be obtained. For conciseness, we will not present the detailed calculations from the third iteration onwards in the chapter, but tabulate the bias, weights and MSE for the first and last five iterations in Table **2.3**. If necessary, readers are encouraged to try several more iterations following the detailed calculations above to have a deeper understanding about the process of training a linear regression model. Besides, (Fig. **2.3**) depicts that MSE decreases with the increase of learning iterations and finally stabilizes.

Table 2.3. The bias, weights and MSE values for the first and last five iterations.

Iteration	b	w_1	w_2	*MSE*
1	0.03107	0.02055	0.02187	2.5576
2	0.06106	0.04041	0.04299	2.3865
3	0.09001	0.05959	0.06340	2.2270
4	0.11797	0.07814	0.08312	2.0782
5	0.14495	0.09606	0.10217	1.9394
...	...	...	...	...
499,996	0.88000	2.37765	-0.97765	3.272×10^{-19}

Iteration	b	w_1	w_2	*MSE*
499,997	0.88000	2.37765	-0.97765	3.271×10^{-19}
499,998	0.88000	2.37765	-0.97765	3.271×10^{-19}
499,999	0.88000	2.37765	-0.97765	3.271×10^{-19}
500,000	0.88000	2.37765	-0.97765	3.271×10^{-19}

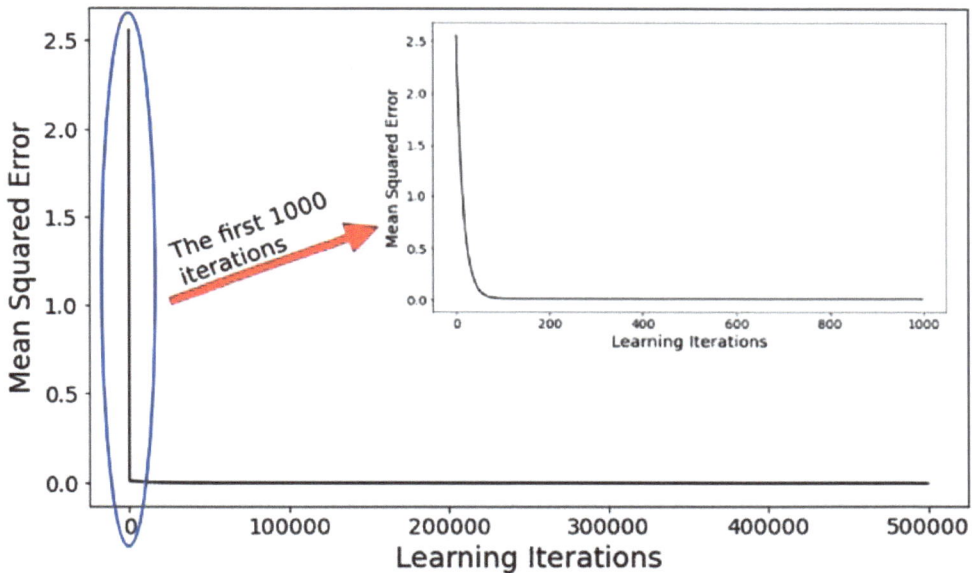

Fig. (2.3). Mean squared error (MSE) *vs.* learning iterations.

As demonstrated in Table **2.3** and Fig. (**2.3**), MSE finally stabilizes at a very tiny MSE value, 3.271×10^{-19}, suggesting that we have trained a good model and the corresponding optimal bias and weights are determined. The resulting linear regression model can be written as:

$$Y = b + \sum_{j=1}^{2} w_j \cdot (\text{normalized } X_j)$$

Here, $b = 0.88, w_1 = 2.37765$ and $w_2 = -0.97765$

As Max-min normalization was performed during the training process, it needs to be reflected in the final model as well. That is why normalized X_j is shown here.

Now, we can use this trained linear regression model to make predictions for previously unseen data (*i.e.,* new data). For instance, there is a new house with 1200 sqft and 3 bedrooms. To predict the price of the house, normalization needs to be applied first using the maximum and minimum values of each respective feature from the training dataset. Recall that the maximum and minimum of size_sqft are 1600 and 740; the maximum and minimum of num_bedrooms are 5 and 2. So, the normalized X_1 for size_sqft and normalized X_2 for num_bedrooms will be:

$$\text{normalized } X_1 = \frac{1200 - 740}{1600 - 740} = 0.5349$$

$$\text{normalized } X_2 = \frac{3 - 2}{5 - 2} = 0.3333$$

Next, plug the normalized feature values into the equation of the linear regression model:

$$Y = b + \sum_{j=1}^{2} w_j \cdot \left(\text{normalized } X_j \right)$$
$$= 0.88 + 2.37765 \times 0.5349 + (-0.97765) \times 0.3333 = 1.826$$

Therefore, for the house with 1200 sqft and 3 bedrooms, the sale price is predicted to be 1.826 million dollars.

2.4. SAMPLE CODES AND COMPARISON

Following the mathematics and numerical example discussed in Sections 2.2 and 2.3, we have implemented the linear regression machine learning model with the aforementioned small dataset from scratch in Python. Readers are encouraged to have their Jupyter Notebook (or other Python IDE) ready and execute the codes along with reading. The complete code file can be downloaded from our shared folder in Google Drive:

https://drive.google.com/drive/folders/1FqJvo4ZPazNbEH_GlHFoodqvegnQmHcn?usp=share_link

Firstly, only the pandas and numpy libraries are imported.

```python
import pandas as pd
import numpy as np
```

Secondly, a **loss_MSE** function is created for calculating the MSE between the known true output values and predicted output values by the linear regression model. See the docstring of the loss_MSE function to understand its usage.

```python
def loss_MSE(X, Y, b, W1, W2): # Mean Squared Error
    """

    Find the Mean Squared Error between true outputs and pre-
dicted outputs
    Inputs: X - list, the input feature values
            Y - list, the true output values
            b - float/int, bias
            W1 - float/int, weight for the 1st feature (i.e.,
size_sqft)
            W2 - float/int, weight for the 2nd feature (i.e.,
num_bedrooms)
    Outputs: MSE - float
    """

    X1 = [val[0] for val in X]
    X2 = [val[1] for val in X]
    m = len(X)
    total_loss = 0
    for i in range(m):
        total_loss = total_loss + (Y[i] - (b + X1[i]*W1 +
X2[i]*W2))**2
    MSE = total_loss / m
    return MSE
```

Thirdly, an **update_bias_weights** is created to update the values of bias and weights based on the gradient descent optimization algorithm. The equations (2.5) to (2.11), which we derived in Section 2.2, are well translated into Python codes in this function. See the docstring of the update_bias_weights function to understand its usage.

```python
def update_bias_weights(X, Y, b, W1, W2, learning_rate):
    """
    Update the bias and weights based on Gradient Descent
    Inputs: X - list, the input feature values
            Y - list, the true output values
            b - float/int, bias
            W1 - float/int, weight for the 1st feature (i.e.,
size_sqft)
            W2 - float/int, weight for the 2nd feature (i.e.,
num_bedrooms)
            learning_rate - float, the learning rate used in
Gradient Descent
    Outputs: (b, W1, W2) - tuple, the updated bias and weights
    """
    X1 = [val[0] for val in X]
    X2 = [val[1] for val in X]
    m = len(X)
    dL_dW1 = 0
    dL_dW2 = 0
    dL_db  = 0

    for i in range(m):
        dL_db  = dL_db  + 2 * (Y[i] - (b + X1[i]*W1 +
X2[i]*W2)) * (-1)
        dL_dW1 = dL_dW1 + 2 * (Y[i] - (b + X1[i]*W1 +
X2[i]*W2)) * (-X1[i])
        dL_dW2 = dL_dW2 + 2 * (Y[i] - (b + X1[i]*W1 +
X2[i]*W2)) * (-X2[i])

    dL_db  = dL_db/m
    dL_dW1 = dL_dW1/m
    dL_dW2 = dL_dW2/m

    # We subtract because the derivatives point in direction
of steepest ascent
    b  = b  - dL_db  * learning_rate
    W1 = W1 - dL_dW1 * learning_rate
    W2 = W2 - dL_dW2 * learning_rate

    return (b, W1, W2)
```

Fourthly, a **train** function is created to oversee the training process for specific iterations and write the log of loss/MSE history. See the docstring of the train function to understand its usage.

```python
def train(X, Y, b, W1, W2, learning_rate, learning_itera-
tions):
    """
    Train linear regression model for the specified iterations
    Inputs: X - list, the input feature values
            Y - list, the true output values
            b - float/int, bias
            W1 - float/int, weight for the 1st feature (i.e.,
size_sqft)
            W2 - float/int, weight for the 2nd feature (i.e.,
num_bedrooms)
            learning_rate - float, the learning rate used in
Gradient Descent
            learning_iterations - int, the number of times of
training
    Outputs: (loss_history, b, W1, W2) - tuple, return the
loss_history, and the final bias and weights
    """
    loss_history = []

    for i in range(learning_iterations):
        b, W1, W2 = update_bias_weights(X, Y, b, W1, W2,
learning_rate)

        # find MSE after the ith iteration of updating bias
and weights
        loss = loss_MSE(X, Y, b, W1, W2)
        loss_history.append(loss)

        if i < 5 or i >= learning_iterations-5:
            print ("iter={:d} \t b={:.5f} \t W1={:.5f} \t
W2={:.5f} \t MSE={}".format(i+1, b, W1, W2, loss))
    return (loss_history, b, W1, W2)
```

Fifthly, a **max_min_norm** function is created to normalize the values of input features (*i.e., X*). See the docstring of the max_min_norm function to understand its usage.

```python
def max_min_norm(X):
    """

    Normalize dataset by using the Max-min normalization tech-
nique
    Inputs: X - numpy.ndarray, the dataset for normalization
    Outputs: (X_norm, np.array(max_min_vals)) - tuple, return
the normalized dataset,
                                            and the max and
min values of each feature
    """

    X_norm = X.copy().astype(float)
    max_min_vals = []
    for col in range(0, X_norm.shape[1]):
        X_max = X_norm[:, col].max()
        X_min = X_norm[:, col].min()
        X_range = X_max - X_min
        X_norm[:, col] = (X_norm[:, col] - X_min) / X_range
        max_min_vals.append({"X_max":X_max, "X_min":X_min,
 "X_range":X_range})
    return (X_norm, np.array(max_min_vals))
```

Sixthly, we store the small dataset as a numpy array, invoke the max_min_norm function for normalization, initialize bias and weights, set learning rate and iterations and then invoke the train function to start building our first linear regression model, after decomposing and fully understanding every single step of the process.

```
# The small dataset
data = np.array([[1600,5,2.28],
                 [1200,4,1.5],
                 [740,2,0.88]])
col_names = ['size_sqft', 'num_bedrooms', 'sale_price_mil-
lion']
print(pd.DataFrame(data, columns=col_names), "\n")

X = data[:, :-1] # all rows, all columns except the last col-
umn
Y = data[:, -1]  # all rows, last column only

X, max_min_vals = max_min_norm(X) # normalize the input fea-
tures
X = X.tolist()
Y = Y.tolist()

# Initialize bias and weights
initial_b  = 0
initial_W1 = 0
initial_W2 = 0

# Set learing rate and iterations
learning_rate = 0.01
learning_iterations = 500000

# Start the training of linear regression model
loss_history, b, W1, W2 = train(X, Y, initial_b, initial_W1,
initial_W2, learning_rate, learning_iterations)
```

```
     size_sqft  num_bedrooms  sale_price_million
0      1600.0           5.0                 2.28
1      1200.0           4.0                 1.50
2       740.0           2.0                 0.88


iter=1      b=0.03107   W1=0.02055    W2=0.02187      MSE=2.5575697626286185
iter=2      b=0.06106   W1=0.04041    W2=0.04299      MSE=2.386536425797163
iter=3      b=0.09001   W1=0.05959    W2=0.06340      MSE=2.227004062632732
iter=4      b=0.11797   W1=0.07814    W2=0.08312      MSE=2.0781991850671244
iter=5      b=0.14495   W1=0.09606    W2=0.10217      MSE=1.9394003261916515
iter=499996    b=0.88000   W1=2.37765    W2=-0.97765     MSE=3.271661739987268e-19
iter=499997    b=0.88000   W1=2.37765    W2=-0.97765     MSE=3.271412898125512e-19
iter=499998    b=0.88000   W1=2.37765    W2=-0.97765     MSE=3.2711650159687197e-19
iter=499999    b=0.88000   W1=2.37765    W2=-0.97765     MSE=3.2709145253923147e-19
iter=500000    b=0.88000   W1=2.37765    W2=-0.97765     MSE=3.2706657119492734e-19
```

Finally, the trained linear regression model is utilized to predict the price of the house (new data) with 1200 sqft and 3 bedrooms:

```
new_data = np.array([[1200,3]], dtype = float)

# Max-min normalization
for col in range(0, new_data.shape[1]):
    new_data[:, col] = ((new_data[:, col]
                         - max_min_vals[col]['X_min'])
                         / max_min_vals[col]['X_range'])

# Use the final bias and weights values
predicted_price = b + W1*new_data[0][0] + W2*new_data[0][1]

print(f'''For the house with 1200 sqft and 3 bedrooms,
the sale price is predicted to be {np.round(pre-
dicted_price,3)} million.''')
```
```
For the house with 1200 sqft and 3 bedrooms,
the sale price is predicted to be 1.826 million.
```

We then compare the above results with those from the off-the-shelf linear regression model offered by the scikit-learn library. These include the final bias and weights after training, and the predicted price for the house (new data) with 1200 sqft and 3 bedrooms. The codes are as follows:

```
import numpy as np
from sklearn.preprocessing import MinMaxScaler
from sklearn.linear_model import LinearRegression

# The small dataset
data = np.array([[1600,5,2.28],
                 [1200,4,1.5],
                 [740,2,0.88]])
X = data[:, :-1] # all rows, all columns except the last col-
umn
Y = data[:, -1]  # all rows, last column only

scaler = MinMaxScaler()
scaler.fit(X)
X = scaler.transform(X) # update to Normalized X

reg = LinearRegression().fit(X, Y)

print(f"The optimal bias found by sklearn: {np.round(reg.in-
tercept_,5)}")
print(f"The optimal weights found by sklearn:
{np.round(reg.coef_,5)}")
```
```
The optimal bias found by sklearn: 0.88
The optimal weights found by sklearn: [ 2.37765 -0.97765]
```

```
new_data = np.array([[1200,3]], dtype = float)
new_data = scaler.transform(new_data)

print(f'''For the house with 1200 sqft and 3 bedrooms,
the sale price is predicted to be {np.round(reg.pre-
dict(new_data),3)} million.''')
```

```
For the house with 1200 sqft and 3 bedrooms,
the sale price is predicted to be [1.826] million.
```

As can be seen from the results using scikit-learn linear regression model, the final bias and weights values are the same as those given by our own linear regression model (*i.e.,* $b = 0.88$, $w_1 = 2.37765$ and $w_2 = -0.97765$). Furthermore, the predicted price for the previously unseen house with 1200 sqft and 3 bedrooms is also the same as that produced by our own model (*i.e., 1.826 million*).

CONCLUSION

In this chapter, we discussed the concept of linear regression, a popular machine learning algorithm used for predicting numerical values. To make the material more accessible, we kept abstract mathematical theories to a minimum. Instead, we focused on a concrete numerical example with a small dataset for predicting the sale price of houses, walking through it step by step. We also provided sample codes and a comparison with the linear regression model from the off-the-shelf library, scikit-learn. By the end of the chapter, readers should have a well-rounded understanding of how linear regression machine learning works behind the scenes, how the mathematics relates to the implementation and performance of the algorithm, and be better equipped to apply it in their projects.

REFERENCES

[1] X. Yan, and X.G. Su, *Linear regression analysis: Theory and computing.* World Scientific Publishing: Singapore, Singapore, 2009.
     http://dx.doi.org/10.1142/6986
[2] D.C. Montgomery, E.A. Peck, and G.G. Vining, *Introduction to Linear Regression Analysis.,* 6th ed Standards Information Network, 2021.
[3] R.J. Casson, and L.D.M. Farmer, "Understanding and checking the assumptions of linear regression: a primer for medical researchers", *Clin. Exp. Ophthalmol.,* vol. 42, no. 6, pp. 590-596, 2014.
     http://dx.doi.org/10.1111/ceo.12358 PMID: 24801277

[4] M.H. Kutner, J. Neter, C.J. Nachtsheim, and W. Wasserman, McGraw Hill Higher Education *Applied linear statistical models (int'l ed),* 4th ed Maidenhead: England, 2004.

[5] Z. Wang, S.A. Irfan, C. Teoh, and P.H. Bhoyar, *Regularization" in Numerical Machine Learning.* Bentham Science, 2023.

[6] Z. Wang, S.A. Irfan, C. Teoh, and P.H. Bhoyar, *Logistic Regression" in Numerical Machine Learning.* Bentham Science, 2023.

## CHAPTER 3

Regularization

Abstract: This chapter delves into L1 and L2 regularization techniques within the context of linear regression, focusing on minimizing overfitting risks while maintaining a concise presentation of mathematical theories. We explore these techniques through a concrete numerical example with a small dataset for predicting house sale prices, providing a step-by-step walkthrough of the process. To further enhance comprehension, we supply sample codes and draw comparisons with the Lasso and Ridge models implemented in the scikit-learn library. By the end of this chapter, readers will acquire a well-rounded understanding of L1 and L2 regularization in the context of linear regression, their implications on model implementation and performance, and be equipped with the knowledge to apply these methods in practical use.

Keywords: L1 Regularization, L2 Regularization, Linear Regression, Numerical Example, Small Dataset, Housing Price Prediction, Scikit-Learn, Lasso, Ridge

3.1. INTRODUCTION TO L1 AND L2 REGULARIZATION

Regularization is the process of adding an extra penalty to a more complicated model with larger values of weights to prevent overfitting. A problem known as overfitting happens when a machine learning model is made specifically for training datasets and is unable to generalize well to previously unseen datasets. Introducing regularization techniques into machine learning models is essential for achieving better generalization and improved performance on new data. By penalizing overly complex models, regularization helps lead to more accurate and stable predictions. Some popular regularization methods include L1 and L2 regularization, which differ in the way they penalize the model's complexity. Regularization has proven to be a critical component in the development of robust and reliable models, particularly when dealing with high-dimensional data or noisy datasets. It enables practitioners to build more efficient models, capable of adapting to new and diverse situations while reducing the risk of overfitting and maintaining interpretability.

This chapter focuses on L1 and L2 regularization, which are demonstrated in detail by making necessary changes from the original linear regression model discussed in Chapter 2. Bear in mind, however, that L1 and L2 regularization can also be applied to other machine learning models (*e.g.*, logistic regression), as well as deep learning neural networks.

Zhiyuan Wang, Sayed Ameenuddin Irfan, Christopher Teoh & Priyanka Hriday Bhoyar

The names of L1 and L2 regularization come from the corresponding L1 and L2 norms of the weight vector W.

The L1 norm is defined as:

$$\|W\|_1 = \sum_{j=1}^{n} |w_j| = |w_1| + |w_2| + \cdots + |w_n|$$

The L2 norm is defined as:

$$\|W\|_2 = \left(\sum_{j=1}^{n} w_j^2\right)^{1/2} = (w_1^2 + w_2^2 + \cdots + w_n^2)^{1/2}$$

Here, w_j is the weight of the jth feature, and n is the number of input features.

Note that $\|W\|$, without subscript, is also conventionally used to represent the L2 norm of the weight vector W.

A linear regression model with the L1 regularization is known as Lasso (least absolute shrinkage and selection operator) regression [1, 2], whereas a linear regression model with the L2 regularization is called Ridge regression [3, 4].

3.2. MATHEMATICS OF L1 REGULARIZATION FOR LINEAR REGRESSION

The general equation of linear regression if having more than one independent variable X (*i.e.*, input feature) is as follows:

$$Y = b + \sum_{j=1}^{n} w_j X_j \tag{3.1}$$

Here,

Y is the output
b is the bias
n is the number of input features
w_j is the weight of the jth feature
X_j is input value of the jth feature

The goal of linear regression is to find the best-fit linear equation model that maps the relationship between input X and output Y, in the form of Equation (3.1) with the optimal weights and bias, which produces the least error (synonymously known as loss in machine learning) between the known true output Y values and predicted output Y values by the model.

Fig. (3.1). Illustration of notations using an exemplary training dataset.

Let us use lowercase x_i to denote the feature values of the ith sample (out of the total m rows of samples from training dataset), then x_{ij} will be the value of the jth feature (out of the total n input features) at the ith sample, as shown in Fig. (**3.1**). Lowercase y_i is used to represent the known output value (*i.e.*, true output value) of the ith sample, and $\hat{y}_i$ is used to denote the corresponding predicted output value by the linear equation model. Equation (3.1) is then updated to Equation (3.2).

$$\hat{y}_i = b + \sum_{j=1}^{n} w_j x_{ij} \qquad\qquad (3.2)$$

Here,

$i \in [1, m]$
m is the number of training samples
x_{ij} is the value of the jth feature at the ith sample

b is the bias
n is the number of input features
w_j is the weight of the jth feature
$\hat{y}_i$ is the predicted value for the ith sample

Up to this step, everything is the same as the original linear regression discussed in Chapter 2. The only difference brought by L1 regularization is the change of loss function. Recall that in the original linear regression, the mean squared error (MSE) function is employed to quantify the loss (L) between true output values and predicted output values. Now in the linear regression with L1 regularization, one penalty term, $\lambda\|W\|_1$, is introduced to the loss function, as follows:

$$L = \frac{1}{2} \cdot MSE + \lambda\|W\|_1 = \frac{1}{2} \cdot \frac{\sum_{i=1}^{m} (y_i - \hat{y}_i)^2}{m} + \lambda\|W\|_1 \qquad (3.3)$$

Here,

L is the loss between true and predicted outputs

m is the number of training samples

y_i is the true value for the ith sample
$\hat{y}_i$ is the predicted value for the ith sample

λ is the penalty coefficient

$\|W\|_1$ is the L1 norm of weights,

$$\|W\|_1 = \sum_{j=1}^{n} |w_j| = |w_1| + |w_2| + \cdots + |w_n|$$

Essentially what $\lambda\|W\|_1$ does is to add an extra penalty to complicated models with larger values of weights. Note that an optional constant $\frac{1}{2}$ is added before the MSE term. The purpose of doing so is purely for mathematical convenience, such that when taking the partial derivatives of L with respect to b and w_j later, the value 2 coming from the power in $(y_i - \hat{y}_i)^2$ can get cancelled out with the constant $\frac{1}{2}$. Adding or removing the $\frac{1}{2}$ de facto does not matter because the nature of the problem (*i.e.*, minimizing loss) is unaffected by such a constant.

Next, the Gradient Descent optimization algorithm is used to find the optimal bias and weights by iteratively tweaking their values a tiny bit at a time in the direction of reducing the loss. In order to carry out the optimization, we first need to find the partial derivative of the mean loss (L) with respect to the bias and weights, namely, $\frac{\partial L}{\partial b}$ and $\frac{\partial L}{\partial w_j}$, denoting the contribution to the mean loss by the bias and each of the weights. This can be done by applying the chain rule, shown in Equations (3.4) to (3.9).

$$\frac{\partial L}{\partial b} = \frac{\partial \left(\frac{1}{2} \cdot \frac{\sum_{i=1}^{m} (y_i - \hat{y}_i)^2}{m}\right)}{\partial b} + \frac{\partial (\lambda \|W\|_1)}{\partial b}$$

$$= \frac{\partial \left(\frac{1}{2} \cdot \frac{\sum_{i=1}^{m} (y_i - \hat{y}_i)^2}{m}\right)}{\partial \hat{y}_i} \cdot \frac{\partial \hat{y}_i}{\partial b} + 0 \tag{3.4}$$

$$\frac{\partial \hat{y}_i}{\partial b} = 1 \tag{3.5}$$

$$\therefore \frac{\partial L}{\partial b} = \frac{\sum_{i=1}^{m} (y_i - \hat{y}_i)(-1)}{m} \tag{3.6}$$

$$\frac{\partial \hat{y}_i}{\partial w_j} = x_{ij} \tag{3.7}$$

If $w_j \geq 0$ then :

$$\frac{\partial L}{\partial w_j} = \frac{\partial \left(\frac{1}{2} \cdot \frac{\sum_{i=1}^{m} (y_i - \hat{y}_i)^2}{m}\right)}{\partial w_j} + \frac{\partial (\lambda \|W\|_1)}{\partial w_j}$$

$$= \frac{\partial \left(\frac{1}{2} \cdot \frac{\sum_{i=1}^{m} (y_i - \hat{y}_i)^2}{m}\right)}{\partial \hat{y}_i} \cdot \frac{\partial \hat{y}_i}{\partial w_j}$$

$$+ \frac{\partial \left(\lambda(|w_1| + |w_2| + \cdots |w_j| + \cdots + |w_n|)\right)}{\partial w_j}$$

$$= \frac{\sum_{i=1}^{m} (y_i - \hat{y}_i)(-1)(x_{ij})}{m} + \lambda \tag{3.8}$$

If $w_j < 0$ then :

$$\frac{\partial L}{\partial w_j} = \frac{\partial \left(\frac{1}{2} \cdot \frac{\sum_{i=1}^{m} (y_i - \hat{y}_i)^2}{m}\right)}{\partial w_j} + \frac{\partial(\lambda \|W\|_1)}{\partial w_j}$$

$$= \frac{\partial \left(\frac{1}{2} \cdot \frac{\sum_{i=1}^{m} (y_i - \hat{y}_i)^2}{m}\right)}{\partial \hat{y}_i} \cdot \frac{\partial \hat{y}_i}{\partial w_j}$$

$$+ \frac{\partial\big(\lambda(|w_1| + |w_2| + \cdots |w_j| + \cdots + |w_n|)\big)}{\partial w_j}$$

$$= \frac{\sum_{i=1}^{m} (y_i - \hat{y}_i)(-1)(x_{ij})}{m} - \lambda \qquad (3.9)$$

Here, $j\epsilon[1, n]$ and n is the number of features.

Subsequently, in the same step as that of the original linear regression, gradient descent is used to update the bias, b (Equation 3.10) and the weights, w (Equation 3.11).

$$b_{\text{new}} = b_{\text{old}} - \frac{\partial L}{\partial b} \cdot \alpha \qquad (3.10)$$

$$w_{j\,\text{new}} = w_{j\,\text{old}} - \frac{\partial L}{\partial w_j} \cdot \alpha \qquad (3.11)$$

Here, α is the learning rate (typically a small value, *e.g.*, 0.1, 0.01, 0.001).

Note that for L1 regularization, when w_j is positive, the constant λ (always ≥ 0) is added in the $\frac{\partial L}{\partial w_j}$ expression (*i.e.*, $\frac{\partial L}{\partial w_j}$ will be larger), and thus push the new w_j to be less positive (*i.e.*, closer to zero) in gradient descent of updating weights (Equation 3.11). On the contrary, when w_j is negative, the constant λ (always ≥ 0) is subtracted in the $\frac{\partial L}{\partial w_j}$ expression (*i.e.*, $\frac{\partial L}{\partial w_j}$ will be smaller), and thus push the new w_j to be less negative (*i.e.*, closer to zero) in the gradient descent of updating weights (Equation 3.11). In other words, the introduced λ by L1 regularization has the overall constant effect of pushing w_j towards 0. This is also why L1 regularization can be used as a feature selection method.

It is worth noting that the mathematical notations and Python codes in this chapter are somewhat similar to those in Chapters 2 and 4 of this book [5, 6]. However, the focuses of Chapters 2 and 4 are on linear regression and logistic regression, respectively, whereas the focus of this chapter is on regularization.

3.3. NUMERICAL EXAMPLE OF L1 REGULARIZATION FOR LINEAR REGRESSION

Same as the original linear regression discussed in Chapter 2, suppose we have a small training dataset presented in (Table **3.1**) with only 3 samples (*i.e.*, $m = 3$), which pertains to the sale price of houses in millions of dollars (abbreviated as **sale_price_million**) based on 2 input features (*i.e.*, $n = 2$), namely, the size of a house in square feet (abbreviated as **size_sqft**) and the total number of bedrooms in the house (abbreviated as **num_bedrooms**). In other words, for this example, X is size_sqft and num_bedrooms, and Y is sale_price_million. Our task is to build a best-fit linear regression model that maps the X and Y under L1 regularization.

Table 3.1. The small dataset for linear regression under regularization.

size_sqft	num_bedrooms	sale_price_million
1600	5	2.28
1200	4	1.5
740	2	0.88

Next, normalize the feature values (*i.e.*, the values of size_sqft and num_bedrooms columns) to bring them to a common scale between 0 and 1, using Max-min normalization, as shown in Equation (3.12). Without normalization, some feature(s) might dominate the machine learning process.

$$normalized\ x_{ij} = \frac{x_{ij} - min_{k \in [1,m]} x_{kj}}{max_{k \in [1,m]} x_{kj} - min_{k \in [1,m]} x_{kj}} \tag{3.12}$$

The maximum and minimum of size_sqft are 1600 and 740, respectively. Likewise, the maximum and minimum of num_bedrooms are 5 and 2, respectively. The output values (*i.e.*, sale_price_million) are left as they are, without any normalization. The small dataset after Max-min normalization on the features is presented in (Table **3.2**).

Table 3.2. The small dataset after Max-min normalization for linear regression under regularization.

size_sqft	num_bedrooms	sale_price_million
1	1	2.28
0.5349	0.6667	1.5
0	0	0.88

Now, let us start the machine learning process to build a linear regression model with L1 regularization.

Initialize the bias:

$$b = 0$$

Initialize the weight for feature size_sqft:

$$w_1 = 0$$

Initialize the weight for feature num_bedrooms:

$$w_2 = 0$$

Set the learning rate:

$$\alpha = 0.001$$

Set the penalty coefficient:

$$\lambda = 0.1$$

Note that for simplicity of writing and expression, all the following x_{ij} refers to the *normalized* x_{ij} by default, unless otherwise stated.

3.3.1. Start the First Iteration of Learning

Take the input values of the first training sample and calculate the predicted $\hat{y}_1$:

$$\hat{y}_1 = b + \sum_{j=1}^{n} w_j x_{1j} = b + w_1 x_{11} + w_2 x_{12} = 0 + 0 \times 1 + 0 \times 1 = 0$$

Take the input values of the second training sample and calculate the predicted $\hat{y}_2$:

$$\hat{y}_2 = b + \sum_{j=1}^{n} w_j x_{2j} = b + w_1 x_{21} + w_2 x_{22} = 0 + 0 \times 0.5349 + 0 \times 0.6667 = 0$$

Take the input values of the third training sample and calculate the predicted $\hat{y}_3$:

$$\hat{y}_3 = b + \sum_{j=1}^{n} w_j x_{3j} = b + w_1 x_{31} + w_2 x_{32} = 0 + 0 \times 0 + 0 \times 0 = 0$$

Calculate the value of $\frac{\partial L}{\partial b}$:

$$\frac{\partial L}{\partial b} = \frac{\sum_{i=1}^{m} (y_i - \hat{y}_i)(-1)}{m}$$
$$= \frac{(2.28 - 0) \times (-1) + (1.5 - 0) \times (-1) + (0.88 - 0) \times (-1)}{3}$$
$$= -1.5533$$

Calculate the value of $\frac{\partial L}{\partial w_1}$; since $w_1 = 0$, which satisfies the condition of $w_1 \geq 0$, a positive λ is added:

$$\frac{\partial L}{\partial w_1} = \frac{\sum_{i=1}^{m} (y_i - \hat{y}_i)(-1)(x_{i1})}{m} + \lambda$$

$$= \frac{(2.28 - 0) \times (-1) \times 1 + (1.5 - 0) \times (-1) \times 0.5349 + (0.88 - 0) \times (-1) \times 0}{3} + 0.1$$

$$= -0.9274$$

Calculate the value of $\frac{\partial L}{\partial w_2}$; since $w_2 = 0$, which satisfies the condition of $w_2 \geq 0$, a positive λ is added:

$$\frac{\partial L}{\partial w_2} = \frac{\sum_{i=1}^{m} (y_i - \hat{y}_i)(-1)(x_{i2})}{m} + \lambda$$

$$= ((2.28 - 0) \times (-1) \times 1 + (1.5 - 0) \times (-1) \times 0.6667 + (0.88 - 0) \times (-1) \times 0)/3 + 0.1$$

$$= -0.9933$$

Update the b value:

$$b_{new} = b_{old} - \frac{\partial L}{\partial b} \cdot \alpha = 0 - (-1.5533) \times 0.001 = 0.001553$$

Update the w_1 value:

$$w_{1\,new} = w_{1\,old} - \frac{\partial L}{\partial w_1} \cdot \alpha = 0 - (-0.9274) \times 0.001 = 0.0009274$$

Update the w_2 value:

$$w_{2\,new} = w_{2\,old} - \frac{\partial L}{\partial w_2} \cdot \alpha = 0 - (-0.9933) \times 0.001 = 0.0009933$$

3.3.2. End the First Iteration of Learning

Now after the very first iteration of learning, there is a set of newly updated bias and weights, *i.e.*, $b = 0.001553, w_1 = 0.0009274$ and $w_2 = 0.0009933$. With these, the latest MSE can be calculated as follows:

$$MSE = \frac{\sum_{i=1}^{m}(y_i - \hat{y}_i)^2}{m}$$

$$= \frac{[2.28 - (0.001553 + 0.0009274 \times 1 + 0.0009933 \times 1)]^2}{3}$$

$$+ \frac{[1.5 - (0.001553 + 0.0009274 \times 0.5349 + 0.0009933 \times 0.6667)]^2}{3}$$

$$+ \frac{[0.88 - (0.001553 + 0.0009274 \times 0 + 0.0009933 \times 0)]^2}{3} = 2.7320$$

So, the latest MSE after the first iteration of learning with L1 regularization is 2.7320. Next, let us continue with the second iteration with the updated bias and weights determined above.

3.3.3. Start the Second Iteration of Learning

Take the input values of the first training sample and calculate the predicted $\hat{y}_1$:

$$\hat{y}_1 = b + \sum_{j=1}^{n} w_j x_{1j} = b + w_1 x_{11} + w_2 x_{12}$$
$$= 0.001553 + 0.0009274 \times 1 + 0.0009933 \times 1 = 0.003474$$

Take the input values of the second training sample and calculate the predicted $\hat{y}_2$:

$$\hat{y}_2 = b + \sum_{j=1}^{n} w_j x_{2j} = b + w_1 x_{21} + w_2 x_{22}$$
$$= 0.001553 + 0.0009274 \times 0.5349 + 0.0009933 \times 0.6667 = 0.002711$$

Take the input values of the third training sample and calculate the predicted $\hat{y}_3$:

$$\hat{y}_3 = b + \sum_{j=1}^{n} w_j x_{3j} = b + w_1 x_{31} + w_2 x_{32}$$
$$= 0.001553 + 0.0009274 \times 0 + 0.0009933 \times 0 = 0.001553$$

Calculate the value of $\frac{\partial L}{\partial b}$:

$$\frac{\partial L}{\partial b} = \frac{\sum_{i=1}^{m} (y_i - \hat{y}_i)(-1)}{m}$$

$$= ((2.28 - 0.003474) \times (-1) + (1.5 - 0.002711) \times (-1)$$
$$+ (0.88 - 0.001553) \times (-1))/3$$

$$= -1.5508$$

Calculate the value of $\frac{\partial L}{\partial w_1}$; since $w_1 = 0.0009274$, which satisfies the condition of $w_1 \geq 0$, a positive λ is added:

$$\frac{\partial L}{\partial w_1} = \frac{\sum_{i=1}^{m} (y_i - \hat{y}_i)(-1)(x_{i1})}{m} + \lambda$$

$$= \frac{(2.28 - 0.003474) \times (-1) \times 1}{3} + \frac{(1.5 - 0.002711) \times (-1) \times 0.5349}{3}$$
$$+ \frac{(0.88 - 0.001553) \times (-1) \times 0}{3} + 0.1$$

$$= -0.9258$$

Calculate the value of $\frac{\partial L}{\partial w_2}$; since $w_2 = 0.0009933$, which satisfies the condition of $w_2 \geq 0$, a positive λ is added:

$$\frac{\partial L}{\partial w_2} = \frac{\sum_{i=1}^{m} (y_i - \hat{y}_i)(-1)(x_{i2})}{m} + \lambda$$

$$= \frac{(2.28 - 0.003474) \times (-1) \times 1}{3} + \frac{(1.5 - 0.002711) \times (-1) \times 0.6667}{3}$$
$$+ \frac{(0.88 - 0.001553) \times (-1) \times 0}{3} + 0.1$$

$$= -0.9916$$

Update the b value:

$$b_{\text{new}} = b_{\text{old}} - \frac{\partial L}{\partial b} \cdot \alpha = 0.001553 - (-1.5508) \times 0.001 = 0.003104$$

Update the w_1 value:

$$w_{1 \text{ new}} = w_{1 \text{ old}} - \frac{\partial L}{\partial w_1} \cdot \alpha = 0.0009274 - (-0.9258) \times 0.001 = 0.001853$$

Update the w_2 value:

$$w_{2 \text{ new}} = w_{2 \text{ old}} - \frac{\partial L}{\partial w_2} \cdot \alpha = 0.0009933 - (-0.9916) \times 0.001 = 0.001985$$

3.3.4. End the Second Iteration of Learning

At the end of the second iteration of learning with L1 regularization, we get a set of newly updated bias and weights, *i.e.*, $b = 0.003104$, $w_1 = 0.001853$ and $w_2 = 0.001985$. With these, the latest MSE can be calculated as follows:

$$
\begin{aligned}
MSE &= \frac{\sum_{i=1}^{m}(y_i - \hat{y}_i)^2}{m} \\
&= \frac{[2.28 - (0.003104 + 0.001853 \times 1 + 0.001985 \times 1)]^2}{3} \\
&+ \frac{[1.5 - (0.003104 + 0.001853 \times 0.5349 + 0.001985 \times 0.6667)]^2}{3} \\
&+ \frac{[0.88 - (0.003104 + 0.001853 \times 0 + 0.001985 \times 0)]^2}{3} = 2.7232
\end{aligned}
$$

Compared with the previous MSE = 2.7320 after the first iteration, it is noticed that the MSE is reduced to 2.7232, indicating that the performance of the linear regression model has been improving, though slowly, due to the small learning rate.

Further, the same learning process is set to repeat a total of 500,000 times to keep updating the bias and weights under the L1 regularization, until the mean loss between the true and predicted output values stabilizes; only then are the optimal bias and weights said to be obtained. For conciseness, we will not present the detailed calculations from the third iteration onwards in the chapter, but tabulate the bias, weights and MSE for the first and last five iterations in Table **3.3**. If necessary, readers are encouraged to try several more iterations to have a deeper understanding of the process of training a linear regression model with L1 regularization. Besides, Fig. (**3.2**) depicts the overall trend that MSE generally decreases with the increase of learning iterations and finally stabilizes. However, it is also worth mentioning that MSE plummets at the beginning and achieves the minimum (0.0367) at the 2658th iteration. At this point, the L1 regularization mechanism considers that it has reached the stage of overfitting (*i.e.*, the model would perform very well on the training dataset, but not generalize well on previously unseen data) and then rectifies it to make the model less specific to the training data. This is also reflected in Fig. (**3.2**), in which MSE for the training dataset starts to rise a bit gradually after the minimum and finally stabilizes at 0.0636.

Table 3.3. The bias, weights and MSE values for the first and last five iterations for training the L1 regularized linear regression model.

Iteration	*b*	*w₁*	*w₂*	*MSE*
1	0.001553	0.0009274	0.0009933	2.7320
2	0.003104	0.001853	0.001985	2.7232
3	0.004652	0.002777	0.002975	2.7143
4	0.006198	0.003700	0.003963	2.7055
5	0.007741	0.004621	0.004949	2.6967
...	...	...	...	...
499,996	1.1466	0.7949	0.00004110	0.0636
499,997	1.1466	0.7949	0.00003797	0.0636
499,998	1.1466	0.7949	0.00003485	0.0636
499,999	1.1466	0.7949	0.00003172	0.0636
500,000	1.1466	0.7949	0.00002860	0.0636

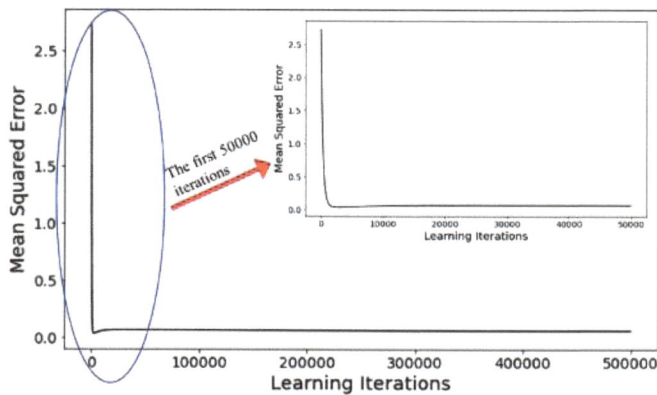

Fig. (3.2). Mean squared error (MSE) *vs.* learning iteration for training the L1 regularized linear regression model.

As can be seen from (Table **3.3**) and Fig. (**3.2**), MSE finally stabilizes at 0.0636, which suggests that we have trained a good linear regression model under L1 regularization. The final obtained bias and weights are $b = 1.1466$, $w_1 = 0.7949$ and $w_2 = 0.00002860$. One important highlight of L1 regularization is that it shrinks the weights of the features it deems less important, often to zero, effectively serving as a method for feature selection. However, it is worth noting that these "less important" features are determined by the model and data, and may or may not align with domain-specific knowledge or broader context. The resulting linear regression model can be written as:

$$Y = b + \sum_{j=1}^{2} w_j \cdot \left(\text{normalized } X_j\right)$$

Here, $b = 1.1466$, $w_1 = 0.7949$ and $w_2 = 0.00002860$.

As Max-min normalization was performed during the training process, it needs to be reflected in the final model as well. That is why normalized X_j is shown here.

Now, we can use this trained linear regression model to make predictions for previously unseen data (*i.e.*, new data). For instance, there is a new house with 1200 sqft and 3 bedrooms. To predict the price of the house, normalization needs to be applied first using the maximum and minimum values of each respective feature from the training dataset. Recall that the maximum and minimum of size_sqft are 1600 and 740; the maximum and minimum of num_bedrooms are 5 and 2. So, the normalized X_1 for size_sqft and normalized X_2 for num_bedrooms will be:

$$\text{normalized } X_1 = \frac{1200 - 740}{1600 - 740} = 0.5349$$

$$\text{normalized } X_2 = \frac{3 - 2}{5 - 2} = 0.3333$$

Next, plug the normalized feature values into the equation of linear regression model:

$$Y = b + \sum_{j=1}^{2} w_j \cdot \left(\text{normalized } X_j\right)$$
$$= 1.1466 + 0.7949 \times 0.5349 + 0.00002860 \times 0.3333 = 1.572$$

Therefore, for the house with 1200 sqft and 3 bedrooms, the sale price is predicted to be 1.572 million dollars.

3.4. SAMPLE CODES AND COMPARISON OF L1 REGULARIZATION FOR LINEAR REGRESSION

Following the mathematics and numerical example discussed in Sections 3.2 and 3.3, we have implemented the L1 regularized linear regression machine learning model with the aforementioned small dataset from scratch in Python. The code is similar to that of the original linear regression discussed in Chapter 2. The difference lies in the function, update_bias_weights, because of the addition of the L1 regularization term (*i.e.*, $\lambda\|W\|_1$) to the loss function. Readers are encouraged to have their Jupyter Notebook (or other Python IDE) ready and try the codes along with reading. The complete code file can be downloaded from our shared folder in Google Drive:

https://drive.google.com/drive/folders/1FqJvo4ZPazNbEH_GlHFoodqvegnQmHcn?usp=share_link

Firstly, only the pandas and numpy libraries are imported.

```python
import pandas as pd
import numpy as np
```

Secondly, a **loss_MSE** function is created for calculating the MSE between the known true output values and predicted output values by the linear regression model. See the docstring of the loss_MSE function to understand its usage.

```python
def loss_MSE(X, Y, b, W1, W2): # Mean Squared Error
    """
    Find the Mean Squared Error between true outputs and pre-
dicted outputs
    Inputs: X - list, the input feature values
            Y - list, the true output values
            b - float/int, bias
            W1 - float/int, weight for the 1st feature (i.e.,
size_sqft)
            W2 - float/int, weight for the 2nd feature (i.e.,
num_bedrooms)
    Outputs: MSE - float
    """
    X1 = [val[0] for val in X]
    X2 = [val[1] for val in X]
    m = len(X)
    total_loss = 0
    for i in range(m):
        total_loss = total_loss + (Y[i] - (b + X1[i]*W1 +
X2[i]*W2))**2
    MSE = total_loss / m
    return MSE
```

Thirdly, an **update_bias_weights** is created to update the values of bias and weights based on the gradient descent optimization algorithm. The equations (3.4) to (3.11), which we derived in Section 3.2, are well translated into Python codes in this function. See the docstring of the update_bias_weights function to understand its usage.

```python
def update_bias_weights(X, Y, b, W1, W2, learning_rate, pen-
alty_coef):
    """

    Update the bias and weights based on Gradient Descent
    Inputs: X - list, the input feature values
            Y - list, the true output values
            b - float/int, bias
            W1 - float/int, weight for the 1st feature
            W2 - float/int, weight for the 2nd feature
            learning_rate - float, used in Gradient Descent
            penalty_coef - float, the penalty coefficient that
multiplies the L1 norm
    Outputs: (b, W1, W2) - tuple, the updated bias and weights
    """

    X1 = [val[0] for val in X]
    X2 = [val[1] for val in X]
    m = len(X)
    dL_dW1 = 0
    dL_dW2 = 0
    dL_db  = 0

    for i in range(m):
        dL_db  = dL_db  + 1 * (Y[i] - (b + X1[i]*W1 +
X2[i]*W2)) * (-1)
        dL_dW1 = dL_dW1 + 1 * (Y[i] - (b + X1[i]*W1 +
X2[i]*W2)) * (-X1[i])
        dL_dW2 = dL_dW2 + 1 * (Y[i] - (b + X1[i]*W1 +
X2[i]*W2)) * (-X2[i])

    dL_db  = dL_db/m

    if W1 >= 0:
        dL_dW1 = dL_dW1/m + penalty_coef
    else:
        dL_dW1 = dL_dW1/m - penalty_coef

    if W2 >= 0:
        dL_dW2 = dL_dW2/m + penalty_coef
    else:
        dL_dW2 = dL_dW2/m - penalty_coef

    b  = b  - dL_db  * learning_rate
    W1 = W1 - dL_dW1 * learning_rate
    W2 = W2 - dL_dW2 * learning_rate

    return (b, W1, W2)
```

Fourthly, a **train** function is created to oversee the training process for specific iterations and write the log of loss/MSE history. See the docstring of the train function to understand its usage.

```python
def train(X, Y, b, W1, W2, learning_rate, learning_iterations,
penalty_coef):
    """
    Train linear regression model for the specified iterations
    Inputs: X - list, the input feature values
            Y - list, the true output values
            b - float/int, bias
            W1 - float/int, weight for the 1st feature (i.e.,
size_sqft)
            W2 - float/int, weight for the 2nd feature (i.e.,
num_bedrooms)
            learning_rate - float, the learning rate used in
Gradient Descent
            learning_iterations - int, the number of times of
training
    Outputs: (loss_history, b, W1, W2) - tuple, return the
loss_history, and the final bias and weights
    """

    loss_history = []

    for i in range(learning_iterations):
        b, W1, W2 = update_bias_weights(X, Y, b, W1, W2,
learning_rate, penalty_coef)

        # find MSE after the ith iteration of updating bias
and weights
        loss = loss_MSE(X, Y, b, W1, W2)
        loss_history.append(loss)

        if i < 5 or i >= learning_iterations-5:
            print ("iter={:d} \t b={:.7f} \t W1={:.7f} \t
W2={:.8f} \t MSE={:.6f}".format(i+1, b, W1, W2, loss))
    return (loss_history, b, W1, W2)
```

Fifthly, a **max_min_norm** function is created to normalize the values of input features (*i.e., X*). See the docstring of the max_min_norm function to understand its usage.

```python
def max_min_norm(X):
    """

    Normalize dataset by using the Max-min normalization tech-
nique
    Inputs: X - numpy.ndarray, the dataset for normalization
    Outputs: (X_norm, np.array(max_min_vals)) - tuple, return
the normalized dataset,

                                              and the max and
min values of each feature
    """

    X_norm = X.copy().astype(float)
    max_min_vals = []
    for col in range(0, X_norm.shape[1]):
        X_max = X_norm[:, col].max()
        X_min = X_norm[:, col].min()
        X_range = X_max - X_min
        X_norm[:, col] = (X_norm[:, col] - X_min) / X_range
        max_min_vals.append({"X_max":X_max, "X_min":X_min,
 "X_range":X_range})
    return (X_norm, np.array(max_min_vals))
```

Sixthly, we store the small dataset as a numpy array, invoke the max_min_norm function for normalization, initialize bias and weights, set learning rate, iterations and penalty coefficient that multiplies the L1 regularization term, then invoke the train function to start building our first L1 regularized linear regression model, after decomposing and fully understanding every single step of the process.

```
# The small dataset
data = np.array([[1600,5,2.28],
                 [1200,4,1.5],
                 [740,2,0.88]])
col_names = ['size_sqft', 'num_bedrooms', 'sale_price_mil-
lion']
print(pd.DataFrame(data, columns=col_names), "\n")

X = data[:, :-1] # all rows, all columns except the last col-
umn
Y = data[:, -1]  # all rows, last column only

X, max_min_vals = max_min_norm(X) # normalize the input fea-
tures
X = X.tolist()
Y = Y.tolist()

# Initialize bias and weights
initial_b  = 0
initial_W1 = 0
initial_W2 = 0

# Set learing rate and iterations
learning_rate = 0.001
learning_iterations = 500000

# Set penalty coefficient
penalty_coef = 0.1

# Start the training of linear regression model
loss_history, b, W1, W2 = train(X, Y, initial_b, initial_W1,
initial_W2, learning_rate, learning_iterations, penalty_coef)
```

```
       size_sqft  num_bedrooms  sale_price_million
0       1600.0          5.0                  2.28
1       1200.0          4.0                  1.50
2        740.0          2.0                  0.88
```

```
iter=1    b=0.0015533     W1=0.0009274     W2=0.00099333    MSE=2.732037
iter=2    b=0.0031041     W1=0.0018532     W2=0.00198491    MSE=2.723171
iter=3    b=0.0046523     W1=0.0027774     W2=0.00297472    MSE=2.714334
iter=4    b=0.0061979     W1=0.0036999     W2=0.00396278    MSE=2.705526
iter=5    b=0.0077409     W1=0.0046208     W2=0.00494909    MSE=2.696748
iter=499996      b=1.1465907      W1=0.7948922      W2=0.00004110     MSE=0.063597
iter=499997      b=1.1465908      W1=0.7948922      W2=0.00003797     MSE=0.063598
iter=499998      b=1.1465908      W1=0.7948922      W2=0.00003485     MSE=0.063598
iter=499999      b=1.1465908      W1=0.7948923      W2=0.00003172     MSE=0.063599
iter=500000      b=1.1465909      W1=0.7948923      W2=0.00002860     MSE=0.063599
```

Finally, the trained linear regression model is utilized to predict the price of the house (new data) with 1200 sqft and 3 bedrooms:

```python
new_data = np.array([[1200,3]], dtype = float)

# Max-min normalization
for col in range(0, new_data.shape[1]):
    new_data[:, col] = ((new_data[:, col]
                            - max_min_vals[col]['X_min'])
                            / max_min_vals[col]['X_range'])

# Use the final bias and weights values
predicted_price = b + W1*new_data[0][0] + W2*new_data[0][1]

print(f'''For the house with 1200 sqft and 3 bedrooms,
the sale price is predicted to be {np.round(pre-
dicted_price,3)} million.''')
```

```
For the house with 1200 sqft and 3 bedrooms,
the sale price is predicted to be 1.572 million.
```

We then compare the above results with those from the off-the-shelf L1 regularized linear regression model (*i.e.*, Lasso) offered by the scikit-learn library. These include the final bias and weights after training, the final MSE, and the predicted price for the house (new data) with 1200 sqft and 3 bedrooms. The codes are as follows:

```python
import numpy as np
from sklearn.preprocessing import MinMaxScaler
from sklearn.linear_model import Lasso

# The small dataset
data = np.array([[1600,5,2.28],
                 [1200,4,1.5],
                 [740,2,0.88]])
X = data[:, :-1] # all rows, all columns except the last column
Y = data[:, -1]  # all rows, last column only

scaler = MinMaxScaler()
scaler.fit(X)
X = scaler.transform(X) # update to Normalized X

l1_reg = Lasso(alpha=0.1) # alpha is the penalty coefficient
l1_reg.fit(X, Y)

print(f"The optimal bias found by sklearn:
{np.round(l1_reg.intercept_,4)}")
print(f"The optimal weights found by sklearn:
{np.round(l1_reg.coef_,4)}")

from sklearn.metrics import mean_squared_error
print("\nMSE found by sklearn:", np.round(mean_squared_er-
ror(Y, l1_reg.predict(X)),4))
```

```
The optimal bias found by sklearn: 1.1466
The optimal weights found by sklearn: [0.795 0.   ]

MSE found by sklearn: 0.0636
```

```
new_data = np.array([[1200,3]], dtype = float)
new_data = scaler.transform(new_data)

print(f'''For the house with 1200 sqft and 3 bedrooms,
the sale price is predicted to be {np.round(l1_reg.pre-
dict(new_data),3)} million.''')
```

```
For the house with 1200 sqft and 3 bedrooms,
the sale price is predicted to be [1.572] million.
```

As can be seen from the results using the scikit-learn L1 regularized linear regression model (*i.e.*, Lasso), the final bias, weights, and MSE values are the same as or extremely close to those given by our own L1 regularized linear regression model (*i.e.*, $b = 1.1466$, $w_1 = 0.7949$, $w_2 = 0.00002860$, and $MSE = 0.0636$). Furthermore, the predicted price for the previously unseen house with 1200 sqft and 3 bedrooms is also the same as that produced by our own model (*i.e.*, 1.572 million).

3.5. MATHEMATICS OF L2 REGULARIZATION FOR LINEAR REGRESSION

The L2 regularized linear regression starts again with the general equation of linear regression when having more than one independent variable X (*i.e.*, input feature), as follows:

$$Y = b + \sum_{j=1}^{n} w_j X_j \tag{3.13}$$

Here,

Y is the output
b is the bias
n is the number of input features
w_j is the weight of the jth feature
X_j is input value of the jth feature

Let us use lowercase x_i to denote the feature values of the ith sample (out of the total m rows of samples from the training dataset), then x_{ij} will be the value of the jth feature (out of the total n input features) at the ith sample, as shown in Fig. (**3.1**). Lowercase y_i is used to represent the known output value (*i.e.*, true output value) of the ith sample, and $\hat{y}_i$ is used to denote the corresponding predicted output value by the linear equation model. Equation (3.13) is then updated to Equation (3.14).

$$\hat{y}_i = b + \sum_{j=1}^{n} w_j x_{ij} \tag{3.14}$$

Here,

$i \in [1, m]$
m is the number of training samples
x_{ij} is the value of the jth feature at the ith sample

b is the bias
n is the number of input features
w_j is the weight of the jth feature
$\hat{y}_i$ is the predicted value for the ith sample

Up to this step, everything is the same as the original linear regression discussed in Chapter 2. The key difference brought by L2 regularization is the introduction of the penalty term $\lambda \|W\|_2^2$ (*i.e.*, penalty coefficient multiplies the squared L2 norm of weights) to the loss function, as follows:

$$L = m \cdot MSE + \lambda \|W\|_2^2 = m \cdot \frac{\sum_{i=1}^{m} (y_i - \hat{y}_i)^2}{m} + \lambda \|W\|_2^2$$
$$= \left(\sum_{i=1}^{m} (y_i - \hat{y}_i)^2 \right) + \lambda \|W\|_2^2 \tag{3.15}$$

Here,

L is the loss between true and predicted outputs

m is the number of training samples

y_i is the true value for the ith sample
$\hat{y}_i$ is the predicted value for the ith sample

λ is the penalty coefficient

$\|W\|_2^2$ is the squared L2 norm of weights,

$$\|W\|_2^2 = \sum_{j=1}^{n} w_j^2 = w_1^2 + w_2{}^2 + \cdots + w_n{}^2$$

A gradient descent optimization algorithm is utilized to find the optimal bias and weights by iteratively tweaking their values a tiny bit at a time in the direction of reducing the loss. Before that, we need to find the partial derivative of the mean loss (L) with respect to the bias and weights, namely, $\frac{\partial L}{\partial b}$ and $\frac{\partial L}{\partial w_j}$, denoting the contribution to the mean loss by the bias and each of the weights.

$$\frac{\partial L}{\partial b} = \frac{\partial(\sum_{i=1}^{m} (y_i - \hat{y}_i)^2)}{\partial b} + \frac{\partial(\lambda\|W\|_2^2)}{\partial b}$$
$$= \frac{\partial(\sum_{i=1}^{m} (y_i - \hat{y}_i)^2)}{\partial \hat{y}_i} \cdot \frac{\partial \hat{y}_i}{\partial b} + 0 \tag{3.16}$$

$$\frac{\partial \hat{y}_i}{\partial b} = 1 \tag{3.17}$$

$$\therefore \frac{\partial L}{\partial b} = \sum_{i=1}^{m} 2(y_i - \hat{y}_i)(-1) \tag{3.18}$$

$$\frac{\partial \hat{y}_i}{\partial w_j} = x_{ij} \tag{3.19}$$

$$\frac{\partial L}{\partial w_j} = \frac{\partial(\sum_{i=1}^{m} (y_i - \hat{y}_i)^2)}{\partial w_j} + \frac{\partial(\lambda\|W\|_2^2)}{\partial w_j}$$
$$= \frac{\partial(\sum_{i=1}^{m} (y_i - \hat{y}_i)^2)}{\partial \hat{y}_i} \cdot \frac{\partial \hat{y}_i}{\partial w_j}$$
$$+ \frac{\partial\left(\lambda(w_1^2 + w_2{}^2 + \cdots w_j{}^2 + \cdots + w_n{}^2)\right)}{\partial w_j}$$
$$= \left(\sum_{i=1}^{m} 2(y_i - \hat{y}_i)(-1)(x_{ij})\right) + 2\lambda w_j \tag{3.20}$$

Here, $j \in [1, n]$ and n is the number of features.

Subsequently, gradient descent is used to update the bias, b (Equation 3.21) and the weights, w (Equation 3.22).

$$b_{\text{new}} = b_{\text{old}} - \frac{\partial L}{\partial b} \cdot \alpha \qquad (3.21)$$

$$w_{j \text{ new}} = w_{j \text{ old}} - \frac{\partial L}{\partial w_j} \cdot \alpha \qquad (3.22)$$

Here, α is the learning rate (typically a small value, *e.g.*, $0.1, 0.01, 0.001$).

3.6 NUMERICAL EXAMPLE OF L2 REGULARIZATION FOR LINEAR REGRESSION

Same as the original linear regression discussed in Chapter 2 and the L1 regularized linear regression discussed in Section 3.3 of the current chapter, we employ a small training dataset presented in (Table **3.1**) with only 3 samples (*i.e.*, $m = 3$), which pertains to the sale price of houses in millions of dollars (abbreviated as **sale_price_million**) based on 2 input features (*i.e.*, $n = 2$), namely, the size of house in square feet (abbreviated as **size_sqft**) and the total number of bedrooms in house (abbreviated as **num_bedrooms**). In other words, for this example, X is size_sqft and num_bedrooms, and Y is sale_price_million. Our task is to build a best-fit linear regression model that maps the X and Y under L2 regularization.

Next, normalize the feature values (*i.e.*, the values of size_sqft and num_bedrooms columns) to bring them to a common scale between 0 and 1, using Max-min normalization, as shown in Equation (3.12). The small dataset after Max-min normalization on the features is presented in (Table **3.2**).

Now, let us start the machine learning process to build a linear regression model with L2 regularization.

Initialize the bias:

$$b = 0$$

Initialize the weight for feature size_sqft:

$$w_1 = 0$$

Initialize the weight for feature num_bedrooms:

$$w_2 = 0$$

Set the learning rate:

$$\alpha = 0.001$$

Set the penalty coefficient:

$$\lambda = 0.1$$

Note that for simplicity of writing and expression, all the following x_{ij} refers to the *normalized* x_{ij} by default, unless otherwise stated.

3.6.1. Start the First Iteration of Learning

Take the input values of the first training sample and calculate the predicted $\hat{y}_1$:

$$\hat{y}_1 = b + \sum_{j=1}^{n} w_j x_{1j} = b + w_1 x_{11} + w_2 x_{12} = 0 + 0 \times 1 + 0 \times 1 = 0$$

Take the input values of the second training sample and calculate the predicted $\hat{y}_2$:

$$\hat{y}_2 = b + \sum_{j=1}^{n} w_j x_{2j} = b + w_1 x_{21} + w_2 x_{22} = 0 + 0 \times 0.5349 + 0 \times 0.6667 = 0$$

Take the input values of the third training sample and calculate the predicted $\hat{y}_3$:

$$\hat{y}_3 = b + \sum_{j=1}^{n} w_j x_{3j} = b + w_1 x_{31} + w_2 x_{32} = 0 + 0 \times 0 + 0 \times 0 = 0$$

Calculate the value of $\frac{\partial L}{\partial b}$:

$$\frac{\partial L}{\partial b} = \sum_{i=1}^{m} 2(y_i - \hat{y}_i)(-1)$$

$$= 2 \times (2.28 - 0) \times (-1) + 2 \times (1.5 - 0) \times (-1) + 2 \times (0.88 - 0) \times (-1)$$

$$= -9.3200$$

Calculate the value of $\frac{\partial L}{\partial w_1}$:

$$\frac{\partial L}{\partial w_1} = \left(\sum_{i=1}^{m} 2(y_i - \hat{y}_i)(-1)(x_{i1}) \right) + 2\lambda w_1$$

$$= 2 \times (2.28 - 0) \times (-1) \times 1 + 2 \times (1.5 - 0) \times (-1) \times 0.5349 + 2 \times (0.88 - 0) \times (-1) \times 0 + 2 \times 0.1 \times 0$$

$$= -6.1647$$

Calculate the value of $\frac{\partial L}{\partial w_2}$:

$$\frac{\partial L}{\partial w_2} = \left(\sum_{i=1}^{m} 2(y_i - \hat{y}_i)(-1)(x_{i2}) \right) + 2\lambda w_2$$

$$= 2 \times (2.28 - 0) \times (-1) \times 1 + 2 \times (1.5 - 0) \times (-1) \times 0.6667 + 2 \times (0.88 - 0) \times (-1) \times 0 + 2 \times 0.1 \times 0$$

$$= -6.5601$$

Update the b value:

$$b_{\text{new}} = b_{\text{old}} - \frac{\partial L}{\partial b} \cdot \alpha = 0 - (-9.3200) \times 0.001 = 0.009320$$

Update the w_1 value:

$$w_{1\,\text{new}} = w_{1\,\text{old}} - \frac{\partial L}{\partial w_1} \cdot \alpha = 0 - (-6.1647) \times 0.001 = 0.006165$$

Update the w_2 value:

$$w_{2\,\text{new}} = w_{2\,\text{old}} - \frac{\partial L}{\partial w_2} \cdot \alpha = 0 - (-6.5601) \times 0.001 = 0.006560$$

3.6.2. End the First Iteration of Learning

Now after the very first iteration of learning, there is a set of newly updated bias and weights, *i.e.*, $b = 0.009320$, $w_1 = 0.006165$ and $w_2 = 0.006560$. With these, the latest MSE can be calculated as follows:

$$MSE = \frac{\sum_{i=1}^{m} (y_i - \hat{y}_i)^2}{m}$$

$$= \frac{[2.28 - (0.009320 + 0.006165 \times 1 + 0.006560 \times 1)]^2}{3}$$

$$+ \frac{[1.5 - (0.009320 + 0.006165 \times 0.5349 + 0.006560 \times 0.6667)]^2}{3}$$

$$+ \frac{[0.88 - (0.009320 + 0.006165 \times 0 + 0.006560 \times 0)]^2}{3}$$

$$= 2.6853$$

So, the latest MSE after the first iteration of learning with L2 regularization is 2.6853. Next, it will continue with the second iteration.

3.6.3. Start the Second Iteration of Learning

Take the input values of the first training sample and calculate the predicted $\hat{y}_1$:

$$\hat{y}_1 = b + \sum_{j=1}^{n} w_j x_{1j} = b + w_1 x_{11} + w_2 x_{12}$$

$$= 0.009320 + 0.006165 \times 1 + 0.006560 \times 1 = 0.02205$$

Take the input values of the second training sample and calculate the predicted $\hat{y}_2$:

$$\hat{y}_2 = b + \sum_{j=1}^{n} w_j x_{2j} = b + w_1 x_{21} + w_2 x_{22}$$

$$= 0.009320 + 0.006165 \times 0.5349 + 0.006560 \times 0.6667 = 0.01699$$

Take the input values of the third training sample and calculate the predicted $\hat{y}_3$:

$$\hat{y}_3 = b + \sum_{j=1}^{n} w_j x_{3j} = b + w_1 x_{31} + w_2 x_{32}$$

$$= 0.009320 + 0.006165 \times 0 + 0.006560 \times 0 = 0.009320$$

Calculate the value of $\frac{\partial L}{\partial b}$:

$$\frac{\partial L}{\partial b} = \sum_{i=1}^{m} 2(y_i - \hat{y}_i)(-1)$$

$$= 2 \times (2.28 - 0.02205) \times (-1) + 2 \times (1.5 - 0.01699) \times (-1) + 2 \times (0.88 - 0.009320) \times (-1)$$

$$= -9.2233$$

Calculate the value of $\frac{\partial L}{\partial w_1}$:

$$\frac{\partial L}{\partial w_1} = \left(\sum_{i=1}^{m} 2(y_i - \hat{y}_i)(-1)(x_{i1}) \right) + 2\lambda w_1$$

$$= 2 \times (2.28 - 0.02205) \times (-1) \times 1 + 2 \times (1.5 - 0.01699) \times (-1) \times 0.5349 + 2 \times (0.88 - 0.009320) \times (-1) \times 0 + 2 \times 0.1 \times 0.006165$$

$$= -6.1012$$

Calculate the value of $\frac{\partial L}{\partial w_2}$:

$$\frac{\partial L}{\partial w_2} = \left(\sum_{i=1}^{m} 2(y_i - \hat{y}_i)(-1)(x_{i2}) \right) + 2\lambda w_2$$

$$= 2 \times (2.28 - 0.02205) \times (-1) \times 1 + 2 \times (1.5 - 0.01699) \times (-1) \times 0.6667 + 2 \times (0.88 - 0.009320) \times (-1) \times 0 + 2 \times 0.1 \times 0.006560$$

$$= -6.4920$$

Update the b value:

$$b_{\text{new}} = b_{\text{old}} - \frac{\partial L}{\partial b} \cdot \alpha = 0.009320 - (-9.2233) \times 0.001 = 0.01854$$

Update the w_1 value:

$$w_{1\,new} = w_{1\,old} - \frac{\partial L}{\partial w_1} \cdot \alpha = 0.006165 - (-6.1012) \times 0.001 = 0.01227$$

Update the w_2 value:

$$w_{2\,new} = w_{2\,old} - \frac{\partial L}{\partial w_2} \cdot \alpha = 0.006560 - (-6.4920) \times 0.001 = 0.01305$$

3.6.4. End the Second Iteration of Learning

At the end of the second iteration of learning with L2 regularization, we get a set of newly updated bias and weights, *i.e.*, $b = 0.01854, w_1 = 0.01227$ and $w_2 = 0.01305$. With these, the latest MSE can be calculated, as follows:

$$
\begin{aligned}
MSE &= \frac{\sum_{i=1}^{m} (y_i - \hat{y}_i)^2}{m} \\
&= \frac{[2.28 - (0.01854 + 0.01227 \times 1 + 0.01305 \times 1)]^2}{3} \\
&+ \frac{[1.5 - (0.01854 + 0.01227 \times 0.5349 + 0.01305 \times 0.6667)]^2}{3} \\
&+ \frac{[0.88 - (0.01854 + 0.01227 \times 0 + 0.01305 \times 0)]^2}{3} \\
&= 2.6307
\end{aligned}
$$

Compared with the previous $MSE = 2.6853$ after the first iteration, it is noticed that the MSE is reduced to 2.6307, indicating that the performance of the linear regression model has been improving, though slowly, due to the small learning rate.

Further, the same learning process is set to repeat a total of 500,000 times to keep updating the bias and weights under the L2 regularization, until the mean loss between the true and predicted output values stabilizes; only then are the optimal bias and weights said to be obtained. For conciseness, we will not present the detailed calculations from the third iteration onwards in the chapter, but tabulate the bias, weights and MSE for the first and last five iterations in (Table **3.4**). If necessary, readers are encouraged to try several more iterations to have a deeper understanding of the process of training a linear regression model with L2 regularization. Besides, Fig. (**3.3**) depicts that MSE decreases with the increase of learning iterations and finally stabilizes.

Table 3.4. The bias, weights and MSE values for the first and last five iterations for training the L2 regularized linear regression model.

Iteration	b	w_1	w_2	*MSE*
1	0.009320	0.006165	0.006560	2.6853
2	0.01854	0.01227	0.01305	2.6307
3	0.02767	0.01830	0.01948	2.5773
4	0.03670	0.02428	0.02583	2.5250
5	0.04564	0.03019	0.03213	2.4737
...	...	...	...	...
499,996	0.8907	0.7100	0.5390	0.01222
499,997	0.8907	0.7100	0.5390	0.01222
499,998	0.8907	0.7100	0.5390	0.01222
499,999	0.8907	0.7100	0.5390	0.01222
500,000	0.8907	0.7100	0.5390	0.01222

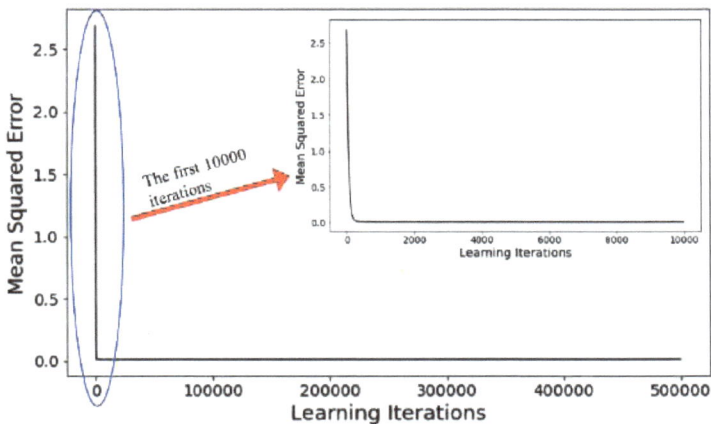

Fig. (3.3). Mean squared error (MSE) *vs.* learning iteration for training the L2 regularized linear regression model.

As can be seen from (Table **3.4**) and Fig. (**3.3**), MSE finally stabilizes at a small value, 0.01222, suggesting that we have trained a good linear regression model with L2 regularization, in which the optimal bias and weights are $b = 0.8907$, $w_1 = 0.71$ and $w_2 = 0.539$. The resulting linear regression model can be written as:

$$Y = b + \sum_{j=1}^{2} w_j \cdot \left(\text{normalized } X_j \right)$$

Here, $b = 0.8907$, $w_1 = 0.71$ and $w_2 = 0.539$.

As Max-min normalization was performed during the training process, it needs to be reflected in the final model as well. That is why normalized X_j is shown here.

Now, we can use this trained linear regression model to make predictions for previously unseen data (*i.e.*, new data). For instance, there is a new house with 1200 sqft and 3 bedrooms. To predict the price of the house, normalization needs to be applied first using the maximum and minimum values of each respective feature from the training dataset. Recall that the maximum and minimum of size_sqft are 1600 and 740; the maximum and minimum of num_bedrooms are 5 and 2. So, the normalized X_1 for size_sqft and normalized X_2 for num_bedrooms will be:

$$\text{normalized } X_1 = \frac{1200 - 740}{1600 - 740} = 0.5349$$

$$\text{normalized } X_2 = \frac{3 - 2}{5 - 2} = 0.3333$$

Next, plug the normalized feature values into the equation of the linear regression model:

$$Y = b + \sum_{j=1}^{2} w_j \cdot \left(\text{normalized } X_j \right)$$
$$= 0.8907 + 0.71 \times 0.5349 + 0.539 \times 0.3333 = 1.45$$

Therefore, for the house with 1200 sqft and 3 bedrooms, the sale price is predicted to be 1.45 million dollars.

3.7. SAMPLE CODES AND COMPARISON OF L2 REGULARIZATION FOR LINEAR REGRESSION

Following the mathematics and numerical example discussed in Sections 3.5 and 3.6, we have implemented the L2 regularized linear regression machine learning model with the aforementioned small dataset from scratch in Python. The code is similar to that of the original linear regression discussed in Chapter 2. The difference lies in the function, update_bias_weights, because of the addition of the L2 regularization term (*i.e.*, $\lambda \|W\|_2^2$) to the loss function. Readers are encouraged to have their Jupyter Notebook (or other Python IDE) ready and try the codes along with reading. The complete code file can be downloaded from our shared folder in Google Drive:

https://drive.google.com/drive/folders/1FqJvo4ZPazNbEH_GlHFoodqvegnQmHc n?usp=share_link

Firstly, only the pandas and numpy libraries are imported.

```python
import pandas as pd
import numpy as np
```

Secondly, a **loss_MSE** function is created for calculating the MSE between the known true output values and predicted output values by the linear regression model. See the docstring of the loss_MSE function to understand its usage.

```python
def loss_MSE(X, Y, b, W1, W2): # Mean Squared Error
    """
    Find the Mean Squared Error between true outputs and pre-
dicted outputs
    Inputs: X - list, the input feature values
            Y - list, the true output values
            b - float/int, bias
            W1 - float/int, weight for the 1st feature (i.e.,
size_sqft)
            W2 - float/int, weight for the 2nd feature (i.e.,
num_bedrooms)
    Outputs: MSE - float
    """
    X1 = [val[0] for val in X]
    X2 = [val[1] for val in X]
    m = len(X)
    total_loss = 0
    for i in range(m):
        total_loss = total_loss + (Y[i] - (b + X1[i]*W1 +
X2[i]*W2))**2
    MSE = total_loss / m
    return MSE
```

Thirdly, an **update_bias_weights** is created to update the values of bias and weights based on gradient descent optimization algorithm. The Equations (3.16) to (3.22), which we derived in Section 3.5, are well translated into Python codes in this function. See the docstring of the update_bias_weights function to understand its usage.

```python
def update_bias_weights(X, Y, b, W1, W2, learning_rate, pen-
alty_coef):
    """
    Update the bias and weights based on Gradient Descent
    Inputs: X - list, the input feature values
            Y - list, the true output values
            b - float/int, bias
            W1 - float/int, weight for the 1st feature (i.e.,
size_sqft)
            W2 - float/int, weight for the 2nd feature (i.e.,
num_bedrooms)
            learning_rate - float, the learning rate used in
Gradient Descent
            penalty_coef - float, the penalty coefficient that
multiplies the L2 term
    Outputs: (b, W1, W2) - tuple, the updated bias and weights
    """
    X1 = [val[0] for val in X]
    X2 = [val[1] for val in X]
    m = len(X)
    dL_dW1 = 0
    dL_dW2 = 0
    dL_db  = 0

    for i in range(m):
        dL_db  = dL_db  + 2 * (Y[i] - (b + X1[i]*W1 +
X2[i]*W2)) * (-1)
        dL_dW1 = dL_dW1 + 2 * (Y[i] - (b + X1[i]*W1 +
X2[i]*W2)) * (-X1[i])
        dL_dW2 = dL_dW2 + 2 * (Y[i] - (b + X1[i]*W1 +
X2[i]*W2)) * (-X2[i])

    dL_db  = dL_db
    dL_dW1 = dL_dW1 + (2 * penalty_coef * W1)
    dL_dW2 = dL_dW2 + (2 * penalty_coef * W2)

    b  = b  - dL_db  * learning_rate
    W1 = W1 - dL_dW1 * learning_rate
    W2 = W2 - dL_dW2 * learning_rate

    return (b, W1, W2)
```

Fourthly, a **train** function is created to oversee the training process for specific iterations and write the log of loss/MSE history. See the docstring of the train function to understand its usage.

```python
def train(X, Y, b, W1, W2, learning_rate, learning_iterations,
penalty_coef):
    """

    Train linear regression model for the specified iterations
    Inputs: X - list, the input feature values
            Y - list, the true output values
            b - float/int, bias
            W1 - float/int, weight for the 1st feature (i.e.,
size_sqft)
            W2 - float/int, weight for the 2nd feature (i.e.,
num_bedrooms)
            learning_rate - float, the learning rate used in
Gradient Descent
            learning_iterations - int, the number of times of
training
    Outputs: (loss_history, b, W1, W2) - tuple, return the
loss_history, and the final bias and weights
    """

    loss_history = []

    for i in range(learning_iterations):
        b, W1, W2 = update_bias_weights(X, Y, b, W1, W2,
learning_rate, penalty_coef)

        # find MSE after the ith iteration of updating bias
and weights
        loss = loss_MSE(X, Y, b, W1, W2)
        loss_history.append(loss)

        if i < 5 or i >= learning_iterations-5:
            print ("iter={:d} \t b={:.5f} \t W1={:.5f} \t
W2={:.5f} \t MSE={}".format(i+1, b, W1, W2, loss))
    return (loss_history, b, W1, W2)
```

Fifthly, a **max_min_norm** function is created to normalize the values of input features (*i.e.*, *X*). See the docstring of the max_min_norm function to understand its usage.

```python
def max_min_norm(X):
    """

    Normalize dataset by using the Max-min normalization tech-
nique
    Inputs: X - numpy.ndarray, the dataset for normalization
    Outputs: (X_norm, np.array(max_min_vals)) - tuple, return
the normalized dataset,
                                            and the max and
min values of each feature
    """

    X_norm = X.copy().astype(float)
    max_min_vals = []
    for col in range(0, X_norm.shape[1]):
        X_max = X_norm[:, col].max()
        X_min = X_norm[:, col].min()
        X_range = X_max - X_min
        X_norm[:, col] = (X_norm[:, col] - X_min) / X_range
        max_min_vals.append({"X_max":X_max, "X_min":X_min,
"X_range":X_range})
    return (X_norm, np.array(max_min_vals))
```

Sixthly, we store the small dataset as a numpy array, invoke the max_min_norm function for normalization, initialize bias and weights, set learning rate, iterations and penalty coefficient that multiplies the L1 regularization term, then invoke the train function to start building our first L1 regularized linear regression model, after decomposing and fully understanding every single step of the process.

```
# The small dataset
data = np.array([[1600,5,2.28],
                 [1200,4,1.5],
                 [740,2,0.88]])
col_names = ['size_sqft', 'num_bedrooms', 'sale_price_mil-
lion']
print(pd.DataFrame(data, columns=col_names), "\n")

X = data[:, :-1] # all rows, all columns except the last col-
umn
Y = data[:, -1]  # all rows, last column only

X, max_min_vals = max_min_norm(X) # normalize the input fea-
tures
X = X.tolist()
Y = Y.tolist()

# Initialize bias and weights
initial_b  = 0
initial_W1 = 0
initial_W2 = 0

# Set learing rate and iterations
learning_rate = 0.001
learning_iterations = 500000

# Set penalty coefficient
penalty_coef = 0.1

# Start the training of linear regression model
loss_history, b, W1, W2 = train(X, Y, initial_b, initial_W1,
initial_W2, learning_rate, learning_iterations, penalty_coef)
```

```
    size_sqft  num_bedrooms  sale_price_million
0     1600.0          5.0                  2.28
1     1200.0          4.0                  1.50
2      740.0          2.0                  0.88
```

```
iter=1    b=0.00932   W1=0.00616      W2=0.00656      MSE=2.6852541963795
iter=2    b=0.01854   W1=0.01227      W2=0.01305      MSE=2.630717277484433
iter=3    b=0.02767   W1=0.01830      W2=0.01948      MSE=2.577299090027449
iter=4    b=0.03670   W1=0.02428      W2=0.02583      MSE=2.5249766308904253
iter=5    b=0.04564   W1=0.03019      W2=0.03213      MSE=2.473727370498438
iter=499996      b=0.89066   W1=0.70996      W2=0.53900      MSE=0.0122176028514185
iter=499997      b=0.89066   W1=0.70996      W2=0.53900      MSE=0.0122176028514185
iter=499998      b=0.89066   W1=0.70996      W2=0.53900      MSE=0.0122176028514185
iter=499999      b=0.89066   W1=0.70996      W2=0.53900      MSE=0.0122176028514185
iter=500000      b=0.89066   W1=0.70996      W2=0.53900      MSE=0.0122176028514185
```

Finally, the trained linear regression model is utilized to predict the price of the house (new data) with 1200 sqft and 3 bedrooms:

```python
new_data = np.array([[1200,3]], dtype = float)

# Max-min normalization
for col in range(0, new_data.shape[1]):
    new_data[:, col] = ((new_data[:, col]
                         - max_min_vals[col]['X_min'])
                         / max_min_vals[col]['X_range'])

# Use the final bias and weights values
predicted_price = b + W1*new_data[0][0] + W2*new_data[0][1]

print(f'''For the house with 1200 sqft and 3 bedrooms,
the sale price is predicted to be {np.round(pre-
dicted_price,3)} million.''')
```

```
For the house with 1200 sqft and 3 bedrooms,
the sale price is predicted to be 1.45 million.
```

We then compare the above results with those from the off-the-shelf L2 regularized linear regression model (*i.e.*, Ridge) offered by the scikit-learn library. These include the final bias and weights after training, the final MSE, and the predicted price for the house (new data) with 1200 sqft and 3 bedrooms. The codes are as follows:

```python
import numpy as np
from sklearn.preprocessing import MinMaxScaler
from sklearn.linear_model import Ridge

# The small dataset
data = np.array([[1600,5,2.28],
                 [1200,4,1.5],
                 [740,2,0.88]])
X = data[:, :-1] # all rows, all columns except the last column
Y = data[:, -1]  # all rows, last column only

scaler = MinMaxScaler()
scaler.fit(X)
X = scaler.transform(X) # update to Normalized X

l2_reg = Ridge(alpha=0.1) # alpha is the penalty coefficient
l2_reg.fit(X, Y)

print(f"The optimal bias found by sklearn:
{np.round(l2_reg.intercept_,4)}")
print(f"The optimal weights found by sklearn:
{np.round(l2_reg.coef_,4)}")

from sklearn.metrics import mean_squared_error
print("\nMSE found by sklearn:", np.round(mean_squared_er-
ror(Y, l2_reg.predict(X)),5))
```

```
The optimal bias found by sklearn: 0.8907
The optimal weights found by sklearn: [0.71  0.539]

MSE found by sklearn: 0.01222
```

```
new_data = np.array([[1200,3]], dtype = float)
new_data = scaler.transform(new_data)

print(f'''For the house with 1200 sqft and 3 bedrooms,
the sale price is predicted to be {np.round(l2_reg.pre-
dict(new_data),3)} million.''')
```

```
For the house with 1200 sqft and 3 bedrooms,
the sale price is predicted to be [1.45] million.
```

As can be seen from the results using scikit-learn L2 regularized linear regression model (*i.e.*, Ridge), the final bias, weights, and MSE values are the same as those given by our own L1 regularized linear regression model (*i.e.*, $b = 0.8907$, $w_1 = 0.71$ and $w_2 = 0.539$, and $MSE = 0.01222$). Furthermore, the predicted price for the previously unseen house with 1200 sqft and 3 bedrooms is also the same as that produced by our own model (*i.e.*, 1.45 million).

CONCLUSION

In this chapter, we discussed the concepts of L1 and L2 regularization in the context of linear regression. To make the material more accessible, we kept abstract mathematical theories to a minimum. Instead, we focused on a concrete numerical example with a small dataset for predicting the sale price of houses, walking through it step by step. We also provided sample codes and comparisons with the Lasso and Ridge models from the off-the-shelf library, scikit-learn. By the end of the chapter, readers should have a well-rounded understanding of how L1 and L2 regularization works behind the scenes in preventing the risk of overfitting, how the mathematics relates to the implementation and performance of the techniques, and be better equipped to apply them in their projects.

REFERENCES

[1] R. Tibshirani, "Regression shrinkage and selection *via* the lasso", *J. R. Stat. Soc. B,* vol. 58, no. 1, pp. 267-288, 1996.
      http://dx.doi.org/10.1111/j.2517-6161.1996.tb02080.x
[2] G. James, D. Witten, T. Hastie, and R. Tibshirani, *An introduction to statistical learning: With applications in R.,* 1st ed Springer: New York, NY, 2013.
      http://dx.doi.org/10.1007/978-1-4614-7138-7
[3] M.H.J. Gruber, *Improving efficiency by shrinkage: The James-stein and ridge regression estimators.* Routledge, 2017.
      http://dx.doi.org/10.1201/9780203751220

[4] C.M. Bishop, *Pattern Recognition and Machine Learning.* Springer: New York, NY, 2006.

[5] Z. Wang, S.A. Irfan, C. Teoh, and P.H. Bhoyar, *Linear Regression" in Numerical Machine Learning.* Bentham Science, 2023.

[6] Z. Wang, S.A. Irfan, C. Teoh, and P.H. Bhoyar, *Logistic Regression" in Numerical Machine Learning.* Bentham Science, 2023.

## CHAPTER 4

Logistic Regression

Abstract: This chapter delves into logistic regression, a widely used machine learning algorithm for classification tasks, with a focus on maintaining accessibility by minimizing abstract mathematical concepts. We present a concrete numerical example employing a small dataset to predict the ease of selling houses in the property market, guiding readers through each step of the process. Additionally, we supply sample codes and draw comparisons with the logistic regression model available in the scikit-learn library. Upon completion of this chapter, readers will have gained a comprehensive understanding of the inner workings of logistic regression, its relationship to algorithm implementation and performance, and the knowledge necessary to apply it to practical applications.

Keywords: Logistic Regression, Classification, Numerical Example, Small Dataset, Scikit-Learn

4.1. INTRODUCTION TO LOGISTIC REGRESSION

Logistic regression is a supervised machine learning algorithm for modeling the probability of a discrete output given input features [1, 2]. Despite its name, logistic regression is more of a classification model than a regression model. It is commonly used to model a dichotomous (binary) output, *i.e.,* anything with two possible values/classes/labels, such as true/false, yes/no, 1/0, on/off, good/bad, malignant/ benign, and pass/fail, to name a few. The foundation of logistic regression lies in its ability to model the relationship between input features and a categorical outcome by utilizing the logistic function, also known as the sigmoid function. This function ensures that the predicted probabilities lie within the range of 0 and 1, making it suitable for classification tasks. Logistic regression has gained immense popularity due to its simplicity, interpretability, and efficiency in various real-world applications. Some of these applications include spam filtering, customer churn prediction, medical diagnosis, and credit risk assessment.

Unlike linear regression, logistic regression does not require the assumption of a linear relationship between the independent (X) and dependent (Y) variables. Besides, the errors between the true and predicted outputs need not conform to a normal distribution. Moreover, the spread of the errors (*i.e.,* the variance of the errors) need not be constant along the values of dependent variables; that is, homoscedasticity is not required. However, there are still several essential assumptions for logistic regression [3, 4]. Firstly, when there is more than one independent variable (X), it requires little or no correlation between the independent

Zhiyuan Wang, Sayed Ameenuddin Irfan, Christopher Teoh & Priyanka Hriday Bhoyar

variables (*i.e.,* little or no multicollinearity). Secondly, it assumes that the independent variable(s) have a linear relationship with the logarithm of the odds; odds is just another way of expressing probability (P) and is defined as the ratio of the probability of an event occurring to the probability of an event not occurring (*i.e.,* $\frac{P}{1-P}$). Thirdly, by default, logistic regression is used to solve binary classification problems, requiring the dependent variable (Y) to be dichotomous. On the other hand, it is worth mentioning that with some modifications and improvements like the one-*vs*-rest (OvR) method, logistic regression can be scaled up for solving multi-class classification problems. Nevertheless, multi-class classification is outside the scope of the present chapter as it focuses on binary classification using the logistic regression algorithm.

4.2. MATHEMATICS OF LOGISTIC REGRESSION

Mathematically, the linear regression discussed in Chapter 2 can be upgraded to logistic regression after introducing a sigmoid function for mapping the linear output to probability and employing a different loss function.

In comparison with Equation (2.2) in Chapter 2 for linear regression, the only change made to Equation (4.1) here is to use a variable Z (rather than Y) to represent the linear output, which is just an intermediate result in the process of logistic regression.

$$Z = b + \sum_{j=1}^{n} w_j X_j \qquad (4.1)$$

Here,

Z is the intermediate linear output
b is the bias
n is the number of input features
w_j is the weight of the jth feature
X_j is input value of the jth feature

The sigmoid function for mapping the intermediate linear output to probability is defined as Equation (4.2) and plotted in Fig. (**4.1**).

$$Y = \frac{1}{1 + e^{-Z}} \qquad (4.2)$$

Here,

Z is the intermediate linear output from the linear Equation (4.1)
Y is the mapped probability

As can be seen from Fig. (**4.1**), the sigmoid function maps the linear output Z into a probability Y that is in the range of 0 to 1. The default threshold is 0.5, meaning that if $Y \geq 0.5$, it will be rounded up to 1 and predicted as class 1; whereas, if $Y < 0.5$, it will be rounded down to 0 and predicted as class 0.

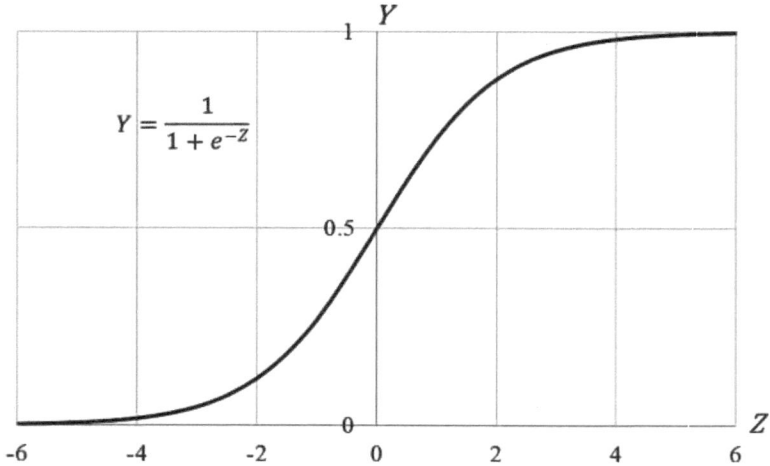

Fig. (4.1). Plot of the sigmoid function.

Fig. (4.2). Illustration of notations using an exemplary training dataset.

Similar to the notations used in Chapter 2 for linear regression, lowercase x_i is used to denote the feature values of the ith sample (out of the total m rows of samples from the training dataset), then x_{ij} will be the value of the jth feature (out of the total n input features) at the ith sample, as shown in Fig. (**4.2**). Lowercase y_i is used to represent the known output (*i.e.*, true output) of the ith sample, and $\hat{y}_i$ is used to denote the corresponding predicted output (*i.e.*, the mapped probability after the sigmoid function) by the logistic regression model. The general term Equations (4.1) and (4.2) are updated to Equations (4.3) and (4.4), respectively.

$$z_i = b + \sum_{j=1}^{n} w_j x_{ij} \qquad (4.3)$$

Here,

$i \in [1, m]$; m is the number of training samples
x_{ij} is the value of the jth feature at the ith sample

b is the bias
n is the number of input features
w_j is the weight of the jth feature
z_i is the intermediate linear output for the ith sample

$$\hat{y}_i = \frac{1}{1 + e^{-z_i}} \qquad (4.4)$$

Here,

$i \in [1, m]$; m is the number of training samples

z_i is the intermediate linear output for the ith sample

$\hat{y}_i$ is the predicted output (*i.e.*, the mapped probability) for the ith sample

Cross-entropy loss function (also known as logistic loss or log loss function) is employed in logistic regression to quantify the error between the true and predicted outputs, which is defined in Equation (4.5).

$$L_i = -[y_i \log(\hat{y}_i) + (1 - y_i) \log(1 - \hat{y}_i)] \qquad (4.5)$$

Here,

$i \in [1, m]$; m is the number of training samples

L_i is the loss for the ith sample

y_i is the true output for the ith sample
$\hat{y}_i$ is the predicted output (*i.e.*, the mapped probability) for the ith sample
log used is the natural logarithm (*i.e.*, to the base e)

The mean loss of all samples is defined in Equation (4.6).

$$L = \frac{1}{m} \sum_{i=1}^{m} L_i \tag{4.6}$$

Here,

L_i is the loss for the ith sample

L is the mean loss
m is the number of training samples

Gradient descent optimization algorithm is utilized to find the optimal bias and weights by iteratively tweaking their values a tiny bit at a time in the direction of reducing the loss. Before that, we need to find the partial derivative of the mean loss (L) with respect to the bias and weights, namely, $\frac{\partial L}{\partial b}$ and $\frac{\partial L}{\partial w_j}$, denoting the contribution to the mean loss by the bias and each of the weights. This can be done by applying the chain rule, shown in Equations (4.7) to (4.12):

$$\frac{\partial L_i}{\partial \hat{y}_i} = -\frac{y_i}{\hat{y}_i} + \frac{1 - y_i}{1 - \hat{y}_i} \tag{4.7}$$

$$\frac{\partial \hat{y}_i}{\partial z_i} = \frac{e^{-z_i}}{(1 + e^{-z_i})^2} = \hat{y}_i(1 - \hat{y}_i) \tag{4.8}$$

$$\frac{\partial z_i}{\partial b} = 1 \tag{4.9}$$

$$\therefore \frac{\partial L}{\partial b} = \frac{1}{m} \sum_{i=1}^{m} \frac{\partial L_i}{\partial b} = \frac{1}{m} \sum_{i=1}^{m} \left(\frac{\partial L_i}{\partial \hat{y}_i} \cdot \frac{\partial \hat{y}_i}{\partial z_i} \cdot \frac{\partial z_i}{\partial b} \right)$$

$$= \frac{1}{m} \sum_{i=1}^{m} \left[\left(-\frac{y_i}{\hat{y}_i} + \frac{1 - y_i}{1 - \hat{y}_i} \right) \cdot \hat{y}_i (1 - \hat{y}_i) \cdot 1 \right]$$

$$= \frac{1}{m} \sum_{i=1}^{m} (\hat{y}_i - y_i) \tag{4.10}$$

$$\frac{\partial z_i}{\partial w_j} = x_{ij} \tag{4.11}$$

$$\therefore \frac{\partial L}{\partial w_j} = \frac{1}{m} \sum_{i=1}^{m} \frac{\partial L_i}{\partial w_j} = \frac{1}{m} \sum_{i=1}^{m} \left(\frac{\partial L_i}{\partial \hat{y}_i} \cdot \frac{\partial \hat{y}_i}{\partial z_i} \cdot \frac{\partial z_i}{\partial w_j} \right)$$

$$= \frac{1}{m} \sum_{i=1}^{m} \left[\left(-\frac{y_i}{\hat{y}_i} + \frac{1 - y_i}{1 - \hat{y}_i} \right) \cdot \hat{y}_i (1 - \hat{y}_i) \cdot x_{ij} \right]$$

$$= \frac{1}{m} \sum_{i=1}^{m} (\hat{y}_i - y_i) x_{ij} \tag{4.12}$$

Here, $j \epsilon [1, n]$ and n is the number of features.

Subsequently, gradient descent is used to update the bias, b (Equation 4.13) and the weights, w (Equation 4.14).

$$b_{\text{new}} = b_{\text{old}} - \frac{\partial L}{\partial b} \cdot \alpha \tag{4.13}$$

$$w_{j\,\text{new}} = w_{j\,\text{old}} - \frac{\partial L}{\partial w_j} \cdot \alpha \tag{4.14}$$

Here, α is the learning rate (typically a small value, *e.g.*, 0.1, 0.01, 0.001).

It is worth noting that the mathematical notations and Python codes in this chapter are somewhat similar to those in Chapters 2 and 3 of this book [5, 6]. However, the focuses of Chapters 2 and 3 are on linear regression and regularization, respectively, whereas the focus of this chapter is on logistic regression.

4.3. NUMERICAL EXAMPLE OF LOGISTIC REGRESSION

Suppose we have a small training dataset presented in Table **4.1** with only 3 samples (*i.e.,* $m = 3$), which has two features, namely, the size of a house in square feet (abbreviated as **size_sqft**) and the total number of bedrooms in the house (abbreviated as **num_bedrooms**), as well as one output about whether it is easy to sell the house (abbreviated as **is_easy_sell**) in the property market. The output is dichotomous with only two possible values/classes/labels (*i.e.,* 0 and 1), where 0 means No (not easy to sell) and 1 means Yes (easy to sell). In other words, for this example, X is size_sqft and num_bedrooms, and Y is is_easy_sell. Our task is to build a logistic regression model that maps the X and Y.

Table 4.1. The small dataset for logistic regression.

size_sqft	num_bedrooms	is_easy_sell
1600	5	1
1200	4	1
740	2	0

Next, normalize the feature values (*i.e.,* the values of size_sqft and num_bedrooms columns) to bring them to a common scale between 0 and 1, using Max-min normalization. as shown in Equation (4.15). Without normalization, some feature(s) might dominate the machine learning process.

$$normalized \ x_{ij} = \frac{x_{ij} - min_{k \in [1,m]} x_{kj}}{max_{k \in [1,m]} x_{kj} - min_{k \in [1,m]} x_{kj}} \tag{4.15}$$

The maximum and minimum of size_sqft are 1600 and 740, respectively. Likewise, the maximum and minimum of num_bedrooms are 5 and 2, respectively. The output labels (*i.e.,* is_easy_sell) are left as they are, without any normalization. The small dataset after Max-min normalization on the features is presented in Table **4.2**.

Table 4.2. The small dataset after Max-min normalization for logistic regression.

size_sqft	num_bedrooms	is_easy_sell
1	1	1
0.5349	0.6667	1
0	0	0

Now, let us start the machine learning process to build a logistic regression model.

Initialize the bias:

$$b = 0$$

Initialize the weight for feature size_sqft:

$$w_1 = 0$$

Initialize the weight for feature num_bedrooms:

$$w_2 = 0$$

Set the learning rate:

$$\alpha = 0.1$$

Note that for simplicity of writing and expression, all the following x_{ij} refers to the *normalized* x_{ij} by default, unless otherwise stated.

4.3.1. Start the First Iteration of Learning

Take the input values of the first training sample and calculate the predicted $\hat{y}_1$:

$$z_1 = b + \sum_{j=1}^{n} w_j x_{1j} = b + w_1 x_{11} + w_2 x_{12} = 0 + 0 \times 1 + 0 \times 1 = 0$$

$$\hat{y}_1 = \frac{1}{1 + e^{-z_1}} = 0.5$$

Take the input values of the second training sample and calculate the predicted $\hat{y}_2$:

$$z_2 = b + \sum_{j=1}^{n} w_j x_{2j} = b + w_1 x_{21} + w_2 x_{22} = 0 + 0 \times 0.5349 + 0 \times 0.6667 = 0$$

$$\hat{y}_2 = \frac{1}{1 + e^{-z_2}} = 0.5$$

Take the input values of the third training sample and calculate the predicted $\hat{y}_3$:

$$z_3 = b + \sum_{j=1}^{n} w_j x_{3j} = b + w_1 x_{31} + w_2 x_{32} = 0 + 0 \times 0 + 0 \times 0 = 0$$

$$\hat{y}_3 = \frac{1}{1 + e^{-z_3}} = 0.5$$

Calculate the value of $\frac{\partial L}{\partial b}$:

$$\frac{\partial L}{\partial b} = \frac{1}{m} \sum_{i=1}^{m} (\hat{y}_i - y_i)$$

$$= \frac{1}{3}[(0.5 - 1) + (0.5 - 1) + (0.5 - 0)]$$

$$= -0.1667$$

Calculate the value of $\frac{\partial L}{\partial w_1}$:

$$\frac{\partial L}{\partial w_1} = \frac{1}{m} \sum_{i=1}^{m} (\hat{y}_i - y_i) x_{i1}$$

$$= \frac{1}{3}[(0.5 - 1) \times 1 + (0.5 - 1) \times 0.5349 + (0.5 - 0) \times 0]$$

$$= -0.2558$$

Calculate the value of $\frac{\partial L}{\partial w_2}$:

$$\frac{\partial L}{\partial w_2} = \frac{1}{m} \sum_{i=1}^{m} (\hat{y}_i - y_i) x_{i2}$$

$$= \frac{1}{3} [(0.5 - 1) \times 1 + (0.5 - 1) \times 0.6667 + (0.5 - 0) \times 0]$$

$$= -0.2778$$

Update the b value:

$$b_{new} = b_{old} - \frac{\partial L}{\partial b} \cdot \alpha = 0 - (-0.1667) \times 0.1 = 0.01667$$

Update the w_1 value:

$$w_{1\ new} = w_{1\ old} - \frac{\partial L}{\partial w_1} \cdot \alpha = 0 - (-0.2558) \times 0.1 = 0.02558$$

Update the w_2 value:

$$w_{2\ new} = w_{2\ old} - \frac{\partial L}{\partial w_2} \cdot \alpha = 0 - (-0.2778) \times 0.1 = 0.02778$$

4.3.2. End the First Iteration of Learning

Now after the very first iteration of learning, there is a set of newly updated bias and weights, *i.e.*, $b = 0.01667$, $w_1 = 0.02558$ and $w_2 = 0.02778$. With these, the latest cross-entropy loss can be calculated as follows:

$$z_1 = b + \sum_{j=1}^{n} w_j x_{1j} = b + w_1 x_{11} + w_2 x_{12}$$
$$= 0.01667 + 0.02558 \times 1 + 0.02778 \times 1 = 0.07003$$

$$\hat{y}_1 = \frac{1}{1 + e^{-z_1}} = 0.5175$$

$$L_1 = -[y_1 \log(\hat{y}_1) + (1 - y_1) \log(1 - \hat{y}_1)]$$
$$= -[1 \times \log(0.5175) + 0 \times \log(1 - 0.5175)] = 0.6587$$

$$z_2 = b + \sum_{j=1}^{n} w_j x_{2j} = b + w_1 x_{21} + w_2 x_{22}$$
$$= 0.01667 + 0.02558 \times 0.5349 + 0.02778 \times 0.6667$$
$$= 0.04887$$

$$\hat{y}_2 = \frac{1}{1 + e^{-z_2}} = 0.5122$$

$$L_2 = -[y_2 \log(\hat{y}_2) + (1 - y_2) \log(1 - \hat{y}_2)]$$
$$= -[1 \times \log(0.5122) + 0 \times \log(1 - 0.5122)] = 0.6690$$

$$z_3 = b + \sum_{j=1}^{n} w_j x_{3j} = b + w_1 x_{31} + w_2 x_{32}$$
$$= 0.01667 + 0.02558 \times 0 + 0.02778 \times 0 = 0.01667$$

$$\hat{y}_3 = \frac{1}{1 + e^{-z_3}} = 0.5042$$

$$L_3 = -[y_3 \log(\hat{y}_3) + (1 - y_3) \log(1 - \hat{y}_3)]$$
$$= -[0 \times \log(0.5042) + 1 \times \log(1 - 0.5042)] = 0.7016$$

$$L = \frac{1}{m} \sum_{i=1}^{m} L_i = \frac{1}{3}(0.6587 + 0.6690 + 0.7016) = 0.6764$$

So, the latest cross-entropy loss after the first iteration of learning is 0.6764. Next, let us continue with the second iteration with the updated bias and weights determined above.

4.3.3. Start the Second Iteration of Learning

Take the input values of the first training sample and calculate the predicted $\hat{y}_1$:

$$z_1 = b + \sum_{j=1}^{n} w_j x_{1j} = b + w_1 x_{11} + w_2 x_{12}$$
$$= 0.01667 + 0.02558 \times 1 + 0.02778 \times 1 = 0.07003$$

$$\hat{y}_1 = \frac{1}{1 + e^{-z_1}} = 0.5175$$

Take the input values of the second training sample and calculate the predicted $\hat{y}_2$:

$$z_2 = b + \sum_{j=1}^{n} w_j x_{2j} = b + w_1 x_{21} + w_2 x_{22}$$
$$= 0.01667 + 0.02558 \times 0.5349 + 0.02778 \times 0.6667$$
$$= 0.04887$$

$$\hat{y}_2 = \frac{1}{1 + e^{-z_2}} = 0.5122$$

Take the input values of the third training sample and calculate the predicted $\hat{y}_3$:

$$z_3 = b + \sum_{j=1}^{n} w_j x_{3j} = b + w_1 x_{31} + w_2 x_{32}$$
$$= 0.01667 + 0.02558 \times 0 + 0.02778 \times 0 = 0.01667$$

$$\hat{y}_3 = \frac{1}{1 + e^{-z_3}} = 0.5042$$

Calculate the value of $\frac{\partial L}{\partial b}$:

$$\frac{\partial L}{\partial b} = \frac{1}{m} \sum_{i=1}^{m} (\hat{y}_i - y_i) = \frac{1}{3}[(0.5175 - 1) + (0.5122 - 1) + (0.5042 - 0)]$$
$$= -0.1554$$

Calculate the value of $\frac{\partial L}{\partial w_1}$:

$$\frac{\partial L}{\partial w_1} = \frac{1}{m} \sum_{i=1}^{m} (\hat{y}_i - y_i) x_{i1}$$

$$= \frac{1}{3}[(0.5175 - 1) \times 1 + (0.5122 - 1) \times 0.5349 + (0.5042 - 0) \times 0]$$
$$= -0.2478$$

Calculate the value of $\frac{\partial L}{\partial w_2}$:

$$\frac{\partial L}{\partial w_2} = \frac{1}{m} \sum_{i=1}^{m} (\hat{y}_i - y_i) x_{i2}$$

$$= \frac{1}{3}[(0.5175 - 1) \times 1 + (0.5122 - 1) \times 0.6667 + (0.5042 - 0) \times 0]$$

$$= -0.2692$$

Update the b value:

$$b_{new} = b_{old} - \frac{\partial L}{\partial b} \cdot \alpha = 0.01667 - (-0.1554) \times 0.1 = 0.03221$$

Update the w_1 value:

$$w_{1\ new} = w_{1\ old} - \frac{\partial L}{\partial w_1} \cdot \alpha = 0.02558 - (-0.2478) \times 0.1 = 0.05036$$

Update the w_2 value:

$$w_{2\ new} = w_{2\ old} - \frac{\partial L}{\partial w_2} \cdot \alpha = 0.02778 - (-0.2692) \times 0.1 = 0.05470$$

4.3.4. End the Second Iteration of Learning

At the end of the second iteration of learning, we get a set of newly updated bias and weights, *i.e.,* $b = 0.03221$, $w_1 = 0.05036$ and $w_2 = 0.05470$. With these, the latest cross-entropy loss can be calculated as follows:

$$z_1 = b + \sum_{j=1}^{n} w_j x_{1j} = b + w_1 x_{11} + w_2 x_{12}$$

$$= 0.03221 + 0.05036 \times 1 + 0.05470 \times 1 = 0.1373$$

$$\hat{y}_1 = \frac{1}{1 + e^{-z_1}} = 0.5343$$

$$L_1 = -[y_1 \log(\hat{y}_1) + (1 - y_1) \log(1 - \hat{y}_1)]$$
$$= -[1 \times \log(0.5343) + 0 \times \log(1 - 0.5343)] = 0.6268$$

$$z_2 = b + \sum_{j=1}^{n} w_j x_{2j} = b + w_1 x_{21} + w_2 x_{22}$$
$$= 0.03221 + 0.05036 \times 0.5349 + 0.05470 \times 0.6667$$
$$= 0.09562$$

$$\hat{y}_2 = \frac{1}{1 + e^{-z_2}} = 0.5239$$

$$L_2 = -[y_2 \log(\hat{y}_2) + (1 - y_2) \log(1 - \hat{y}_2)]$$
$$= -[1 \times \log(0.5239) + 0 \times \log(1 - 0.5239)] = 0.6465$$

$$z_3 = b + \sum_{j=1}^{n} w_j x_{3j} = b + w_1 x_{31} + w_2 x_{32}$$
$$= 0.03221 + 0.05036 \times 0 + 0.05470 \times 0 = 0.03221$$

$$\hat{y}_3 = \frac{1}{1 + e^{-z_3}} = 0.5081$$

$$L_3 = -[y_3 \log(\hat{y}_3) + (1 - y_3) \log(1 - \hat{y}_3)]$$
$$= -[0 \times \log(0.5081) + 1 \times \log(1 - 0.5081)] = 0.7095$$

$$L = \frac{1}{m} \sum_{i=1}^{m} L_i = \frac{1}{3}(0.6268 + 0.6465 + 0.7095) = 0.6609$$

Compared with the previous cross-entropy loss = 0.6764 after the first iteration, it is noticed that the loss is now reduced to 0.6609, indicating that the performance of the logistic regression model has been improving!

Further, the same learning process is set to repeat a total of 500,000 times to keep updating the bias and weights until the cross-entropy loss between the true and predicted output values stabilizes and reaches its minimum; only then are the optimal bias and weights said to be obtained. For conciseness, we will not present the detailed calculations from the third iteration onwards in the chapter, but tabulate the bias, weights, and cross-entropy loss for the first and last five iterations in Table **4.3**. If necessary, readers are encouraged to try several more iterations following the detailed calculations above to have a deeper understanding of the process of training a logistic regression model. Besides, Fig. (**4.3**) depicts that cross-entropy loss decreases with the increase of learning iterations and finally stabilizes.

Table 4.3. The bias, weights and cross-entropy loss values for the first and last five iterations.

Iteration	b	w_1	w_2	$loss$
1	0.01667	0.02558	0.02778	0.6764
2	0.03221	0.05036	0.05470	0.6609
3	0.04666	0.07438	0.08081	0.6465
4	0.06010	0.09766	0.10613	0.6331
5	0.07256	0.12024	0.13071	0.6206
...	...	...	...	...
499,996	-8.40173	12.6909	15.4901	1.296×10^{-4}
499,997	-8.40174	12.6909	15.4901	1.296×10^{-4}
499,998	-8.40174	12.6909	15.4901	1.296×10^{-4}
499,999	-8.40174	12.6909	15.4901	1.296×10^{-4}
500,000	-8.40174	12.6909	15.4901	1.296×10^{-4}

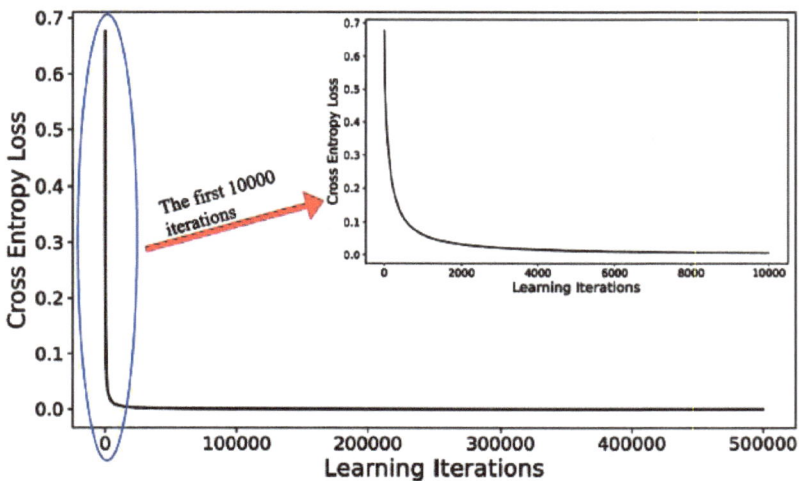

Fig. (4.3). Cross-entropy loss *vs.* learning iterations.

As demonstrated in Table **4.3** and Fig. (**4.3**), cross-entropy loss finally stabilizes at a very tiny value, 1.296×10^{-4}, suggesting that we have trained a good logistic regression model and the corresponding optimal bias and weights are determined. The resulting model can be written as:

$$Z = b + \sum_{j=1}^{n} w_j \cdot (\text{ normalized } X_j)$$

$$Y = \frac{1}{1 + e^{-Z}}$$

Here, $b = -8.40174, w_1 = 12.6909$ and $w_2 = 15.4901$.

As Max-min normalization was performed during the training process, it needs to be reflected in the final model as well. That is why normalized X_j is shown here.

Now, we can use this trained logistic regression model to make predictions for previously unseen data (*i.e.*, new data). For instance, there is a new house with 1200 sqft and 3 bedrooms. To predict whether it is easy to sell the house in the property market, normalization needs to be applied first using the maximum and minimum values of each respective feature from the training dataset. Recall that the maximum and minimum of size_sqft are 1600 and 740; the maximum and minimum of num_bedrooms are 5 and 2. So, the normalized X_1 for size_sqft and normalized X_2 for num_bedrooms will be:

$$\text{normalized } X_1 = \frac{1200 - 740}{1600 - 740} = 0.5349$$

$$\text{normalized } X_2 = \frac{3 - 2}{5 - 2} = 0.3333$$

Next, plug the normalized feature values into the equations of the logistic regression model:

$$Z = b + \sum_{j=1}^{n} w_j \cdot (\text{ normalized } X_j)$$
$$= -8.40174 + 12.6909 \times 0.5349 + 15.4901 \times 0.3333$$
$$= 3.5495$$

$$Y = \frac{1}{1 + e^{-z}} = 0.9721$$

Since $0.9721 \geq 0.5$, the predicted class will be 1, which means it is easy to sell this house with 1200 sqft and 3 bedrooms.

4.4. SAMPLE CODES AND COMPARISON

Following the mathematics and numerical example discussed in Sections 4.2 and 4.3, we have implemented the logistic regression machine learning model with the aforementioned small dataset from scratch in Python. Readers are encouraged to have their Jupyter Notebook (or other Python IDE) ready and execute the codes along with reading. The complete code file can be downloaded from our shared folder in Google Drive:

https://drive.google.com/drive/folders/1FqJvo4ZPazNbEH_GlHFoodqvegnQmHcn?usp=share_link

Firstly, only the pandas and numpy libraries are imported.

```python
import pandas as pd
import numpy as np
```

Secondly, three functions, namely, **sigmoid_func**, **y_hat_calc**, and **cross_ entropy _loss**, are created to calculate the mapped probability by sigmoid function, predicted probability output, and cross-entropy loss, respectively. See the docstrings of the functions to understand their usage.

Thirdly, two functions, namely, **predict_class** and **predict_accuracy**, are created to output the predicted class and compute subset accuracy, respectively. See the docstrings of the functions to understand their usage.

```
def sigmoid_func(z):
    """

    The implementaion of sigmoid function
    Inputs: z - numpy.ndarray, the intermediate linear results
    Outputs: y_hat - numpy.ndarray, the mapped probaility by
sigmoid
    """

    y_hat = 1/(1 + np.exp(-z))
    return y_hat

def y_hat_calc(X, b, W):
    """

    Calculate the predicted outputs, y_hat
    Inputs: X - numpy.ndarray, the input feature values
            b - float/int, bias
            W - numpy.ndarray, weights of features
    Outputs: y_hat.T - numpy.ndarray, the transposed predicted
probaility outputs
    """

    z = np.dot(W.T, X) + b
    y_hat = sigmoid_func(z)
    return y_hat.T

def cross_entropy_loss(Y, y_hat):
    """

    Find the cross-entropy loss between true outputs and pre-
dicted outputs
    Inputs: Y - numpy.ndarray, the true output values
            y_hat - numpy.ndarray, the predicted output values
    Outputs: L - numpy.ndarray, the cross-entropy loss
    """

    L = - np.sum( np.dot(Y.T, np.log(y_hat)) + np.dot((1 -
Y).T, np.log(1 - y_hat)) ) / Y.shape[0]
    return L
```

```python
def predict_class(X, b, W):
    '''
    Calculate the predicted class based on default threshold
0.5
    Inputs: X - numpy.ndarray, the input feature values
            b - float/int, bias
            W - numpy.ndarray, weights of features
    Outputs: numpy.ndarray, the predicted class, 1 or 0
    '''
    return np.where(y_hat_calc(X, b, W) >= 0.5, 1, 0)

def predict_accuracy(Y, X, b, W):
    '''
    Calculate the accuracy between true and predicted outputs
    Inputs: Y - numpy.ndarray, the true output values
            X - numpy.ndarray, the input feature values
            b - float/int, bias
            W - numpy.ndarray, weights of features
    Outputs: float, in range of [0.0, 1.0]
    '''
    return np.sum(Y == predict_class(X, b, W)) / Y.shape[0]
```

Fourthly, an **update_bias_weights** is created to update the values of bias and weights based on the gradient descent optimization algorithm. The Equations (4.7) to (4.14), which we derived in Section 4.2, are well translated into Python codes in this function. See the docstring of the update_bias_weights function to understand its usage.

```python
def update_bias_weights(X, Y, y_hat, b, W, learning_rate):
    """
    Update the bias and weights based on Gradient Descent
    Inputs: X - numpy.ndarray, the input feature values
            Y - numpy.ndarray, the true output values
            y_hat - numpy.ndarray, the predicted output values
            b - float/int, bias
            W - numpy.ndarray, weights of features
            learning_rate - float, the learning rate used in
Gradient Descent
    Outputs: (b, W) - tuple, the updated bias and weights
    """
    dL_db = np.sum(y_hat - Y) / X.shape[1]
    dL_dW = np.dot(X, (y_hat-Y)) / X.shape[1]

    b = b - dL_db * learning_rate
    W = W - dL_dW * learning_rate

    return (b, W)
```

Fifthly, a **train** function is created to oversee the training process for specific iterations and write the log of cross-entropy loss history. See the docstring of the train function to understand its usage.

```python
def train(X, Y, b, W, learning_rate, learning_iterations):
    """
    Train logistic regression model for the specified itera-
tions
    Inputs: X - numpy.ndarray, the input feature values
            Y - numpy.ndarray, the true output values
            b - float/int, bias
            W - numpy.ndarray, weights of features
            learning_rate - float, the learning rate used in
Gradient Descent
            learning_iterations - int, the number of times of
training
    Outputs: (loss_history, b, W) - tuple, return the
loss_history, and the final bias and weights
    """

    loss_history = []
    for i in range(learning_iterations):
        y_hat = y_hat_calc(X, b, W)

        b, W = update_bias_weights(X, Y, y_hat, b, W, learn-
ing_rate)

        # find loss after the ith iteration of updating bias
and weights
        L = cross_entropy_loss(Y, y_hat_calc(X, b, W))
        loss_history.append(L)

        if i < 5 or i >= learning_iterations-5:
            print ("iter={:d} \t b={:.5f} \t W1={:.5f} \t
W2={:.5f} \t loss={}".format(i+1, b, W[0][0], W[1][0], L))

    return (loss_history, b, W)
```

Sixthly, a **max_min_norm** function is created to normalize the values of input features (*i.e., X*). See the docstring of the max_min_norm function to understand its usage.

```python
# The small dataset
data = np.array([[1600,5,1],
                 [1200,4,1],
                 [740,2,0]])
col_names = ['size_sqft', 'num_bedrooms', 'is_easy_sell']
print(pd.DataFrame(data, columns=col_names), "\n")

X = data[:, :-1] # all rows, all columns except the last col-
umn
Y = data[:, -1]  # all rows, last column only

X, max_min_vals = max_min_norm(X) # normalize the input fea-
tures
X = X.T
Y = Y.reshape(-1,1)

# Initialize bias and weights
initial_b = 0
initial_W1 = 0
initial_W2 = 0

# Set learing rate and iterations
learning_rate = 0.1
learning_iterations = 500000

# Start the training of logistic regression model
loss_history, b, W = train(X, Y, initial_b, np.array([[ini-
tial_W1],[initial_W2]]), learning_rate, learning_iterations)
```

Seventhly, we store the small dataset as a numpy array, invoke the max_min_norm function for normalization, initialize bias and weights, set learning rate and iterations and then invoke the train function to start building our first logistic regression model after decomposing and fully understanding every single step of the process.

```python
def max_min_norm(X):
    """
    Normalize dataset by using the Max-min normalization tech-
nique
    Inputs: X - numpy.ndarray, the dataset for normalization
    Outputs: (X_norm, np.array(max_min_vals)) - tuple, return
the normalized dataset, and the max and min values of each
feature
    """
    X_norm = X.copy().astype(float)
    max_min_vals = []
    for col in range(0, X_norm.shape[1]):
        X_max = X_norm[:, col].max()
        X_min = X_norm[:, col].min()
        X_range = X_max - X_min
        X_norm[:, col] = (X_norm[:, col] - X_min) / X_range
        max_min_vals.append({"X_max":X_max, "X_min":X_min,
"X_range":X_range})
    return (X_norm, np.array(max_min_vals))
```

	size_sqft	num_bedrooms	is_easy_sell
0	1600	5	1
1	1200	4	1
2	740	2	0

```
iter=1      b=0.01667   W1=0.02558      W2=0.02778      loss=0.6764246196944534
iter=2      b=0.03220   W1=0.05036      W2=0.05470      loss=0.6609103694374685
iter=3      b=0.04666   W1=0.07438      W2=0.08081      loss=0.6465026917750528
iter=4      b=0.06010   W1=0.09766      W2=0.10613      loss=0.6331070942469185
iter=5      b=0.07256   W1=0.12024      W2=0.13071      loss=0.6206362623737394
iter=499996     b=-8.40173      W1=12.69092     W2=15.49013     loss=0.00012961536388369103
iter=499997     b=-8.40174      W1=12.69092     W2=15.49013     loss=0.00012961510448407314
iter=499998     b=-8.40174      W1=12.69092     W2=15.49013     loss=0.0001296148450854918
iter=499999     b=-8.40174      W1=12.69093     W2=15.49014     loss=0.00012961458568794696
iter=500000     b=-8.40174      W1=12.69093     W2=15.49014     loss=0.00012961432629147565
```

Eighthly, the accuracy for the training dataset, as well as the predicted probability and the predicted class for each training sample, are calculated and printed out.

```python
print("accuracy for training dataset:", predict_accuracy(Y, X,
b, W))
```
```
accuracy for training dataset: 1.0
```

```python
print("training dataset, probability of belonging to class
1:\n",
        np.round(y_hat_calc(X, b, W),4))
```
```
training dataset, probability of belonging to class 1:
 [[1.000e+00]
 [9.998e-01]
 [2.000e-04]]
```

```python
print("training dataset, predicted class:\n",
        predict_class(X, b, W))
```
```
training dataset, predicted class:
 [[1]
 [1]
 [0]]
```

Finally, the trained logistic regression model is utilized to predict the output (*i.e.,* class) of the house (new data) with 1200 sqft and 3 bedrooms:

```python
new_data = np.array([[1200,3]], dtype = float)

# Max-min normalization
for col in range(0, new_data.shape[1]):
    new_data[:, col] = ((new_data[:, col]
                        - max_min_vals[col]['X_min'])
                        / max_min_vals[col]['X_range'])

new_data = new_data.T

predicted_class = predict_class(new_data, b, W)

print ("For the house with 1200 sqft and 3 bedrooms, predicted
class:",
        '1 (i.e., Yes, easy to sell)' if predicted_class[0][0]
== 1
        else '0 (i.e., No, not easy to sell)')

print ("\n, and probability of belonging to class 1 is",
        np.round(y_hat_calc(new_data, b, W)[0][0], 2))
```
```
For the house with 1200 sqft and 3 bedrooms, predicted class: 1
(i.e., Yes, easy to sell)

, and probability of belonging to class 1 is 0.97
```

We then compare the above results with those from the off-the-shelf logistic regression model offered by the scikit-learn library. These include the accuracy for the training dataset, as well as the predicted probability and the predicted class for each training sample and the house (new data) with 1200 sqft and 3 bedrooms. The codes are as follows:

```python
import numpy as np
from sklearn.linear_model import LogisticRegression
from sklearn.metrics import accuracy_score
from sklearn.preprocessing import MinMaxScaler

# The small dataset
data = np.array([[1600,5,1],
                 [1200,4,1],
                 [740,2,0]])

X = data[:, :-1] # all rows, all columns except the last column
Y = data[:, -1]  # all rows, last column only

scaler = MinMaxScaler()
scaler.fit(X)
X = scaler.transform(X) # update to Normalized X

lgr = LogisticRegression(penalty='none', tol=1.5e-4).fit(X, Y)

print("accuracy for training dataset:", accuracy_score(Y, lgr.predict(X)))
```

accuracy for training dataset: 1.0

```
print("training dataset, probabilities of belonging to class
1:\n",
        np.round(lgr.predict_proba(X)[:,1].reshape(-1,1), 4))
```

```
training dataset, probabilities of belonging to class 1:
 [[1.000e+00]
 [9.998e-01]
 [2.000e-04]]
```

```
print("training dataset, predicted class:\n",
        lgr.predict(X).reshape(-1,1))
```

```
training dataset, predicted class:
 [[1]
 [1]
 [0]]
```

```
new_data = np.array([[1200,3]], dtype = float)
new_data = scaler.transform(new_data)

print ("For the house with 1200 sqft and 3 bedrooms, predicted
class:",
        '1 (i.e., Yes, easy to sell)' if lgr.pre-
dict(new_data)[0] == 1
        else '0 (i.e., No, not easy to sell)')

print ("\n, and probability of belonging to class 1 is",
        np.round(lgr.predict_proba(new_data)[0][1], 2))
```

```
For the house with 1200 sqft and 3 bedrooms, predicted class: 1
(i.e., Yes, easy to sell)
```

```
, and probability of belonging to class 1 is 0.97
```

As can be seen from the results using the scikit-learn logistic regression model, the accuracy for the training dataset, as well as the predicted probability and the predicted class for each training sample, are the same as those given by our own logistic regression model. Furthermore, the predicted class for the previously unseen house with 1200 sqft and 3 bedrooms is also the same as that produced by our own model.

CONCLUSION

In this chapter, we discussed the concept of logistic regression, a popular machine learning algorithm used for classification tasks. To make the material more accessible, we kept abstract mathematical theories to a minimum. Instead, we focused on a concrete numerical example with a small dataset to predict whether it is easy to sell houses in the property market, walking through it step by step. We also provided sample codes and a comparison with the logistic regression model from the off-the-shelf library, scikit-learn. By the end of the chapter, readers should have a well-rounded understanding of how logistic regression machine learning works behind the scenes, how the mathematics relates to the implementation and performance of the algorithm, and be better equipped to apply it in their projects.

REFERENCES

[1] J.K. Mandal, and D. Bhattacharya, Eds., "Emerging technology in modelling and graphics", *Proceedings of IEM graph, 2018, 1st ed. Singapore, Singapore: Springer, 2019.*
[2] S. Raschka, *Python Machine Learning.* Packt Publishing: Birmingham, England, 2015.
[3] J.C. Stoltzfus, "Logistic regression: a brief primer", *Acad. Emerg. Med.,* vol. 18, no. 10, pp. 1099-1104, 2011.
     http://dx.doi.org/10.1111/j.1553-2712.2011.01185.x PMID: 21996075
[4] A.C. Mueller, and S. Guido, *Introduction to machine learning with python: A guide for data scientists.* O'Reilly Media: Sebastopol, CA, 2016.
[5] Z. Wang, S.A. Irfan, C. Teoh, and P.H. Bhoyar, *Linear Regression" in Numerical Machine Learning.* Bentham Science, 2023.
[6] Z. Wang, S.A. Irfan, C. Teoh, and P.H. Bhoyar, *Regularization" in Numerical Machine Learning.* Bentham Science, 2023.

## CHAPTER 5

Decision Tree

Abstract: In this chapter, we explore the concept of decision trees, prioritizing accessibility by minimizing abstract mathematical theories. We examine a concrete numerical example using a small dataset to predict the suitability of playing tennis based on weather conditions, guiding readers through the process step-by-step. Moreover, we provide sample codes and compare them with the decision tree classification model found in the scikit-learn library. Upon completing this chapter, readers will have gained a comprehensive understanding of the inner workings of decision tree machine learning, the relationship between the underlying principles, and the implementation and performance of the algorithm, preparing them to apply their knowledge to practical scenarios.

Keywords: Decision Tree, Classification, Numerical Example, Small Dataset, Scikit-Learn

5.1. INTRODUCTION TO DECISION TREE

A decision tree is a diagrammatic representation of a set of choices and the results of those choices [1]. Decision tree algorithms have become a popular choice for both classification and regression tasks in machine learning due to their inherent advantages. These include their ease of interpretability, as the decision-making process is explicitly laid out in the tree structure, and their efficient training process. Decision trees can handle missing values, automatically select relevant features, and easily manage both numerical and categorical data. Furthermore, they are robust to outliers and noise in the data. Some of the common applications of decision trees include customer segmentation, fraud detection, medical diagnosis, and risk management. Due to their comprehensible nature and ability to visualize complex decision-making processes, decision trees have found widespread adoption in various industries and research fields. Decision tree is a diagram showing the several paths to reach a choice under specific constraints. Each branch symbolizes the decision space, and its leaf nodes are the outcomes. One node, called the root node, is the starting point for the decision tree, and many more branches, including decision nodes and leaf nodes.

For example, as shown in Fig. (**5.1**), consider a situation where one needs to decide whether to go to outdoor sports. The decision tree for this problem may look like this:

Root node: "Should I go to outdoor sports?"

Zhiyuan Wang, Sayed Ameenuddin Irfan, Christopher Teoh & Priyanka Hriday Bhoyar

Decision node: "Is weather good to support outdoor sports?"

If yes, leaf node: "Go to play"

If no, leaf node: "Do not go to play"

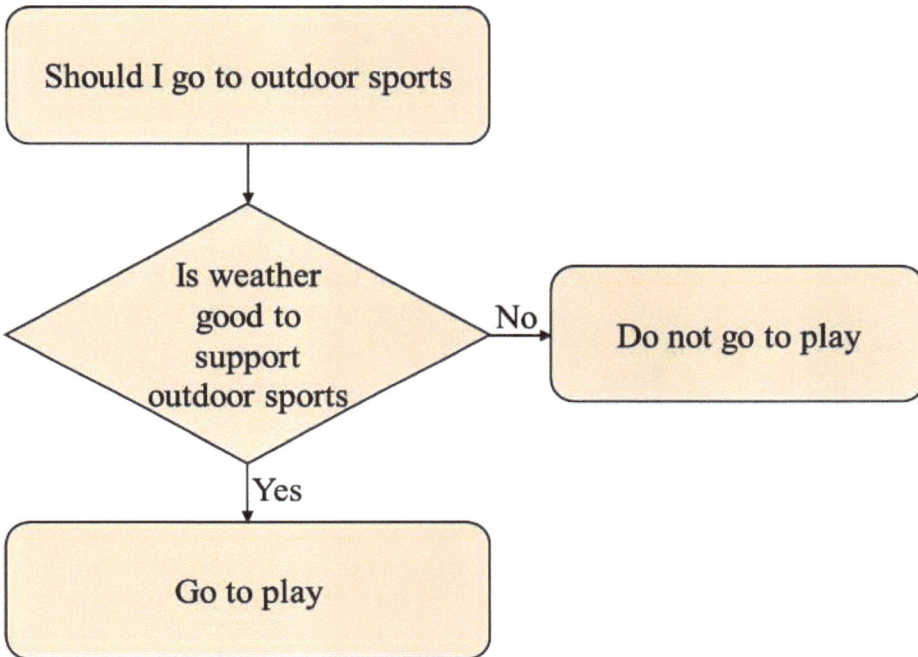

Fig. (5.1). A simple decision tree example.

In this example, the decision node represents the weather condition outside. If the condition is met (*i.e.*, the weather is good), the tree leads to the outcome of going to play. If the condition is not met (*i.e.*, the weather is not good), the tree leads to the outcome of not going to play.

Now the question might be how to decide which leaf node to select as the root node and decision node. For better decision-making, we use Hunt's algorithm, which helps to give a clear understanding of splitting and choosing the important parameter for root nodes.

5.2. ALGORITHM OF DECISION TREE

In the context of decision tree learning, a heuristic known as Hunt's algorithm is utilized to determine the optimal split for each node in the tree [2]. It is a procedure that iteratively analyzes each feature and the possible value of the feature as a candidate split. Then it chooses the one that yields the most significant increase in information gain (discussed later).

Here is the general process of the Hunt algorithm:

- Calculate the entropy of the current node. Entropy is a measure of the impurity or uncertainty of the data at the node. It is calculated based on the frequencies of the different classes in the data.
- Consider each feature and each possible value of that feature as a candidate split. Calculate the information gain of each candidate split by comparing the entropy of the current node to the entropy of the child nodes that would result from the split.
- Select the split that results in the greatest information gain.
- Repeat the process for each child node, until the desired depth of the tree is reached, or all nodes are pure (*i.e.*, contain only data belonging to a single class).
- Hunt's algorithm is a popular choice for decision tree learning due to its simplicity and efficiency in constructing a decision tree from a dataset. Hunt's algorithm has also served as a foundation for the development of other decision tree algorithms [3], such as ID3 (Iterative Dichotomiser 3), C4.5 (an extension of ID3 that can handle continuous attributes, missing values, and pruning), and CART (Classification and Regression Trees).

As aforementioned, the impurity of a node in a decision tree can be measured using entropy, shown in Equation (5.1). Entropy is calculated based on the frequencies of the different classes in the data. If the data at a node is completely pure, with all data belonging to a single class, then the entropy is zero. On the other hand, if the data is equally divided among all classes, then the entropy is at its maximum.

$$Entropy = \sum_{i=1}^{n} -P_i log_2 P_i \tag{5.1}$$

Here, P_i is the proportion of class i in the node.

Hunt's algorithm recursively splits the data into smaller and smaller subsets until each subset contains data belonging to a single class. At each split, the algorithm considers every feature and every possible value of that feature as a candidate split and selects the split that results in the greatest information gain. Once the tree has been built, it can be used to make predictions by following the splits in the tree to arrive at a leaf node, which represents a class prediction.

In decision tree learning, information gain (IG) is a measure that determines how well a given feature splits the training samples. It is used to decide which feature to split on at each step in building the tree. The metric that is commonly used to calculate information gain is entropy, which is a measure of the "disordered" or "random" nature of a group of samples. Equation (5.2) shows the mathematical formulation for information gain.

$$Information\ Gain = Entropy(parent)\text{-}Weighted\ sum\ of\ Entropy(children) \quad \textbf{(5.2)}$$

Here, the $Entropy(parent)$ for parent node, calculated using Equation (5.1), is the entropy of the set of samples before the split, and the $Entropy(children)$, calculated using Equation (5.1), for child nodes are the entropies of the two groups of samples created by the split. The weight assigned to each child node is simply the ratio of $\dfrac{\text{number of samples in child node}}{\text{number of samples in parent code}}$.

A decision tree has several advantages [4], including interpretability, as the decision-making process is explicitly laid out in the tree structure, efficient training, and the ability to handle missing values and automatically select relevant features, which is why it is a popular machine learning algorithm in practice.

5.3. NUMERICAL EXAMPLE OF DECISION TREE

Let us consider a small categorical dataset with 5 training samples that contain weather outlook and temperature as input features, and an output label indicating whether it is appropriate to play tennis given these conditions. The dataset is presented in Table **5.1**.

Table 5.1. The small dataset for the decision tree.

	Outlook	**Temperature**	**Play_Tennis**
1st sample	rainy	hot	no
2nd sample	rainy	cool	yes

3rd sample	overcast	cool	yes
4th sample	sunny	hot	yes
5th sample	sunny	cool	yes

Both the input features and output labels are encoded using numerical values 0, 1, 2, and so forth. For example, 0 represents overcast in the Outlook column, 1 represents rainy, and 2 represents sunny. Similarly, 0 represents cool in the Temperature column, and 1 represents hot. In the Play_Tennis column, 0 represents no, and 1 represents yes. This encoding is necessary because the decision tree expects the inputs to be numerical rather than categorical. The updated dataset after encoding is presented in Table **5.2**.

Table 5.2. The small dataset after encoding for the decision tree.

	Outlook	Temperature	Play_Tennis
1st sample	1	1	0
2nd sample	1	0	1
3rd sample	0	0	1
4th sample	2	1	1
5th sample	2	0	1

To build a decision tree model, firstly, we need to calculate the entropy of the root node with all 5 training samples using Equation (5.1). As seen from Table **5.2**, of the 5 training samples, 4 samples belong to class 1 (*i.e.*, yes), thus $P_1 = \frac{4}{5}$; and 1 sample belongs to class 0 (*i.e.*, no), thus $P_0 = \frac{1}{5}$.

$$Entropy(root) = \sum_{i=1}^{n} -P_i log_2 P_i = -P_1 log_2 P_1 - P_0 log_2 P_0$$
$$= -\frac{4}{5} log_2 \frac{4}{5} - \frac{1}{5} log_2 \frac{1}{5} = 0.258 + 0.464 = 0.722$$

Secondly, consider each feature and each possible value of that feature as a candidate split. The aim is to find the optimal split that produces the greatest information gain. There are 2 input features, namely, Outlook and Temperature. Let us consider Outlook first, which contains 3 unique values, 0, 1, and 2 (*i.e.*, overcast, rainy, and sunny). We can make a fair split between 0 and 1 by using a split condition, Outlook ≤ 0.5; as such, samples with outlook as overcast will be split into one group, and samples with outlook as rainy or sunny will be split into another group. The visual representation for this split is as follows:

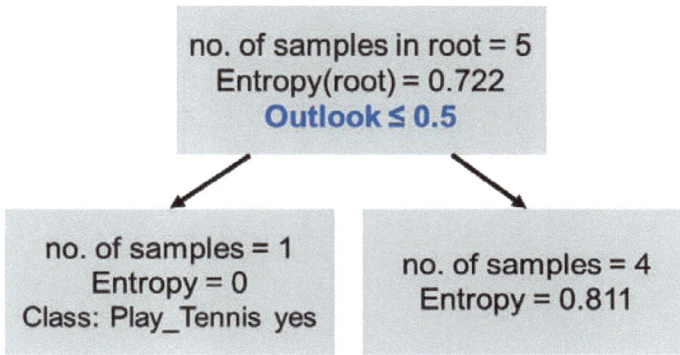

no. of samples in root = 5
Entropy(root) = 0.722
Outlook ≤ 0.5

no. of samples = 1
Entropy = 0
Class: Play_Tennis yes

no. of samples = 4
Entropy = 0.811

There is only 1 sample (*i.e.*, the 3rd sample in Table **5.2**) which satisfies the condition, Outlook ≤ 0.5, and constitutes the child node on the left. Its entropy can be calculated as:

$$Entropy(left\ child\ node) = \sum_{i=1}^{n} -P_i log_2 P_i = -P_1 log_2 P_1 - P_0 log_2 P_0$$

$$= -\frac{1}{1} log_2 \frac{1}{1} - \frac{0}{1} log_2 \frac{0}{1} = 0$$

The remaining 4 samples do not satisfy the condition, Outlook ≤ 0.5, and constitute the child node on the right. Its entropy can be calculated as:

$$Entropy(right\ child\ node) = \sum_{i=1}^{n} -P_i log_2 P_i = -P_1 log_2 P_1 - P_0 log_2 P_0$$

$$= -\frac{3}{4} log_2 \frac{3}{4} - \frac{1}{4} log_2 \frac{1}{4} = 0.811$$

The information gain (IG) for the split using the condition, Outlook ≤ 0.5, is therefore calculated as:

$$IG\ (Outlook\ \le\ 0.5)$$
$$= Entropy(parent) - Weighted\ sum\ of\ Entropy(children)$$
$$= 0.722 - \left(\frac{1}{5} \times 0 + \frac{4}{5} \times 0.811\right) = 0.0732$$

For the feature Outlook, we can also consider another fair split between 1 and 2 by using a split condition, Outlook ≤ 1.5; as such, samples with outlook as overcast or rainy will be split into one group, and samples with outlook as sunny will be split into another group. The visual representation for this split is as follows:

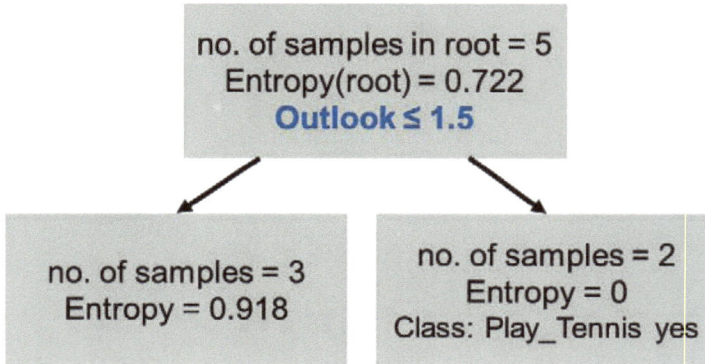

no. of samples in root = 5
Entropy(root) = 0.722
Outlook ≤ 1.5

no. of samples = 3
Entropy = 0.918

no. of samples = 2
Entropy = 0
Class: Play_Tennis yes

3 samples (*i.e.*, the 1st, 2nd, and 3rd samples in Table **5.2**) satisfy the condition, Outlook ≤ 1.5, and constitutes the child node on the left. Its entropy can be calculated as:

$$Entropy(left\ child\ node) = \sum_{i=1}^{n} -P_i log_2 P_i = -P_1 log_2 P_1 - P_0 log_2 P_0$$
$$= -\frac{2}{3} log_2 \frac{2}{3} - \frac{1}{3} log_2 \frac{1}{3} = 0.918$$

The remaining 2 samples do not satisfy the condition, Outlook ≤ 1.5, and constitute the child node on the right. Its entropy can be calculated as:

$$Entropy(right\ child\ node) = \sum_{i=1}^{n} -P_i log_2 P_i = -P_1 log_2 P_1 - P_0 log_2 P_0$$
$$= -\frac{2}{2} log_2 \frac{2}{2} - \frac{0}{2} log_2 \frac{0}{2} = 0$$

The information gain (IG) for the split using the condition, Outlook $\leq$ 1.5, is therefore calculated as:

$$IG\ (Outlook\ \leq\ 1.5)$$
$$= Entropy(parent) - Weighted\ sum\ of\ Entropy(children)$$
$$= 0.722 - \left(\frac{3}{5} \times 0.918 + \frac{2}{5} \times 0\right) = 0.171$$

By now, we have iterated all the possible splits for the feature Outlook. You might wonder why not consider splitting using conditions like, Outlook $\leq$ 0 or Outlook $\leq$ 2. This is because, under these conditions, the total 5 samples will not be split into separate groups; instead, they will all remain in the same group.

Let us now consider another feature, Temperature, which contains 2 unique values, 0 and 1 (*i.e.*, cool and hot). We can make a fair split between 0 and 1 by using a split condition, Temperature ≤ 0.5; as such, samples with a temperature as cool will be split into one group, and samples with a temperature as hot will be split into another group. The visual representation for this split is as follows:

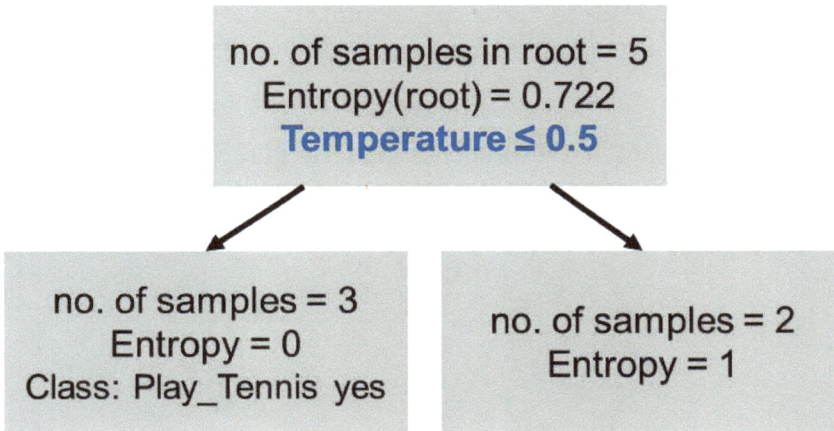

3 samples (*i.e.*, the 2nd, 3rd, and 5th samples in Table **5.2**) satisfy the condition, Temperature $\leq$ 0.5, and constitute the child node on the left. Its entropy can be calculated as:

$$Entropy(left\ child\ node) = \sum_{i=1}^{n} -P_i log_2 P_i = -P_1 log_2 P_1 - P_0 log_2 P_0$$
$$= -\frac{3}{3} log_2 \frac{3}{3} - \frac{0}{3} log_2 \frac{0}{3} = 0$$

The remaining 2 samples do not satisfy the condition, Temperature ≤ 0.5, and constitute the child node on the right. Its entropy can be calculated as:

$$Entropy(right\ child\ node) = \sum_{i=1}^{n} -P_i log_2 P_i = -P_1 log_2 P_1 - P_0 log_2 P_0$$
$$= -\frac{1}{2} log_2 \frac{1}{2} - \frac{1}{2} log_2 \frac{1}{2} = 1$$

The information gain (IG) for the split using the condition, Temperature ≤ 0.5, is therefore calculated as:

$$IG\ (Temperature\ \leq\ 0.5)$$
$$= Entropy(parent) - Weighted\ sum\ of\ Entropy(children)$$
$$= 0.722 - \left(\frac{3}{5} \times 0 + \frac{2}{5} \times 1\right) = 0.322$$

After all the calculations, we find that $IG\ (Temperature\ \leq\ 0.5)$ gives the greatest information gain compared with $IG\ (Outlook\ \leq\ 0.5)$ and $IG\ (Outlook\ \leq\ 1.5)$. Therefore, the split condition, Temperature ≤ 0.5, is used to split the root node containing all 5 samples, visually as follows:

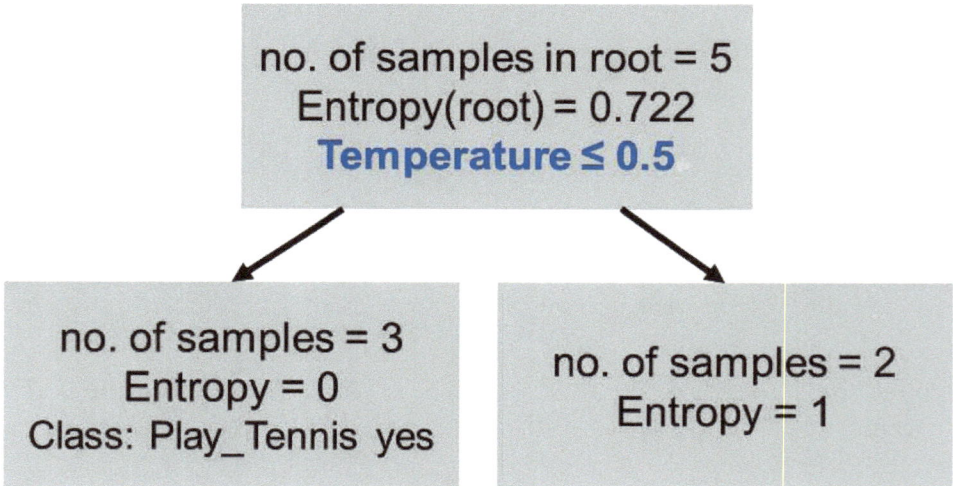

> no. of samples in root = 5
> Entropy(root) = 0.722
> **Temperature ≤ 0.5**

> no. of samples = 3
> Entropy = 0
> Class: Play_Tennis yes

> no. of samples = 2
> Entropy = 1

It is worth noting that the child node on the right includes samples (*i.e.*, the 1st and 4th samples in Table **5.2**) from 2 classes. By default, the decision tree building algorithm does not stop here and will continue to split the node. In this case, there is only one possible candidate split, *i.e.*, split between 1 (*i.e.*, rainy) and 2 (*i.e.*, sunny) for the feature Outlook, because the Temperature value for both samples (*i.e.*, the 1st and 4th samples in Table **5.2**) is 1 (*i.e.*, hot). The visual representation for this split is updated as follows:

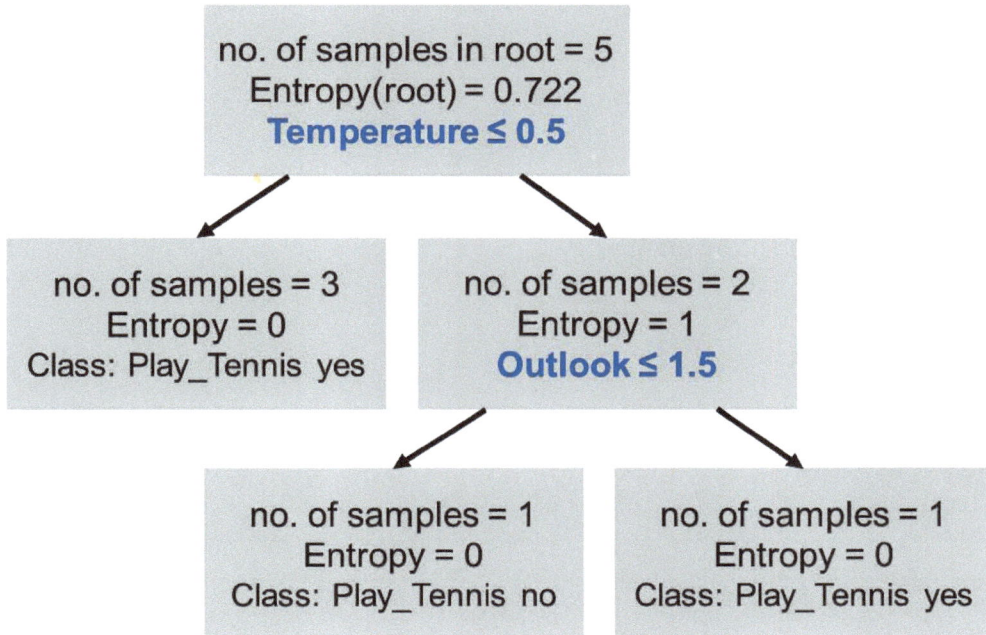

The process of building a decision tree model using this small dataset is now complete.

5.4. SAMPLE CODES AND COMPARISON

Now, let us construct a decision tree model from scratch using Python codes and compare the results obtained above with that from the off-the-shelf decision tree classifier offered by the scikit-learn library.

The complete code file can be downloaded from our shared folder in Google Drive:

https://drive.google.com/drive/folders/1FqJvo4ZPazNbEH_GlHFoodqvegnQmHcn?usp=share_link

```python
import numpy as np
import pandas as pd
```

```python
def entropy(y):
    """

    Calculate the entropy at each node
    Inputs:
        y - numpy.ndarray, array of labels in the node. e.g.,
array([0, 1, 1, 1, 1]) in root node
    Outputs:
        entropy - float, the calculated entropy value
    """

    _, counts = np.unique(y, return_counts=True) # re-
turn_counts : bool, optional.
                                                # If True,
also return the number of times each unique item appears
    probabilities = counts / len(y)
    entropy = np.sum( -(probabilities * np.log2(probabili-
ties)) )
    return entropy
```

```python
def split_data(X, y, feature_idx, value):
    """

    Split the dataset into two subsets (left and right) based
on the given feature index and value
    Inputs:
        X - numpy.ndarray, array of features
        y - numpy.ndarray, array of labels
        feature_idx - int, index of the feature to split on
        value - float, the value to split the dataset
    Outputs:
        X_left, y_left - numpy.ndarray, the subset with fea-
ture values <= value
        X_right, y_right - numpy.ndarray, the subset with fea-
ture values > value
    """

    left_mask = X[:, feature_idx] <= value # mask using True
and False
    right_mask = X[:, feature_idx] > value # mask using True
and False
    return X[left_mask], y[left_mask], X[right_mask],
y[right_mask]
```

```python
def best_split(X, y, n_features):
    best_gain, best_feature, best_value = 0, None, None

    parent_entropy = entropy(y) # # Equation (5.2) in book:
Entropy(parent)

    for feature_idx in range(n_features): # iterate all fea-
tures
        values = np.unique(X[:, feature_idx])
        split_values = (values[:-1] + values[1:]) / 2   # Cal-
culate the middle values between unique feature values
                                                      # e.g.,
values = [0,1,2]; ([0,1] + [1,2])/2 = [1,3]/2 = [0.5, 1.5]

        for value in split_values: # iterate all possible
splits
            X_left, y_left, X_right, y_right = split_data(X,
y, feature_idx, value)

            if len(y_left) == 0 or len(y_right) == 0:
                continue

            left_entropy = entropy(y_left)
            right_entropy = entropy(y_right)

            # Equation (5.2) in book: Weighted sum of En-
tropy(children)
            child_entropy = (len(y_left) / len(y)) * left_en-
tropy + (len(y_right) / len(y)) * right_entropy

            # Equation (5.2) in book
            information_gain = parent_entropy - child_entropy

            if information_gain > best_gain:
                best_gain, best_feature, best_value = infor-
mation_gain, feature_idx, value

    return best_gain, best_feature, best_value
```

```python
# Recursive function to build the decision tree
def build_tree(X, y, n_features, max_depth, depth=0):
    if depth == max_depth or entropy(y) == 0 or len(y) <= 1:
        return {'label': np.argmax(np.bincount(y))} #
bincount: count 0's occurences, 1's occurences, 2's, 3's
                                                 # argmax:
return index of max value

    information_gain, feature, value = best_split(X, y, n_fea-
tures) # returned feature is the index of the feature in fea-
ture_cols
    print(f"best split at depth {depth}: best_gain =
{round(information_gain,3)}, split on {feature_cols[feature]}
<= {value}")

    if information_gain == 0:
        return {'label': np.argmax(np.bincount(y))}

    X_left, y_left, X_right, y_right = split_data(X, y, fea-
ture, value) # real split happens here after figure out which
split give best gain
    # print("X_left, y_left\n", X_left, y_left)
    # print("X_right, y_right\n", X_right, y_right)

    return {
        'feature': feature,
        'value': value,
        'left': build_tree(X_left, y_left, n_features,
max_depth, depth + 1),
        'right': build_tree(X_right, y_right, n_features,
max_depth, depth + 1),
    }
```

```
def predict(tree, x):
    """
    Make predictions for a single instance using the decision
tree
    Inputs:
        tree - dict, the decision tree structure
        x - numpy.ndarray, a single feature instance
    Outputs:
        prediction - int, the predicted label for the input
instance
    """
    if 'label' in tree: # i.e., reached the leaf node
        return tree['label']

    feature = tree['feature']
    value = tree['value']

    # navigate to the left or right subtree (like how we ex-
plored binary tree)
    if x[feature] <= value:
        return predict(tree['left'], x)
    else:
        return predict(tree['right'], x)
```

```
data = np.array([["rainy","hot","no"],
                 ["rainy","cool","yes"],
                 ["overcast","cool","yes"],
                 ["sunny","hot","yes"],
                 ["sunny","cool","yes"]])

col_names = ["Outlook","Temperature","Play_Tennis"]
data = pd.DataFrame(data, columns=col_names)
print("Original data:\n", data, "\n")
```

```
Original data:

    Outlook Temperature Play_Tennis
0     rainy         hot          no
1     rainy        cool         yes
2  overcast        cool         yes
3     sunny         hot         yes
4     sunny        cool         yes
```

```python
def label_encode_dataframe(data):
    """

    Perform label encoding on a pandas DataFrame by replacing
    categorical values with integer labels
    Inputs:
        data - pandas.DataFrame, the input DataFrame with cat-
    egorical values
    Outputs:
        encoded_data - pandas.DataFrame, the DataFrame with
    integer labels instead of categorical values
    """

    encoded_data = data.copy()
    for column in encoded_data.columns:
        unique_values = sorted(encoded_data[column].unique())
        value_to_int = {value: idx for idx, value in enumer-
    ate(unique_values)}
        encoded_data[column] = encoded_data[col-
    umn].map(value_to_int)
    return encoded_data

data = label_encode_dataframe(data)
print("Encoded data:\n", data, "\n")
```

Encoded data:

	Outlook	Temperature	Play_Tennis
0	1	1	0
1	1	0	1
2	0	0	1
3	2	1	1
4	2	0	1

```python
feature_cols = ["Outlook", "Temperature"]
X = data[fea-
ture_cols].to_numpy()
y = data["Play_Tennis"].to_numpy()

tree = build_tree(X, y, n_features=len(feature_cols),
max_depth=3)
```

best split at depth 0: best_gain = 0.322, split on Temperature <= 0.5

best split at depth 1: best_gain = 1.0, split on Outlook <= 1.5

```
import pprint
pprint.pprint(tree)
```

```
{'feature': 1,
 'left': {'label': 1},
 'right': {'feature': 0,
          'left': {'label': 0},
          'right': {'label': 1},
          'value': 1.5},
 'value': 0.5}
```

```
# Make predictions
predictions = [predict(tree, x) for x in X]
print("\nPredictions:", predictions, "\n")

# Calculate the accuracy
accuracy = np.sum(predictions == y) / len(y)
print("Accuracy:", accuracy, "\n")
```

```
Predictions: [0, 1, 1, 1, 1]


Accuracy: 1.0
```

We then compare the above results and our manually calculated results from Section 5.3 with those from the off-the-shelf decision tree model offered by the scikit-learn library.

```python
import numpy as np
import pandas as pd
from sklearn import metrics
from sklearn import tree
from sklearn import preprocessing
from sklearn.tree import DecisionTreeClassifier
import matplotlib.pyplot as plt

data = np.array([["rainy","hot","no"],
                 ["rainy","cool","yes"],
                 ["overcast","cool","yes"],
                 ["sunny","hot","yes"],
                 ["sunny","cool","yes"]])
col_names = ["Outlook","Temperature","Play_Tennis"]
data = pd.DataFrame(data, columns=col_names)
print(data, "\n")
```

	Outlook	Temperature	Play_Tennis
0	rainy	hot	no
1	rainy	cool	yes
2	overcast	cool	yes
3	sunny	hot	yes
4	sunny	cool	yes

```python
#The data can be labbeled using Label encoder from sklearn
string_to_int= preprocessing.LabelEn-
coder()
data=data.apply(string_to_int.fit_transform)
print(data, "\n")
```

	Outlook	Temperature	Play_Tennis
0	1	1	0
1	1	0	1
2	0	0	1
3	2	1	1
4	2	0	1

```
#To divide our data into features and Labels
feature_cols = ["Outlook", "Temperature"]
X = data[feature_cols]
y = data["Play_Tennis"]

# train the machine learning model
dtc = DecisionTreeClassifier(criterion="entropy", ran-
dom_state=100)
dtc.fit(X, y)
```

```
features=["Outlook", "Temperature"]
labels=['Play_Tennis no', 'Play_Tennis yes']

fig, axes = plt.subplots(nrows = 1,ncols = 1,figsize = (4,4),
dpi=200)
tree.plot_tree(dtc,
               feature_names = features,
               class_names=labels,
               filled = True);
# fig.savefig('dtc_small_dataset.png')
```

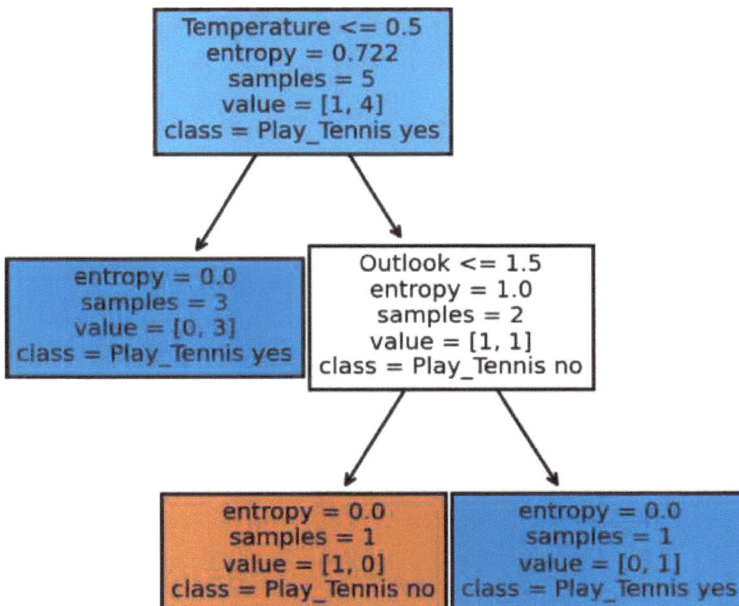

As can be seen from the results of the scikit-learn decision tree classifier and compared with our manually calculated results, the same decision tree is generated with the same entropies for all the nodes.

CONCLUSION

In this chapter, we discussed the concept of a decision tree. To make the material more accessible, we kept abstract mathematical theories to a minimum. Instead, we focused on a concrete numerical example with a small dataset to predict whether it is appropriate to play tennis based on weather conditions, walking through it step by step. We also provided sample codes and a comparison with the decision tree classification model from the off-the-shelf library, scikit-learn. By the end of the chapter, readers should have a well-rounded understanding of how decision tree machine learning works behind the scenes, how the mathematics relates to the implementation and performance of the algorithm, and be better equipped to apply it in their projects.

REFERENCES

[1] P-N. Tan, M. Steinbach, A. Karpatne, and V. Kumar, *Introduction to Data Mining.,* 2nd ed Pearson: Upper Saddle River, NJ, 2017.
[2] J. Han, J. Pei, and H. Tong, *Data Mining: Concepts and Techniques.,* 4th ed Morgan Kaufmann: Oxford, England, 2022.
[3] J.R. Quinlan, *C4.5: Programs for Machine Learning.* Morgan Kaufmann, 2014.
[4] L. Breiman, *Classification and Regression Trees.,* 1st Edition Routledge: New York, 2017. http://dx.doi.org/10.1201/9781315139470

## CHAPTER 6

Gradient Boosting

Abstract: In this chapter, we explore gradient boosting, a powerful ensemble machine learning method, for both regression and classification tasks. With a focus on accessibility, we minimize abstract mathematical theories and instead emphasize two concrete numerical examples with small datasets related to predicting house sale prices and ease of selling houses in the property market. By providing a step-by-step walkthrough, we illuminate the inner workings of gradient boosting and offer sample codes and comparisons to the gradient boosting models available in the scikit-learn library. Upon completing this chapter, readers will possess a comprehensive understanding of gradient boosting's mechanics, its connection to the implementation and performance of the algorithm, and be well-prepared to apply it in real-world projects.

Keywords: Gradient Boosting, Ensemble Learning, Regression, Classification, Numerical Example, Small Dataset, Scikit-Learn

6.1. INTRODUCTION TO GRADIENT BOOSTING

Gradient boosting is a robust ensemble machine learning model that sequentially trains a spate of weak learners to produce a more accurate model at the end [1, 2]. A weak learner, generally a rather simple decision tree, is a rudimentary machine learning model with low prediction accuracy but still better than random guessing. As demonstrated in Fig. (**6.1**), the prediction error of the ensemble model is reduced with each new decision tree added and integrated with all the prior decision trees [3]. Gradient boosting is an efficient and accurate algorithm that has been applied to regression and classification problems in many fields, including engineering, healthcare, natural language processing, and computer vision, among others. One of the key strengths of gradient boosting is its ability to leverage the collective knowledge of multiple weak learners, ultimately generating a more robust and accurate model. This is achieved by iteratively focusing on the areas where previous weak learners have failed to make accurate predictions and subsequently improving upon those areas. As a result, gradient boosting has become a popular choice for tackling complex problems and achieving state-of-the-art performance in various applications, even outperforming other ensemble methods, such as random forests in certain contexts. Its versatility and adaptability make gradient boosting a valuable tool in the arsenal of machine learning practitioners and researchers alike.

The rest of this chapter is organized as follows. Section 6.2 presents the mathematics of gradient boosting for regression, followed by the demonstration of a numerical example in detail and code comparison in Section 6.3. Analogously,

Zhiyuan Wang, Sayed Ameenuddin Irfan, Christopher Teoh & Priyanka Hriday Bhoyar

Section 6.4 presents the mathematics of gradient boosting for classification, followed by the demonstration of a numerical example in detail and code comparison in Section 6.5.

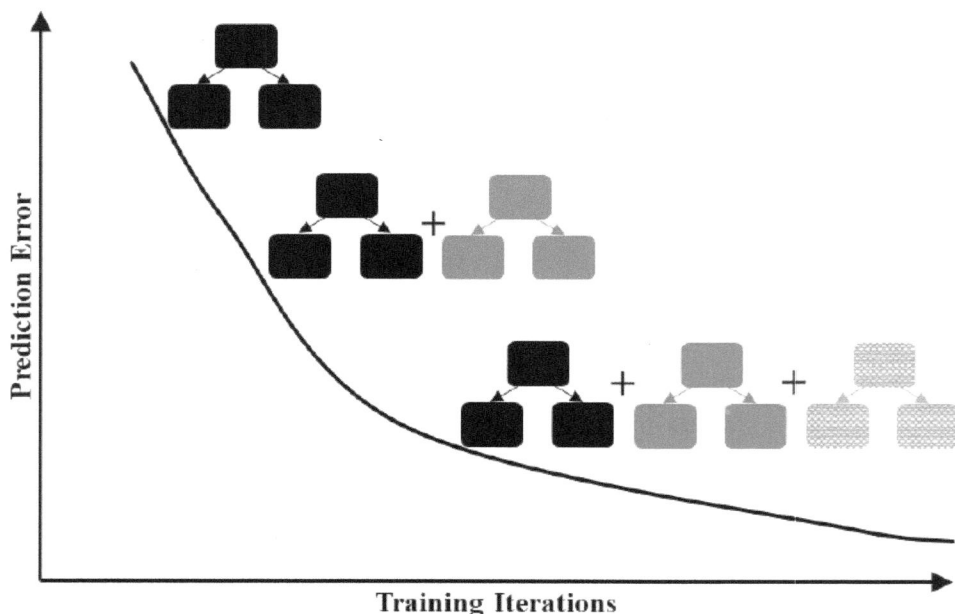

Fig. (6.1). Illustration of gradient boosting.

6.2. MATHEMATICS OF GRADIENT BOOSTING FOR REGRESSION

The basic idea of gradient boosting is to iteratively improve the overall model by fitting the weak learners to the residuals or gradient of the loss function with respect to the previous model's predictions. This process can be viewed as a numerical optimization technique that minimizes the loss function over the training dataset. The algorithm starts by initializing the model with a constant value. The main loop of the algorithm iterates for a predetermined number of iterations (M), and in each iteration, the following four steps are performed. Firstly, the pseudo-residuals are computed by taking the negative gradient of the loss function with respect to the current model's predictions. These pseudo-residuals represent the direction in which the model needs to move to minimize the loss function. Secondly, a weak learner, typically a decision tree, is fit to the pseudo-residuals. The tree is constructed by splitting the input feature space into regions and learning the optimal value for each region to minimize the loss function. Thirdly, the optimal values, denoted by γ, are computed for each region by minimizing the loss function with respect to the previous model's predictions plus the new weak learner's output. Fourthly, the model is updated by adding the weighted output of the new weak learner to the previous model's predictions; the weight here, denoted by α, is a shrinkage parameter that controls the learning rate of gradient boosting. Finally, these four steps are repeated for M iterations, and the final model is a combination of weak learners that can make accurate predictions by collectively minimizing the loss function. Together with the generic pseudocode [4], the mathematics used in gradient boosting for regression is presented in Table **6.1**. Common symbols used throughout the chapter are x_i, denoting the feature values of the ith sample (out of the total n samples from training dataset); y_i and $F(x_i)$, representing the true and predicted output for the ith sample, respectively; m and M, denoting the index of a decision tree and the total number of decision trees in the gradient boosting model; r_{im}, representing the residual of the ith sample in the mth decision tree; R_{jm}, denoting the jth leaf node of the mth decision tree; α, referring to the learning rate when building the model.

Table 6.1 Pseudocode and mathematics of gradient boosting for regression.

Input: Training dataset $\{(x_i, y_i)\}_{i=1}^{n}$ and a differentiable Loss Function $L(y_i, F(x_i)) = \frac{1}{2}[y_i - F(x_i)]^2$

Step 1: Initialize model with a constant value $F_0(x) = \underset{\gamma}{\text{argmin}} \sum_{i=1}^{n} L(y_i, \gamma)$

Step 2: for $m = 1\ to\ M$:

(a) Find pseudo-residuals $r_{im} = -\left[\frac{\partial L(y_i, F(x_i))}{\partial F(x_i)}\right]_{F(x)=F_{m-1}(x)}$ for $i = 1, 2, \dots, n$

(b) Fit the regression tree to the training dataset $\{(x_i, r_{im})\}_{i=1}^{n}$

(c) For $j = 1 \dots J_m$ compute $\gamma_{jm} = \underset{\gamma}{\text{argmin}} \sum_{x_i \in R_{jm}} L(y_i, F_{m-1}(x_i) + \gamma)$

(d) Update $F_m(x_i) = F_{m-1}(x_i) + \alpha(\gamma_{jm} | x_i \in R_{jm})$

Step 3: Output $F_m(x)$

6.3. NUMERICAL EXAMPLE AND CODE COMPARISON OF GRADIENT BOOSTING FOR REGRESSION

Suppose we have a small training dataset presented in Table **6.2** with only 3 samples (*i.e.*, $n = 3$), which pertains to the sale price of houses in millions of dollars (abbreviated as **sale_price_million**) based on 1 input features, the total number of bedrooms in the house (abbreviated as **num_bedrooms**). In other words, for this example, the independent variable X is num_bedrooms, and the dependent variable Y is sale_price_million. Our task is to build a gradient boosting regression model that maps the X and Y.

Table 6.2. The small dataset for gradient boosting regression.

	num_bedrooms (x_i)	sale_price_million (y_i)
$i = 1$	5	2.28
$i = 2$	4	1.5
$i = 3$	2	0.88

Using this small training dataset, we will break down the pseudocode into bite-sized chunks and execute it step by step.

Input: Training dataset $\{(x_i, y_i)\}_{i=1}^{n}$ and a differentiable Loss Function
$L(y_i, F(x_i)) = \frac{1}{2}[y_i - F(x_i)]^2$

For the input step, besides the training dataset, it also requires the loss function to be differentiable. Hence, find the derivative of Loss L with respect to the predicted value $F(x_i)$ as follows:

$$\frac{\partial L(y_i, F(x_i))}{\partial F(x_i)} = [y_i - F(x_i)](-1)$$

Step 1: Initialize model with a constant value $F_0(x) = \underset{\gamma}{\text{argmin}} \sum_{i=1}^{n} L(y_i, \gamma)$.

Here, γ represents the predicted value and $F_0(x)$ is the γ value that minimizes the total loss, $\sum_{i=1}^{n} L(y_i, \gamma)$.

$$\sum_{i=1}^{n} L(y_i, \gamma) = L(y_1, \gamma) + L(y_2, \gamma) + L(y_3, \gamma)$$
$$= \frac{1}{2}[y_1 - \gamma]^2 + \frac{1}{2}[y_2 - \gamma]^2 + \frac{1}{2}[y_3 - \gamma]^2$$

To find the minimum using the first-order derivative:

$$\frac{d \sum_{i=1}^{n} L(y_i, \gamma)}{d\gamma} = 0$$

$$\therefore (y_1 - \gamma)(-1) + (y_2 - \gamma)(-1) + (y_3 - \gamma)(-1) = 0$$

$$\gamma - y_1 + \gamma - y_2 + \gamma - y_3 = 0$$

$$3\gamma = y_1 + y_2 + y_3$$

$$\gamma = \frac{y_1 + y_2 + y_3}{3} = \frac{2.28 + 1.5 + 0.88}{3} = 1.553$$

Bear in mind that $F_0(x)$ is the γ value that minimizes the total loss, so initially $F_0(x) = \gamma = 1.553$, which is a constant value for all samples. *i.e.,*

$$F_0(x_1) = 1.553$$

$$F_0(x_2) = 1.553$$

$$F_0(x_3) = 1.553$$

Note the reason we know we have found the minimum total loss instead of the maximum is the implicit usage of the second-order derivative, $\frac{d^2 \sum_{i=1}^{n} L(y_i, \gamma)}{d\gamma^2}$, which gives a positive number, 3.

Step 2: for $m = 1\ to\ M$:

(a) Find pseudo-residuals $r_{im} = -\left[\dfrac{\partial L(y_i, F(x_i))}{\partial F(x_i)}\right]_{F(x)=F_{m-1}(x)}$ for $i = 1, 2, \ldots, n$

Here, m is the index of decision tree; r_{im} is the residual of the ith sample in the mth decision tree.

$$\frac{\partial L(y_i, F(x_i))}{\partial F(x_i)} = [y_i - F(x_i)](-1)$$

$$-\left[\frac{\partial L(y_i, F(x_i))}{\partial F(x_i)}\right] = [y_i - F(x_i)]$$

$$\therefore r_{im} = [y_i - F(x_i)]_{F(x)=F_{m-1}(x)}$$

When $m = 1$ (*i.e.*, the first decision tree):

$$r_{i1} = [y_i - F(x_i)]_{F(x)=F_0(x)} = y_i - F_0(x_i)$$

By plugging in all the $F_0(x_i)$ values identified from Step 1:

$$r_{11} = y_1 - F_0(x_1) = 2.28 - 1.553 = 0.727$$

$$r_{21} = y_2 - F_0(x_2) = 1.5 - 1.553 = -0.053$$

$$r_{31} = y_3 - F_0(x_3) = 0.88 - 1.553 = -0.673$$

Append the calculated $F_0(x_i)$ and r_{i1} values to the original table:

-	num_bedrooms (x_i)	sale_price_million (y_i)	$F_0(x_i)$	r_{i1}
$i = 1$	5	2.28	1.553	0.727
$i = 2$	4	1.5	1.553	−0.053
$i = 3$	2	0.88	1.553	−0.673

Step 2: for $m = 1\ to\ M$:

(b) Fit the regression tree to the training dataset $\{(x_i, r_{im})\}_{i=1}^{n}$

Here, a simple regression tree is constructed as follows by taking x_i as the input and r_{i1} as the output since $m = 1$. Readers are encouraged to review how to find the best split for the node of a decision tree in Chapter 5.

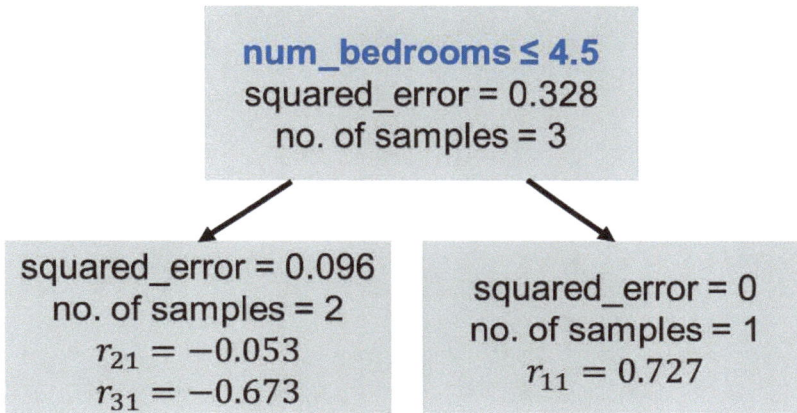

squared_error is used as the measure of the quality/purity of the split. The optimal value of the child node after split is 0 (*i.e.*, the purest child node). *e.g.*, for the root node, it is calculated as follows:

$$\text{mean} = \frac{0.727 + (-0.053) + (-0.673)}{3} = 0.000333$$

$$\text{squared\_error} = \frac{(0.727 - 0.000333)^2 + (-0.053 - 0.000333)^2 + (-0.673 - 0.000333)^2}{3}$$

$$= 0.328$$

Step 2: for $m = 1\ to\ M$:

(c) For $j = 1 \dots J_m$ compute $\gamma_{jm} = \underset{\gamma}{\text{argmin}} \sum_{x_i \in R_{jm}} L(y_i, F_{m-1}(x_i) + \gamma)$

Here, R_{jm} denotes the jth leaf node of the mth tree. In the first decision tree (*i.e.*, $m = 1$), there are only 2 leaf nodes, R_{11} and R_{21}, as shown below.

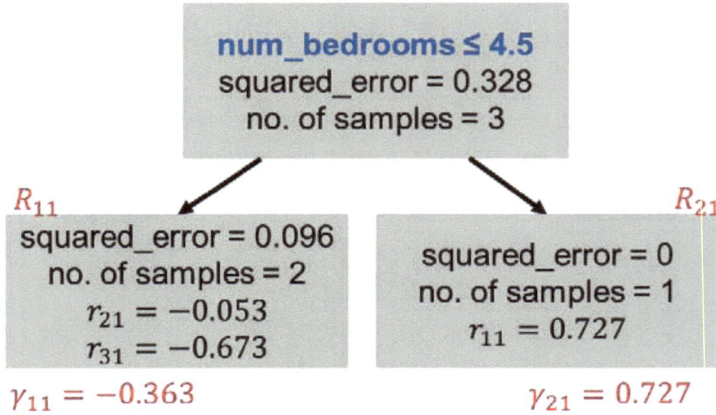

num_bedrooms ≤ 4.5
squared_error = 0.328
no. of samples = 3

R_{11}
squared_error = 0.096
no. of samples = 2
$r_{21} = -0.053$
$r_{31} = -0.673$
$\gamma_{11} = -0.363$

R_{21}
squared_error = 0
no. of samples = 1
$r_{11} = 0.727$
$\gamma_{21} = 0.727$

Correspondingly, γ_{jm} is the gamma value to be calculated for the jth leaf node of the mth tree.

$$\because m = 1, \quad \therefore \gamma_{jm} = \gamma_{j1} = \underset{\gamma}{\text{argmin}} \sum_{x_i \in R_{j1}} L(y_i, F_0(x_i) + \gamma)$$

For $j = 1$, the 1st leaf node, $\gamma_{11} = \underset{\gamma}{\text{argmin}} \sum_{x_i \in R_{11}} L(y_i, F_0(x_i) + \gamma)$, which is to find the γ that minimizes $\sum_{x_i \in R_{11}} L(y_i, F_0(x_i) + \gamma)$.

$\because$ Only the 2nd and 3rd samples (x_2 and x_3) are allocated to the 1st leaf node (R_{11}).

$$\therefore \sum_{x_i \in R_{11}} L(y_i, F_0(x_i) + \gamma) = \frac{1}{2}[y_2 - (F_0(x_2) + \gamma)]^2 + \frac{1}{2}[y_3 - (F_0(x_3) + \gamma)]^2$$

$$= \frac{1}{2}[1.5 - (1.553 + \gamma)]^2 + \frac{1}{2}[0.88 - (1.553 + \gamma)]^2$$

$$= \frac{1}{2}[-0.053 - \gamma]^2 + \frac{1}{2}[-0.673 - \gamma]^2$$

To find the minimum using the first-order derivative:

$$\frac{d \sum_{x_i \in R_{11}} L(y_i, F_0(x_i) + \gamma)}{d\gamma} = 0$$

$$[-0.053 - \gamma](-1) + [-0.673 - \gamma](-1) = 0$$

$$2\gamma = (-0.053) + (-0.673)$$

$$\gamma = \frac{(-0.053) + (-0.673)}{2} = -0.363$$

$$\therefore \gamma_{11} = -0.363$$

As can be seen, intriguingly, the γ value is just the average of the residual values on the first leaf node (*i.e.*, $\frac{r_{21}+r_{31}}{2} = \frac{(-0.053)+(-0.673)}{2} = -0.363$). This happens because of our strategic selection of loss function.

Analogously, the 2nd leaf node follows a similar calculation:

For $j = 2$, the 2nd leaf node, $\gamma_{21} = \underset{\gamma}{\text{argmin}} \sum_{x_i \in R_{21}} L(y_i, F_0(x_i) + \gamma)$, which is to find the γ that minimizes $\sum_{x_i \in R_{21}} L(y_i, F_0(x_i) + \gamma)$

$\because$ Only the 1st sample (x_1) is allocated to the 2nd leaf node (R_{21}).

$$\sum_{x_i \in R_{21}} L(y_i, F_0(x_i) + \gamma)$$

$$= \frac{1}{2}[y_1 - (F_0(x_1) + \gamma)]^2 = \frac{1}{2}[2.28 - (1.553 + \gamma)]^2 = \frac{1}{2}[0.727 - \gamma]^2$$

To find the minimum using the first-order derivative:

$$\frac{d \sum_{x_i \in R_{21}} L(y_i, F_0(x_i) + \gamma)}{d\gamma} = 0$$

$$[0.727 - \gamma](-1) = 0$$

$$\gamma = 0.727$$

$$\therefore \gamma_{21} = 0.727$$

Again, the γ value here can also be considered as the average of the single residual value on the second leaf node (*i.e.*, $\frac{r_{11}}{1} = \frac{0.727}{1} = 0.727$).

Step 2: for $m = 1\ to\ M$:

(d) Update $F_m(x_i) = F_{m-1}(x_i) + \alpha(\gamma_{jm}|x_i \in R_{jm})$

Here, α is the learning rate. We set $\alpha = 0.5$ in this example.

$$\because m = 1, \quad \therefore F_m(x_i) = F_1(x_i) = F_0(x_i) + \alpha(\gamma_{j1}|x_i \in R_{j1})$$

$\because x_1$ is allocated to R_{21} (*i.e.*, $x_1 \in R_{21}$)

$$\therefore F_1(x_1) = F_0(x_1) + 0.5 \times 0.727 = 1.553 + 0.5 \times 0.727 = 1.917$$

$\because x_2$ is allocated to R_{11} (*i.e.*, $x_2 \in R_{11}$)

$$\therefore F_1(x_2) = F_0(x_2) + 0.5 \times (-0.363) = 1.553 + 0.5 \times (-0.363) = 1.372$$

$\because x_3$ is allocated to R_{11} (*i.e.*, $x_3 \in R_{11}$)

$$\therefore F_1(x_3) = F_0(x_3) + 0.5 \times (-0.363) = 1.553 + 0.5 \times (-0.363) = 1.372$$

Update the table with the newly computed $F_1(x_i)$ values:

-	num_bedrooms (x_i)	sale_price_million (y_i)	$F_0(x_i)$	r_{i1}	$F_1(x_i)$
$i = 1$	5	2.28	1.553	0.727	1.917
$i = 2$	4	1.5	1.553	−0.053	1.372
$i = 3$	2	0.88	1.553	−0.673	1.372

By now, we have finished the first decision tree (*i.e.*, $m = 1$) of Step 2.

Assume a total of 2 decision trees (*i.e.*, $M = 2$) are to be built for the gradient boosting model in this simple numerical example. Let's continue the computation for the 2nd decision tree.

Step 2: for $m = 1\ to\ M$:

(a) Find pseudo-residuals $r_{im} = -\left[\dfrac{\partial L(y_i, F(x_i))}{\partial F(x_i)}\right]_{F(x)=F_{m-1}(x)}$ for $i = 1,2,\dots,n$

Here, m is the index of decision tree; r_{im} is the residual of the ith sample in the mth decision tree.

$$\frac{\partial L(y_i, F(x_i))}{\partial F(x_i)} = [y_i - F(x_i)](-1)$$

$$-\left[\frac{\partial L(y_i, F(x_i))}{\partial F(x_i)}\right] = [y_i - F(x_i)]$$

$$\therefore r_{im} = [y_i - F(x_i)]_{F(x)=F_{m-1}(x)}$$

When $m = 2$ (*i.e.*, the second decision tree):

$$r_{i2} = [y_i - F(x_i)]_{F(x)=F_1(x)} = y_i - F_1(x_i)$$

By plugging in all the $F_1(x_i)$ values from the final results of the first decision tree:

$$r_{12} = y_1 - F_1(x_1) = 2.28 - 1.917 = 0.363$$

$$r_{22} = y_2 - F_1(x_2) = 1.5 - 1.372 = 0.128$$

$$r_{32} = y_3 - F_1(x_3) = 0.88 - 1.372 = -0.492$$

Append the calculated r_{i2} values to the table:

-	num_bedrooms (x_i)	sale_price_million (y_i)	$F_0(x_i)$	r_{i1}	$F_1(x_i)$	r_{i2}
$i = 1$	5	2.28	1.553	0.727	1.917	0.363
$i = 2$	4	1.5	1.553	−0.053	1.372	0.128
$i = 3$	2	0.88	1.553	−0.673	1.372	−0.492

Step 2: for $m = 1 \ to \ M$:

(b) Fit the regression tree to the training dataset $\{(x_i, r_{im})\}_{i=1}^{n}$

Here, a simple regression tree is constructed as follows by taking x_i as the input and r_{i1} as the output since $m = 2$.

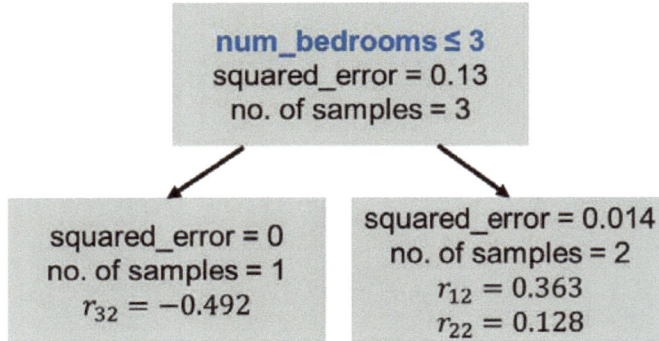

squared_error is a measure of the quality/purity of the split. The optimal value of the child node after split is 0 (*i.e.*, the purest child node). *e.g.*, for the leaf node on the right (*i.e.*, the 2nd leaf node), it is calculated as follows:

$$\text{mean} = \frac{0.363+0.128}{2} = 0.246$$

$$\text{squared\_error} = \frac{(0.363-0.246)^2+(0.128-0.246)^2}{2} = 0.014$$

Step 2: for $m = 1 \ to \ M$:

(c) For $j = 1 \dots J_m$ compute $\gamma_{jm} = \underset{\gamma}{\text{argmin}} \sum_{x_i \in R_{jm}} L(y_i, F_{m-1}(x_i) + \gamma)$

Here, R_{jm} denotes the jth leaf node of the mth tree. In the second decision tree (*i.e.*, $m = 2$), there are only 2 leaf nodes, R_{12} and R_{22} as shown below.

$$\boxed{\begin{array}{c} \textbf{num\_bedrooms} \le 3 \\ \text{squared\_error} = 0.13 \\ \text{no. of samples} = 3 \end{array}}$$

R_{12} ↙   ↘ R_{22}

$$\boxed{\begin{array}{c} \text{squared\_error} = 0 \\ \text{no. of samples} = 1 \\ r_{32} = -0.492 \end{array}}$$

$$\boxed{\begin{array}{c} \text{squared\_error} = 0.014 \\ \text{no. of samples} = 2 \\ r_{12} = 0.363 \\ r_{22} = 0.128 \end{array}}$$

$\gamma_{12} = -0.492$ $\gamma_{22} = 0.246$

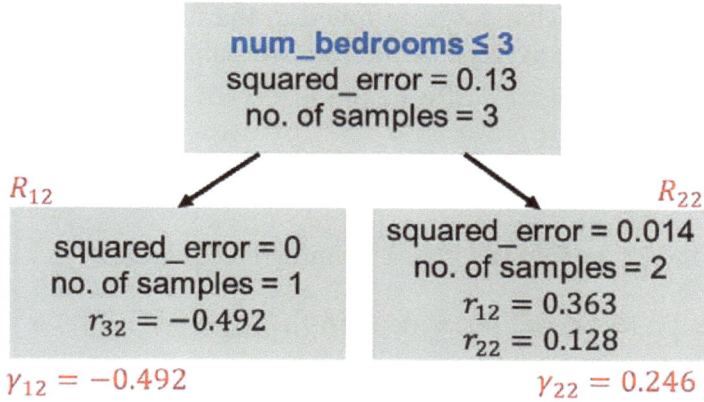

$$\because m = 2, \quad \therefore \gamma_{jm} = \gamma_{j2} = \underset{\gamma}{\mathrm{argmin}} \sum_{x_i \in R_{j2}} L(y_i, F_1(x_i) + \gamma)$$

For $j = 1$, the 1st leaf node, $\gamma_{12} = \underset{\gamma}{\mathrm{argmin}} \sum_{x_i \in R_{12}} L(y_i, F_1(x_i) + \gamma)$, which is to find the γ that minimizes $\sum_{x_i \in R_{12}} L(y_i, F_1(x_i) + \gamma)$.

$\because$ Only the 3rd sample (x_3) is allocated to the 1st leaf node (R_{12}).

$$\therefore \sum_{x_i \in R_{12}} L(y_i, F_1(x_i) + \gamma)$$

$$= \frac{1}{2} [y_3 - (F_1(x_3) + \gamma)]^2$$

$$= \frac{1}{2} [0.88 - (1.372 + \gamma)]^2 = \frac{1}{2} [-0.492 - \gamma]^2$$

To find the minimum using the first-order derivative:

$$\frac{d \sum_{x_i \in R_{12}} L(y_i, F_1(x_i) + \gamma)}{d\gamma} = 0$$

$$[-0.492 - \gamma](-1) = 0$$

$$\gamma = -0.492$$

$$\therefore \gamma_{12} = -0.492$$

Alternatively, based on what we have found in the first iteration, the γ value for each leaf node is just the average of the residual values on the leaf node. We can just apply this relationship to simplify the calculation:

$$\gamma_{12} = \frac{r_{32}}{1} = \frac{-0.492}{1} = -0.492$$

Analogously, the 2nd leaf node follows a similar calculation:

For $j = 2$, the 2nd leaf node, $\gamma_{22} = \underset{\gamma}{\text{argmin}} \sum_{x_i \in R_{22}} L(y_i, F_1(x_i) + \gamma)$, which is to find the γ that minimizes $\sum_{x_i \in R_{22}} L(y_i, F_1(x_i) + \gamma)$.

$\because$ Only the 1st and 2nd samples (x_1 and x_2) are allocated to the 2nd leaf node (R_{22}).

$$\therefore \sum_{x_i \in R_{22}} L(y_i, F_1(x_i) + \gamma)$$

$$= \frac{1}{2}[y_1 - (F_1(x_1) + \gamma)]^2 + \frac{1}{2}[y_2 - (F_1(x_2) + \gamma)]^2$$

$$= \frac{1}{2}[2.28 - (1.917 + \gamma)]^2 + \frac{1}{2}[1.5 - (1.372 + \gamma)]^2$$

$$= \frac{1}{2}[0.363 - \gamma]^2 + \frac{1}{2}[0.128 - \gamma]^2$$

To find the minimum using the first-order derivative:

$$\frac{d \sum_{x_i \in R_{22}} L(y_i, F_1(x_i) + \gamma)}{d\gamma} = 0$$

$$[0.363 - \gamma](-1) + [0.128 - \gamma](-1) = 0$$

$$2\gamma = 0.363 + 0.128$$

$$\gamma = \frac{0.363 + 0.128}{2} = 0.246$$

$$\therefore \gamma_{22} = 0.246$$

Alternatively, based on what we have found in the first iteration, the γ value for each leaf node is just the average of the residual values on the leaf node. We can just apply this relationship to simplify the calculation:

$$\gamma_{22} = \frac{r_{12} + r_{22}}{2} = \frac{0.363 + 0.128}{2} = 0.246$$

Step 2: for $m = 1\ to\ M$:

(d) Update $F_m(x_i) = F_{m-1}(x_i) + \alpha(\gamma_{jm}|x_i \in R_{jm})$

Here, α is the learning rate. We set $\alpha = 0.5$ in this example.

$$\because m = 2, \quad \therefore F_m(x_i) = F_2(x_i) = F_1(x_i) + \alpha(\gamma_{j2}|x_i \in R_{j2})$$

$\because x_1$ is allocated to R_{22} (i.e., $x_1 \in R_{22}$)

$$\therefore F_2(x_1) = F_1(x_1) + 0.5 \times 0.246 = 1.917 + 0.5 \times 0.246 = 2.04$$

$\because x_2$ is allocated to R_{22} (i.e., $x_2 \in R_{22}$)

$$\therefore F_2(x_2) = F_1(x_2) + 0.5 \times 0.246 = 1.372 + 0.5 \times 0.246 = 1.495$$

$\because x_3$ is allocated to R_{12} (i.e., $x_3 \in R_{12}$)

$$\therefore F_2(x_3) = F_1(x_3) + 0.5 \times (-0.492) = 1.372 + 0.5 \times (-0.492) = 1.126$$

Update the table with the newly computed $F_2(x_i)$ values:

-	num_bedrooms (x_i)	sale_price_million (y_i)	$F_0(x_i)$	r_{i1}	$F_1(x_i)$	r_{i2}	$F_2(x_i)$
$i = 1$	5	2.28	1.553	0.727	1.917	0.363	2.04
$i = 2$	4	1.5	1.553	−0.053	1.372	0.128	1.495
$i = 3$	2	0.88	1.553	−0.673	1.372	-0.492	1.126

It is noticed that the final results after the second decision tree (*i.e.*, $F_2(x_i)$ values) are closer to the true y_i values, as compared with $F_1(x_i)$ values, indicating the performance of the gradient boosting regression model has been improving, and we are on the right track!

By now, we have finished the second decision tree (*i.e.*, $m = 2$) of Step 2. Since we assumed the gradient boosting model consists of a total of 2 decision trees only in this example, we have completed the whole Step 2.

Looking back, we used the following expression in the Step 2(d) when $m = 2$:

$$F_2(x_i) = F_1(x_i) + \alpha(\gamma_{j2}|x_i \in R_{j2})$$

Do not forget that we applied this expression in the Step 2(d) when $m = 1$:

$$F_1(x_i) = F_0(x_i) + \alpha(\gamma_{j1}|x_i \in R_{j1})$$

If concatenating them together, we can get this expression:

$$F_2(x_i) = F_0(x_i) + \alpha(\gamma_{j1}|x_i \in R_{j1}) + \alpha(\gamma_{j2}|x_i \in R_{j2})$$

This will be our trained gradient boosting regression model for this simple example!

Here, $(\gamma_{j1}|x_i \in R_{j1})$ and $(\gamma_{j2}|x_i \in R_{j2})$ are the values we can find from the first and second decision trees, respectively. α is the learning rate, and we set it as 0.5 in this example.

Visually, the model is like this:

$$F_2(x) = 1.553 + 0.5 \cdot \quad + 0.5 \cdot$$

Step 3: Output $F_m(x)$

Finally, we come to the 3rd and the last step of the algorithm, making predictions for previously unseen data (*i.e.*, new data) using the trained gradient boosting regression model. For instance, if there is a house with 3 bedrooms, the predicted price by the model will be:

$$F_2(x) = 1.553 + 0.5 \cdot (-0.363) + 0.5 \cdot (-0.492) = 1.126$$

Therefore, for the house with 3 bedrooms, the sale price is predicted to be 1.126 million dollars. As expected, the prediction is not that good at this stage because our model merely got 2 shallow decision trees and was built using only 3 training samples for demonstration. However, it paves the way for building a more complex and accurate model! We now have a much clearer understanding of how it works at each step of the gradient boosting algorithm for regression.

Now, let us compare the results obtained above with that from the off-the-shelf gradient boosting regressor offered by the scikit-learn library.

The complete code file can be downloaded from our shared folder in Google Drive:

https://drive.google.com/drive/folders/1FqJvo4ZPazNbEH_GlHFoodqvegnQmHcn?usp=share_link

```python
import pandas as pd
import numpy as np
from sklearn.ensemble import GradientBoostingRegressor
from sklearn import tree

# The small dataset
data = np.array([[5,2.28],
                 [4,1.5],
                 [2,0.88]])
col_names = ['num_bedrooms', 'sale_price_million']
print(pd.DataFrame(data, columns=col_names), "\n")

X = data[:, 0].reshape(-1, 1) # all rows, 1st column
y = data[:, 1] # all rows, 2nd column
```

```
   num_bedrooms   sale_price_million
0           5.0                 2.28
1           4.0                 1.50
2           2.0                 0.88
```

```
gbr = GradientBoostingRegressor(n_estimators=2,
                                criterion='squared_error',
                                learning_rate=0.5,
                                max_depth=1)
# n_estimators: The number of boosting stages (i.e., trees)
# criterion: The function to measure the quality of a split
# learning_rate: The alpha value
# max_depth: the maximum depth of each tree

gbr.fit(X, y)
```

```
print("training dataset, predicted value:\n",
      np.round( gbr.predict(X), decimals=3 ).reshape(-1,1))
# same as our manually calculated values
```

```
training dataset, predicted value:
[[2.04 ]
 [1.495]
 [1.126]]
```

```
_ = tree.plot_tree(gbr.estimators_[0][0],
                   feature_names=['num_bedrooms'],
                   filled=True)
print("First Decision Tree:")
```

```
First Decision Tree:
```

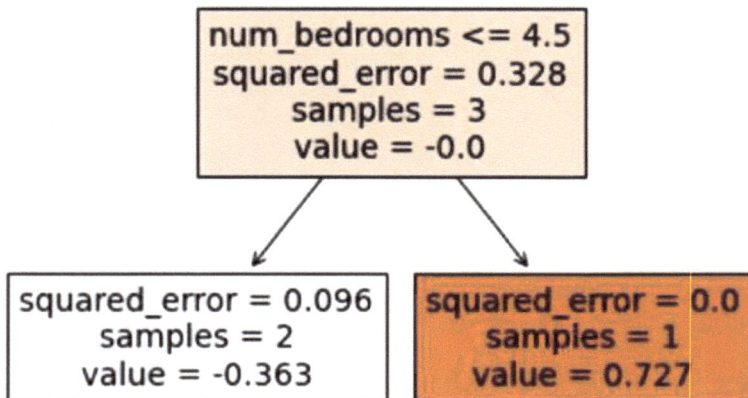

```
_ = tree.plot_tree(gbr.estimators_[1][0],
                      feature_names=['num_bedrooms'],
                      filled=True)
print("Second Decision Tree:")
```

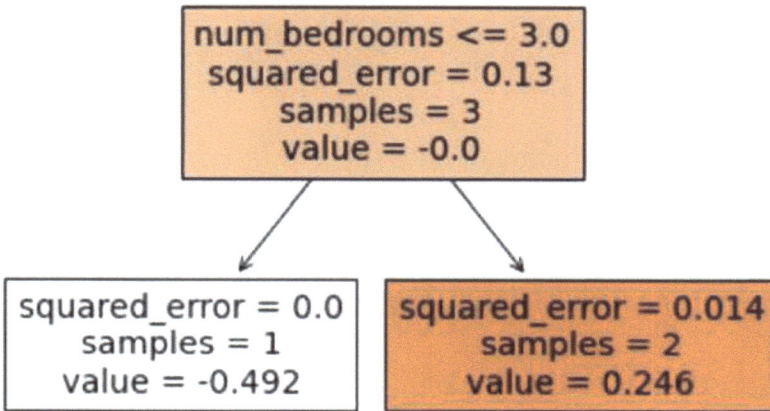

Second Decision Tree:

```
                    num_bedrooms <= 3.0
                    squared_error = 0.13
                       samples = 3
                       value = -0.0


    squared_error = 0.0          squared_error = 0.014
       samples = 1                  samples = 2
     value = -0.492               value = 0.246
```

```
# New house with 3 bedrooms, the predicted price
# by the model will be:
np.round( gbr.predict(np.array([[3]])), decimals=3 )
```

array([1.126])

As can be seen from the results of the scikit-learn gradient boosting regressor and compared with our manually calculated results, the same decision trees are generated, with the same squared_error for all the nodes of the decision trees, and the same gamma values for all the leaf nodes of the decision trees (note that scikit-learn simply uses "value" in the plots of decision trees to represent "gamma value"). Besides, the same predictions for the 3 training samples are obtained (*i.e.*, 2.04 for x_1, 1.495 for x_2, and 1.126 for x_3). Finally, the same prediction for the previously unseen house with 3 bedrooms is obtained (*i.e.*, 1.126).

6.4. MATHEMATICS OF GRADIENT BOOSTING FOR CLASSI-FICATION

To understand the gradient boosting for classification, we must first review two fundamental statistics terminologies, namely, probability and odds. Probability (P) represents the chance that an event occurs. Odds is just an expression of relative probability and is defined as the ratio of the probability of an event occurring to the probability of an event not occurring (*i.e.*, $odds = \frac{P}{1-P}$). For example, suppose there are 2 blue and 1 red balls,

$$P_{blue} = \frac{2}{3} = 0.667$$

$$odds_{blue} = \frac{2}{1} = 2$$

Following the original definition of odds (*i.e.*, $odds = \frac{P}{1-P}$), it can also be written as:

$$odds_{blue} = \frac{P_{blue}}{1 - P_{blue}} = \frac{\frac{2}{3}}{1 - \frac{2}{3}} = 2$$

For the original definition of odds (*i.e.*, $odds = \frac{P}{1-P}$), apply *log* operation on both sides of the equation:

$$log(odds) = log(\frac{P}{1 - P})$$

Note that all the *log* used in the chapter refer to the natural logarithm (*i.e.*, to the base *e*), unless otherwise stated.

The original equation for odds (*i.e.*, $odds = \frac{P}{1-P}$) can be transformed into the following equation by taking P to the left side of the equal sign:

$$P = \frac{1}{1 + \frac{1}{odds}}$$

Since *log* used is a natural logarithm (*i.e.*, to the base *e*), it can be further transformed to:

$$P = \frac{1}{1 + \frac{1}{e^{log(odds)}}}$$

$$P = \frac{1}{1 + e^{-log(odds)}}$$

$$P = \frac{e^{log(odds)}}{1 + e^{log(odds)}}$$

The algorithm of gradient boosting classification is the same as that of gradient boosting regression, except for the different loss functions, as shown in Table **6.3**.

Table 6.3. Pseudocode and mathematics of gradient boosting for classification.

Input: Training dataset $\{(x_i, y_i)\}_{i=1}^n$ and a differentiable Loss Function $L(y_i, F(x_i)) = -y_i F(x_i) + log(1 + e^{F(x_i)})$, $where\ F(x_i) = log(odds_i)$

Step 1: Initialize model with a constant value $F_0(x) = \underset{\gamma}{argmin} \sum_{i=1}^n L(y_i, \gamma)$

Step 2: for $m = 1\ to\ M$:

(a) Find pseudo-residuals $r_{im} = -\left[\frac{\partial L(y_i, F(x_i))}{\partial F(x_i)}\right]_{F(x)=F_{m-1}(x)}$ for $i = 1, 2, \dots, n$

(b) Fit the regression tree to the training dataset $\{(x_i, r_{im})\}_{i=1}^n$

(c) For $j = 1 \dots J_m$ compute $\gamma_{jm} = \underset{\gamma}{argmin} \sum_{x_i \in R_{jm}} L(y_i, F_{m-1}(x_i) + \gamma)$

(d) Update $F_m(x_i) = F_{m-1}(x_i) + \alpha(\gamma_{jm} | x_i \in R_{jm})$

Step 3: Output $F_m(x)$

The loss function employed in gradient boosting classification appears somewhat peculiar at first glance. It essentially starts from the loss function we have seen in Chapter 4 for logistic regression, that is, the cross-entropy loss function!

$$L = -\left[y_i\ log(P_i)\ +\ (1 - y_i)\ log(1 - P_i)\right]$$

Here, P_i is the predicted probability ($\in [0, 1]$) for the ith sample and y_i is the true label (*e.g.,* 0 or 1) for the ith sample.

Then, a series of transformations of the cross-entropy loss function are performed:

$$L = -\left[y_i \log(P_i) + \log(1 - P_i) - y_i \log(1 - P_i)\right]$$

$$L = -\left[y_i\big(\log(P_i) - \log(1 - P_i)\big) + \log(1 - P_i)\right]$$

$$L = -\left[y_i \log\left(\frac{P_i}{1 - P_i}\right) + \log(1 - P_i)\right]$$

$$\because odds = \frac{P}{1-P} \text{ and } P = \frac{e^{\log(odds)}}{1 + e^{\log(odds)}}$$

$$\therefore L = -\left[y_i \log(odds_i) + \log\left(1 - \frac{e^{\log(odds_i)}}{1 + e^{\log(odds_i)}}\right)\right]$$

$$L = -\left[y_i \log(odds_i) + \log\left(\frac{1}{1 + e^{\log(odds_i)}}\right)\right]$$

$$L = -\left[y_i \log(odds_i) + \log(1) - \log\big(1 + e^{\log(odds_i)}\big)\right]$$

$$L = -y_i \log(odds_i) + \log\big(1 + e^{\log(odds_i)}\big)$$

We set $F(x_i) = \log(odds_i)$ to represent the predicted value for the ith sample before it is mapped to the predicted probability by the previously derived equation:

$$P = \frac{1}{1 + e^{-\log(odds)}} = \frac{e^{\log(odds)}}{1 + e^{\log(odds)}}$$

Note: Does this $P = \frac{1}{1+e^{-\log(odds)}}$ remind you of the sigmoid function utilized in Chapter 4 for logistic regression?

Finally, replace all the $\log(odds_i)$ with $F(x_i)$ in the loss function:

$$L = -y_i F(x_i) + \log\big(1 + e^{F(x_i)}\big)$$

So, L has become a function of y_i and $F(x_i)$:

$$L(y_i, F(x_i)) = -y_i F(x_i) + \log\big(1 + e^{F(x_i)}\big)$$

Here, y_i represents the true output (*e.g.*, 0 or 1); and $F(x_i)$ represents the predicted value (this is not the predicted probability in the range of 0 to 1).

Next, as per the Input step of the gradient boosting algorithm, we must check whether the loss function is differentiable with respect to $F(x_i)$:

$$\frac{\partial L(y_i, F(x_i))}{\partial F(x_i)} = -y_i + \frac{1}{1 + e^{F(x_i)}} e^{F(x_i)} = -y_i + \frac{e^{F(x_i)}}{1 + e^{F(x_i)}}$$

$$= -y_i + \frac{e^{\log(odds_i)}}{1 + e^{\log(odds_i)}} = -y_i + P_i$$

Always bear in mind that $P = \frac{e^{\log(odds)}}{1 + e^{\log(odds)}}$ when reading this section of gradient boosting classification.

As can be seen from the first-order differentiation of $L(y_i, F(x_i))$ with respect to $F(x_i)$, it finally leads to a very concise expression (*i.e.*, $-y_i + P_i$), where P_i is the predicted probability ($\in [0, 1]$) for the ith sample, and y_i is the true output (0 or 1) for the ith sample.

6.5. Numerical Example and Code Comparison of Gradient Boosting for Classification

Suppose we have a small training dataset presented in Table **6.4** with only 3 samples (*i.e.*, $n = 3$), which has one feature, the total number of bedrooms in the house (abbreviated as **num_bedrooms**), as well as one output about whether it is easy to sell the house (abbreviated as **is_easy_sell**) in the property market. The output is dichotomous with only two possible outputs (*i.e.*, 0 and 1), where 0 means No (not easy to sell) and 1 means Yes (easy to sell). In other words, for this example, X is num_bedrooms, and Y is is_easy_sell. Our task is to build a gradient boosting classification model that maps the X and Y.

Table 6.4. The small dataset for gradient boosting classification.

-	num_bedrooms (x_i)	is_easy_sell (y_i)
$i = 1$	5	1
$i = 2$	4	0

$i = 3$	2	1

Using this small training dataset, we will break down the pseudocode into bite-sized chunks and execute it step by step.

Input: Training dataset $\{(x_i, y_i)\}_{i=1}^n$ and a differentiable Loss Function $L(y_i, F(x_i)) = -y_i F(x_i) + log(1 + e^{F(x_i)})$, where $F(x_i) = log(odds_i)$

For the input step, we have had the training dataset as presented in Table **6.4** and checked that the loss function is differentiable.

$$\frac{\partial L(y_i, F(x_i))}{\partial F(x_i)} = -y_i + \frac{1}{1 + e^{F(x_i)}} e^{F(x_i)} = -y_i + \frac{e^{F(x_i)}}{1 + e^{F(x_i)}}$$

$$= -y_i + \frac{e^{log(odds_i)}}{1 + e^{log(odds_i)}} = -y_i + P_i$$

Step 1: Initialize model with a constant value $F_0(x) = \arg\min_\gamma \sum_{i=1}^n L(y_i, \gamma)$

Here, γ represents the predicted value and $F_0(x)$ is the γ value that minimizes the total loss, $\sum_{i=1}^n L(y_i, \gamma)$.

$$\sum_{i=1}^n L(y_i, \gamma) = L(y_1, \gamma) + L(y_2, \gamma) + L(y_3, \gamma)$$

$$= -y_1\gamma + log(1 + e^\gamma) - y_2\gamma + log(1 + e^\gamma) - y_3\gamma + log(1 + e^\gamma)$$

To find the minimum using the first-order derivative:

$$\frac{d \sum_{i=1}^n L(y_i, \gamma)}{d\gamma} = 0$$

$$\therefore -y_1 + \frac{e^\gamma}{1 + e^\gamma} - y_2 + \frac{e^\gamma}{1 + e^\gamma} - y_3 + \frac{e^\gamma}{1 + e^\gamma} = 0$$

$$3\frac{e^\gamma}{1 + e^\gamma} = y_1 + y_2 + y_3$$

$$\frac{e^\gamma}{1 + e^\gamma} = \frac{y_1 + y_2 + y_3}{3} = \frac{1 + 0 + 1}{3} = \frac{2}{3}$$

$$3e^\gamma = 2(1 + e^\gamma)$$

$$e^\gamma = 2$$

$$\gamma = log(2) = 0.693$$

Bear in mind that $F_0(x)$ is the γ value that minimizes the total loss, so initially $F_0(x) = \gamma = 0.693$.

$$\because F(x) = log(odds)$$

$\therefore F_0(x) =$ initial $log(odds) = 0.693$, which is a constant value for all samples initially.

Hence,

$$F_0(x_1) = \text{initial } log(odds_1) = 0.693$$

$$F_0(x_2) = \text{initial } log(odds_2) = 0.693$$

$$F_0(x_3) = \text{initial } log(odds_3) = 0.693$$

Find the predicted probability P_i based on the computed initial $log(odds_i)$:

$$\because P_i = \frac{e^{log(odds_i)}}{1 + e^{log(odds_i)}}$$

$$\therefore P_1 = \frac{e^{log(odds_1)}}{1 + e^{log(odds_1)}} = \frac{e^{0.693}}{1 + e^{0.693}} = 0.667$$

$$P_2 = \frac{e^{log(odds_2)}}{1 + e^{log(odds_2)}} = \frac{e^{0.693}}{1 + e^{0.693}} = 0.667$$

$$P_3 = \frac{e^{log(odds_3)}}{1 + e^{log(odds_3)}} = \frac{e^{0.693}}{1 + e^{0.693}} = 0.667$$

Append the $F_0(x) =$ initial $log(odds)$ and P_i to the table:

-	num_bedrooms (x_i)	is_easy_sell (y_i)	$F_0(x_i)$ = initial $log(odds_i)$	P_i
$i = 1$	5	1	0.693	0.667
$i = 2$	4	0	0.693	0.667
$i = 3$	2	1	0.693	0.667

Step 2: for $m = 1\ to\ M$:

(a) Find pseudo-residuals $r_{im} = -\left[\frac{\partial L(y_i, F(x_i))}{\partial F(x_i)}\right]_{F(x)=F_{m-1}(x)}$ for $i = 1, 2, \dots, n$

Here, m is the index of decision tree; r_{im} is the residual of the ith sample in the mth decision tree.

$$\because \frac{\partial L(y_i, F(x_i))}{\partial F(x_i)} = -y_i + P_i$$

$$\therefore -\left[\frac{\partial L(y_i, F(x_i))}{\partial F(x_i)}\right] = y_i - P_i$$

When $m = 1$ (*i.e.*, the first decision tree):

$$r_{i1} = y_i - P_i$$

Here, the P_i must be corresponding to $F_0(x_i)$ since dealing with the first decision tree

By plugging in all the P_i values identified from Step 1:

$$r_{11} = y_1 - P_1 = 1 - 0.667 = 0.333$$

$$r_{21} = y_2 - P_2 = 0 - 0.667 = -0.667$$

$$r_{31} = y_3 - P_3 = 1 - 0.667 = 0.333$$

Append the calculated r_{i1} values to the original table:

-	num_bedrooms (x_i)	is_easy_sell (y_i)	$F_0(x_i)$ = initial $log(odds_i)$	P_i	r_{i1}
i = 1	5	1	0.693	0.667	0.333
i = 2	4	0	0.693	0.667	-0.667
i = 3	2	1	0.693	0.667	0.333

Step 2: for $m = 1\ to\ M$:

(b) Fit the regression tree to the training dataset $\{(x_i, r_{im})\}_{i=1}^n$

Here, a simple regression tree is constructed as follows by taking x_i as the input and r_{i1} as the output since $m = 1$.

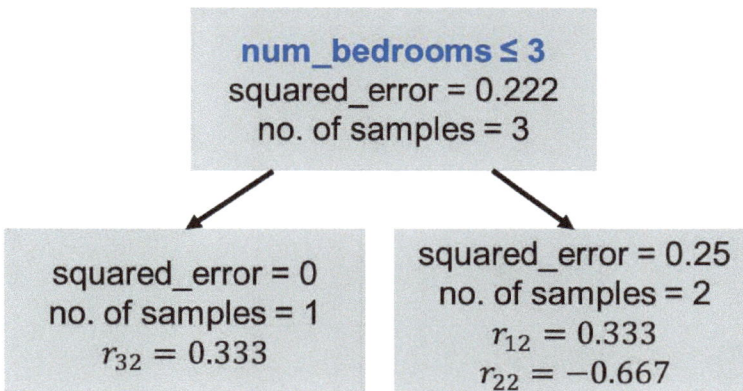

num_bedrooms ≤ 3
squared_error = 0.222
no. of samples = 3

squared_error = 0
no. of samples = 1
$r_{32} = 0.333$

squared_error = 0.25
no. of samples = 2
$r_{12} = 0.333$
$r_{22} = -0.667$

squared_error is used as the measure of the quality/purity of the split. The optimal value of the child node after split is 0 (*i.e.*, the purest child node), *e.g.*, for the leaf node on the right (*i.e.*, the 2nd leaf node), it is calculated as follows:

$$\text{mean} = \frac{0.333+(-0.667)}{2} = -0.167$$

$$\text{squared\_error} = \frac{(0.333-(-0.167))^2+(-0.667-(-0.167))^2}{2} = 0.25$$

Next, before diving into **Step 2(c)**, let us quickly review the Taylor series.

$$f(x) = f(a) + \frac{f'(a)}{1!}(x - a) + \frac{f''(a)}{2!}(x - a)^2 + \frac{f'''(a)}{3!}(x - a)^3 + \; \dots$$

Here, a is a constant number, and x represents the independent variable

Take a simple function, $f(x) = e^x$, for demonstration:

$$f'(x) = e^x \quad f''(x) = e^x \quad f'''(x) = e^x$$

$$\text{Let } a = 0, \text{ then } f(a) = 1, \; f'(a) = 1, f''(a) = 1, f'''(a) = 1$$

Apply the Taylor series formula:

$$\therefore f(x) = 1 + \frac{1}{1!}x + \frac{1}{2!}x^2 + \frac{1}{3!}x^3 + \cdots$$

A quick validation can be conducted for the Taylor series expansion. If using the original function $f(x) = e^x$, when $x = 0.5$, $e^{0.5} = 1.649$. If using the Taylor Series expansion:

$$1 + \frac{1}{1!}x + \frac{1}{2!}x^2 + \frac{1}{3!}x^3 = 1 + 0.5 + \frac{1}{2}0.5^2 + \frac{1}{6}0.5^3 = 1.646$$

As can be seen, a good approximation is obtained when using Taylor Series.

Now, let us continue with the **Step 2(c)** of the gradient boosting classification.

Step 2: for $m = 1 \; to \; M$:

(c) For $j = 1 \dots J_m$ compute $\gamma_{jm} = \underset{\gamma}{\text{argmin}} \sum_{x_i \in R_{jm}} L(y_i, F_{m-1}(x_i) + \gamma)$

Here, R_{jm} denotes the jth leaf node of the mth tree. In the first decision tree (*i.e.*, $m = 1$), there are only 2 leaf nodes, R_{11} and R_{21} as shown below.

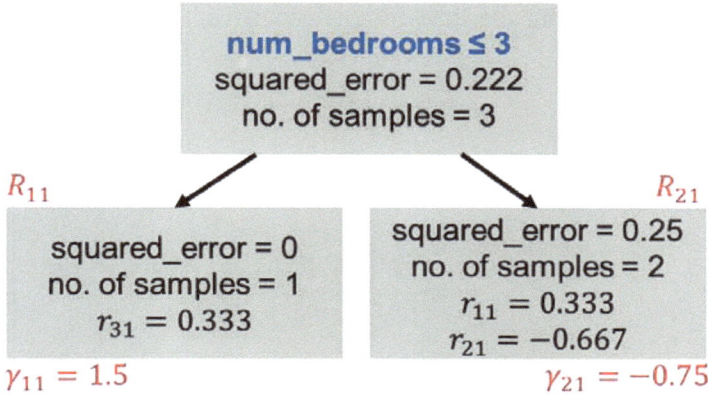

Correspondingly, γ_{jm} is the gamma value to be calculated for the jth leaf node of the mth tree.

$$\because m = 1, \quad \therefore \gamma_{jm} = \gamma_{j1} = \underset{\gamma}{\text{argmin}} \sum_{x_i \in R_{j1}} L(y_i, F_0(x_i) + \gamma)$$

For $j = 1$, the 1st leaf node, $\gamma_{11} = \underset{\gamma}{\text{argmin}} \sum_{x_i \in R_{11}} L(y_i, F_0(x_i) + \gamma)$, which is to find the γ that minimizes $\sum_{x_i \in R_{11}} L(y_i, F_0(x_i) + \gamma)$.

$\because$ Only the 3rd sample (x_3) is allocated to the 1st leaf node (R_{11}).

$$\therefore \sum_{x_i \in R_{11}} L(y_i, F_0(x_i) + \gamma)$$

$$= L(y_3, F_0(x_3) + \gamma) = -y_3(F_0(x_3) + \gamma) + log\left(1 + e^{F_0(x_3) + \gamma}\right)$$

Apply 2nd order Taylor series formula, with the independent variable as $F_0(x_3) + \gamma$ and $a = F_0(x_3)$.

$$L(y_3, F_0(x_3) + \gamma)$$
$$= L(y_3, F_0(x_3)) + L'(y_3, F_0(x_3)) \cdot (F_0(x_3) + \gamma - F_0(x_3))$$
$$+ \frac{L''(y_3, F_0(x_3))}{2!} \cdot (F_0(x_3) + \gamma - F_0(x_3))^2$$

$$\therefore L(y_3, F_0(x_3) + \gamma) = L(y_3, F_0(x_3)) + L'(y_3, F_0(x_3))\gamma + \frac{L''(y_3, F_0(x_3))}{2}\gamma^2$$

To find the minimum using the first-order derivative:

$$\frac{dL(y_3, F_0(x_3) + \gamma)}{d\gamma} = 0$$

$$L'(y_3, F_0(x_3)) + L''(y_3, F_0(x_3))\gamma = 0$$

$$\gamma = \frac{-L'(y_3, F_0(x_3))}{L''(y_3, F_0(x_3))}$$

As derived previously, the first-order differentiation of the loss function:

$$\because \frac{\partial L(y_i, F(x_i))}{\partial F(x_i)} = -y_i + P_i$$

$$\therefore L'(y_i, F(x_i)) = -y_i + P_i$$

$$\therefore L'(y_i, F_0(x_i)) = -y_i + P_i = -r_{i1}$$

Here, the P_i must be corresponding to $F_0(x_i)$ since dealing with the first decision tree.

$$L'(y_3, F_0(x_3)) = -y_3 + P_3 = -r_{31}$$

$$-L'(y_3, F_0(x_3)) = y_3 - P_3 = r_{31}$$

Second-order differentiation is nothing but the first-order differentiation of the first-order derivative. Besides, always bear in mind that $P_i = \frac{e^{log(odds_i)}}{1+e^{log(odds_i)}}$ and $F(x_i) = log(odds_i)$ when reading this section of gradient boosting classification. So, the differentiation with respect to $F(x_i)$ is the same as the differentiation with respect to $log(odds_i)$.

$$L''\big(y_i, F(x_i)\big) = L'\big(\, L'\big(y_i, F(x_i)\big)\,\big) = L'(-y_i + P_i) = L'\left(-y_i + \frac{e^{\log(odds_i)}}{1 + e^{\log(odds_i)}}\right)$$

$$= L'\left(-y_i + \big(1 + e^{\log(odds_i)}\big)^{-1} e^{\log(odds_i)}\right)$$

$$= 0 + (-1)\big(1 + e^{\log(odds_i)}\big)^{-2} e^{\log(odds_i)} e^{\log(odds_i)}$$

$$+ \big(1 + e^{\log(odds_i)}\big)^{-1} e^{\log(odds_i)}$$

$$= \frac{-\big(e^{\log(odds_i)}\big)^2}{(1 + e^{\log(odds_i)})^2} + \frac{e^{\log(odds_i)}}{1 + e^{\log(odds_i)}}$$

$$= \frac{-\big(e^{\log(odds_i)}\big)^2}{(1 + e^{\log(odds_i)})^2} + \frac{\big(1 + e^{\log(odds_i)}\big) e^{\log(odds_i)}}{(1 + e^{\log(odds_i)})^2}$$

$$= \frac{e^{\log(odds_i)}}{(1 + e^{\log(odds_i)})^2} = \frac{e^{\log(odds_i)} \cdot 1}{(1 + e^{\log(odds_i)}) \cdot (1 + e^{\log(odds_i)})}$$

$$= \frac{e^{\log(odds_i)}}{(1 + e^{\log(odds_i)})} \cdot \frac{1}{(1 + e^{\log(odds_i)})} = P_i(1 - P_i)$$

$$\therefore L''\big(y_i, F_0(x_i)\big) = P_i(1 - P_i)$$

Here, the P_i must be corresponding to $F_0(x_i)$ since dealing with the first decision tree.

Do not forget the first order differentiation derived above:

$$L'\big(y_i, F_0(x_i)\big) = -y_i + P_i = -r_{i1}$$

So, finally gamma value for the 1st leaf R_{11}:

$$\gamma = \frac{-L'\big(y_3, F_0(x_3)\big)}{L''\big(y_3, F_0(x_3)\big)} = \frac{r_{31}}{P_3(1 - P_3)} = \frac{0.333}{0.667(1 - 0.667)} = 1.5$$

$$\therefore \gamma_{11} = 1.5$$

Analogously, the 2nd leaf node follows a similar calculation:

For $j = 2$, the 2nd leaf node, $\gamma_{21} = \underset{\gamma}{\text{argmin}} \sum_{x_i \in R_{21}} L(y_i, F_0(x_i) + \gamma)$, which is to find the γ that minimizes $\sum_{x_i \in R_{21}} L(y_i, F_0(x_i) + \gamma)$.

$\because$ Only the 1st and 2nd samples (x_1 and x_2) are allocated to the 2nd leaf node (R_{21}).

$$\sum_{x_i \in R_{21}} L(y_i, F_0(x_i) + \gamma)$$

$$= L(y_1, F_0(x_1) + \gamma) + L(y_2, F_0(x_2) + \gamma)$$

$$= L(y_1, F_0(x_1)) + L'(y_1, F_0(x_1))\gamma + \frac{L''(y_1, F_0(x_1))}{2}\gamma^2 + L(y_2, F_0(x_2))$$
$$+ L'(y_2, F_0(x_2))\gamma + \frac{L''(y_2, F_0(x_2))}{2}\gamma^2$$

To find the minimum using the first-order derivative:

$$\frac{d(L(y_1, F_0(x_1) + \gamma) + L(y_2, F_0(x_2) + \gamma))}{d\gamma} = 0$$

$$L'(y_1, F_0(x_1)) + L''(y_1, F_0(x_1))\gamma + L'(y_2, F_0(x_2)) + L''(y_2, F_0(x_2))\gamma = 0$$

$$\gamma = \frac{[-L'(y_1, F_0(x_1))] + [-L'(y_2, F_0(x_2))]}{L''(y_1, F_0(x_1)) + L''(y_2, F_0(x_2))}$$

As we derived above:

$$L'(y_i, F_0(x_i)) = -y_i + P_i = -r_{i1}$$

$$L''(y_i, F_0(x_i)) = P_i(1 - P_i)$$

$$\therefore \gamma = \frac{[-L'(y_1, F_0(x_1))] + [-L'(y_2, F_0(x_2))]}{L''(y_1, F_0(x_1)) + L''(y_2, F_0(x_2))} = \frac{r_{11} + r_{21}}{P_1(1 - P_1) + P_2(1 - P_2)}$$
$$= \frac{0.333 + (-0.667)}{0.667(1 - 0.667) + 0.667(1 - 0.667)} = -0.75$$

$$\therefore \gamma_{21} = -0.75$$

Let us summarize our findings and simplify the calculations of the γ value for each leaf node. As observed from the final γ expression right above, the numerator is just the sum of residuals of the samples allocated to the leaf node (*e.g.*, $r_{11} + r_{21}$), and the denominator is just the sum of $P_i(1 - P_i)$ of the samples allocated to the leaf node (e.g., $P_1(1 - P_1) + P_2(1 - P_2)$). We can straightway apply these relationships directly from the next decision tree onwards.

Step 2: for $m = 1\ to\ M$:

(d) Update $F_m(x_i) = F_{m-1}(x_i) + \alpha(\gamma_{jm}|x_i \in R_{jm})$

Here, α is the learning rate. We set $\alpha = 0.5$ in this example.

$$\because m = 1, \quad \therefore F_m(x_i) = F_1(x_i) = F_0(x_i) + \alpha(\gamma_{j1}|x_i \in R_{j1})$$

Furthermore, the probability for each sample needs to be updated to be corresponding to $F_1(x_i)$ now:

$$P_i = \frac{e^{log(odds_i)}}{1 + e^{log(odds_i)}} = \frac{e^{F_1(x_i)}}{1 + e^{F_1(x_i)}}$$

$\because x_1 \in R_{21} \quad \therefore F_1(x_1) = F_0(x_1) + 0.5 \times (-0.75) = 0.693 + 0.5 \times (-0.75) = 0.318$

$$P_1 = \frac{e^{log(odds_1)}}{1 + e^{log(odds_1)}} = \frac{e^{F_1(x_1)}}{1 + e^{F_1(x_1)}} = \frac{e^{0.318}}{1 + e^{0.318}} = 0.5788$$

$\because x_2 \in R_{21} \quad \therefore F_1(x_2) = F_0(x_2) + 0.5 \times (-0.75) = 0.693 + 0.5 \times (-0.75) = 0.318$

$$P_2 = \frac{e^{log(odds_2)}}{1 + e^{log(odds_2)}} = \frac{e^{F_1(x_2)}}{1 + e^{F_1(x_2)}} = \frac{e^{0.318}}{1 + e^{0.318}} = 0.5788$$

$\because x_3 \in R_{11} \quad \therefore F_1(x_3) = F_0(x_3) + 0.5 \times (1.5) = 0.693 + 0.5 \times (1.5) = 1.443$

$$P_3 = \frac{e^{log(odds_3)}}{1 + e^{log(odds_3)}} = \frac{e^{F_1(x_3)}}{1 + e^{F_1(x_3)}} = \frac{e^{1.443}}{1 + e^{1.443}} = 0.8089$$

Update the newly computed $F_1(x_i)$ and the corresponding P_i values to the table:

-	num_bedrooms (x_i)	is_easy_sell (y_i)	$F_0(x_i)$ = initial $log(odds_i)$	P_i	r_{i1}	$F_1(x_i)$ = $log(odds_i)$	P_i
$i = 1$	5	1	0.693	0.667	0.333	0.318	0.5788

$i = 2$	4	0	0.693	0.667	-0.667	0.318	0.5788
$i = 3$	2	1	0.693	0.667	0.333	1.443	0.8089

By now, we have finished the first decision tree (*i.e.*, $m = 1$) of Step 2.

Assume a total of 2 decision trees (*i.e.*, $M = 2$) are to be built for the gradient boosting model in this simple numerical example. Let's continue the computation for the 2nd decision tree.

Step 2: for $m = 1\ to\ M$:

(a) Find pseudo-residuals $r_{im} = -\left[\dfrac{\partial L(y_i, F(x_i))}{\partial F(x_i)}\right]_{F(x)=F_{m-1}(x)}$ for $i = 1, 2, \ldots, n$

Here, m is the index of the decision tree; r_{im} is the residual of the ith sample in the mth decision tree.

$$\frac{\partial L(y_i, F(x_i))}{\partial F(x_i)} = -y_i + P_i$$

$$\therefore -\left[\frac{\partial L(y_i, F(x_i))}{\partial F(x_i)}\right] = y_i - P_i$$

When $m = 2$ (*i.e.*, the second decision tree):

$$r_{i2} = y_i - P_i$$

Here, the P_i must be corresponding to $F_1(x_i)$ since dealing with the second decision tree

By plugging in all the $F_1(x_i)$ values from the final results of the first decision tree:

$$r_{12} = y_1 - P_1 = 1 - 0.5788 = 0.4212$$

$$r_{22} = y_2 - P_2 = 0 - 0.5788 = -0.5788$$

$$r_{32} = y_3 - P_3 = 1 - 0.8089 = 0.1911$$

Append the calculated r_{i2} values to the table:

-	num_bed rooms (x_i)	is_easy_s ell (y_i)	$F_0(x_i)$ = initial $log(odds_i)$	P_i	r_{i1}	$F_1(x_i)$ = $log(odds_i)$	P_i	r_{i2}
$i = 1$	5	1	0.693	0.667	0.333	0.318	0.5788	0.4212
$i = 2$	4	0	0.693	0.667	-0.667	0.318	0.5788	-0.5788
$i = 3$	2	1	0.693	0.667	0.333	1.443	0.8089	0.1911

Step 2: for $m = 1\ to\ M$:

(a) Find pseudo-residuals $r_{im} = -\left[\frac{\partial L(y_i, F(x_i))}{\partial F(x_i)}\right]_{F(x) = F_{m-1}(x)}$ for $i = 1, 2, \dots, n$

Here, a simple regression tree is constructed as follows by taking x_i as the input and r_{i1} as the output since $m = 2$.

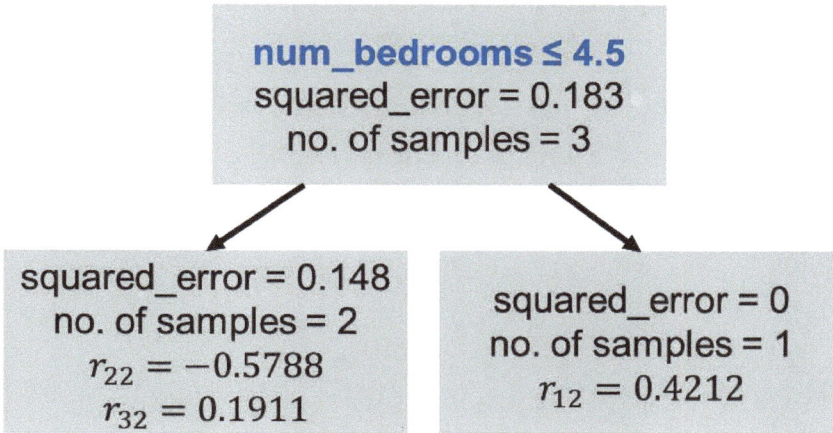

num_bedrooms $\leq$ 4.5
squared_error = 0.183
no. of samples = 3

squared_error = 0.148
no. of samples = 2
$r_{22} = -0.5788$
$r_{32} = 0.1911$

squared_error = 0
no. of samples = 1
$r_{12} = 0.4212$

Step 2: for $m = 1\ to\ M$:

(c) For $j = 1 \dots J_m$ compute $\gamma_{jm} = \underset{\gamma}{\text{argmin}} \sum_{x_i \in R_{jm}} L(y_i, F_{m-1}(x_i) + \gamma)$

Here, R_{jm} denotes the jth leaf node of the mth tree. In the second decision tree (*i.e.*, $m = 2$), there are only 2 leaf nodes, R_{12} and R_{22}, as shown below.

num_bedrooms ≤ 4.5
squared_error = 0.183
no. of samples = 3

R_{12} R_{22}

squared_error = 0.148
no. of samples = 2
$r_{22} = -0.5788$
$r_{32} = 0.1911$
$\gamma_{12} = -0.973$

squared_error = 0
no. of samples = 1
$r_{12} = 0.4212$
$\gamma_{22} = 1.728$

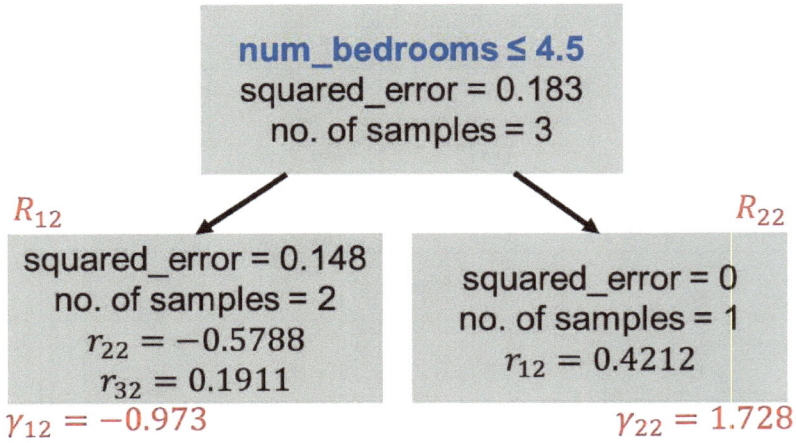

To calculate the γ value for each leaf node, we can straightaway apply the relationships identified from the first decision tree (*i.e.*, the numerator is just the sum of residuals of the samples allocated to the leaf node and the denominator is just the sum of $P_i(1 - P_i)$ of the samples allocated to the leaf node).

$$\gamma_{12} = \frac{r_{22} + r_{32}}{P_2(1 - P_2) + P_3(1 - P_3)} = \frac{-0.5788 + 0.1911}{0.5788(1 - 0.5788) + 0.8089(1 - 0.8089)}$$
$$= -0.973$$

$$\gamma_{22} = \frac{r_{12}}{P_1(1 - P_1)} = \frac{0.4212}{0.5788(1 - 0.5788)} = 1.728$$

Step 2: For $m = 1 \, to \, M$:

(d) Update $F_m(x_i) = F_{m-1}(x_i) + \alpha(\gamma_{jm}|x_i \in R_{jm})$

Here, α is the learning rate. We set $\alpha = 0.5$ in this example.

$$\because m = 2, \quad \therefore F_m(x_i) = F_2(x_i) = F_1(x_i) + \alpha(\gamma_{j2}|x_i \in R_{j2})$$

Furthermore, probability for each sample needs to be updated to be corresponding to $F_2(x_i)$ now:

$$P_i = \frac{e^{log(odds_i)}}{1 + e^{log(odds_i)}} = \frac{e^{F_2(x_i)}}{1 + e^{F_2(x_i)}}$$

Since we assumed the gradient boosting classifier comprises 2 decision trees only in this example, we have completed the whole Step 2 and the model training. Then, in the end, the calculated probability needs to be mapped to class/label (*i.e.*, 0 or 1). Similar to Chapter 4 for logistic regression, the default threshold of 0.5 is then employed. If $P \geq 0.5$, it will be rounded up to 1 and predicted as class 1; whereas, if $P < 0.5$, it will be rounded down to 0 and predicted as class 0.

$$\because x_1 \in R_{22}$$

$$\therefore F_2(x_1) = F_1(x_1) + 0.5 \times 1.728 = 0.318 + 0.5 \times 1.728 = 1.182$$

$$P_1 = \frac{e^{log(odds_1)}}{1 + e^{log(odds_1)}} = \frac{e^{F_2(x_1)}}{1 + e^{F_2(x_1)}} = \frac{e^{1.182}}{1 + e^{1.182}} = 0.7653$$

$$\because P_1 \geq 0.5 \quad \therefore class\ 1$$

$$\because x_2 \in R_{12}$$

$$\therefore F_2(x_2) = F_1(x_2) + 0.5 \times (-0.973) = 0.318 + 0.5 \times (-0.973) = -0.1685$$

$$P_2 = \frac{e^{log(odds_2)}}{1 + e^{log(odds_2)}} = \frac{e^{F_2(x_2)}}{1 + e^{F_2(x_2)}} = \frac{e^{-0.1685}}{1 + e^{-0.1685}} = 0.4579$$

$$\because P_2 < 0.5 \quad \therefore class\ 0$$

$$\because x_3 \in R_{12}$$

$$\therefore F_2(x_3) = F_1(x_3) + 0.5 \times (-0.973) = 1.443 + 0.5 \times (-0.973) = 0.9565$$

$$P_3 = \frac{e^{log(odds_3)}}{1 + e^{log(odds_3)}} = \frac{e^{F_2(x_3)}}{1 + e^{F_2(x_3)}} = \frac{e^{0.9565}}{1 + e^{0.9565}} = 0.7224$$

$$\because P_3 \geq 0.5 \quad \therefore class\ 1$$

Append the newly computed $F_2(x_i)$ and the corresponding P_i values to the table:

	num_bedroo ms (x_i)	is_easy_sell (y_i)	$F_0(x_i)$ = initial $log(odds_i)$	P_i	r_{i1}	$F_1(x_i)$ = $log(odds_i)$	P_i	r_{i2}	$F_2(x_i)$ = $log(odds_i)$	P_i
$t=1$	5	1	0.693	0.667	0.333	0.318	0.5788	0.4212	1.182	0.7653
$t=2$	4	0	0.693	0.667	-0.667	0.318	0.5788	-0.5788	-0.1685	0.4579
$t=3$	2	1	0.693	0.667	0.333	1.443	0.8089	0.1911	0.9565	0.7224

Looking back, we used the following expression in Step 2(d) when $m = 2$:

$$F_2(x_i) = F_1(x_i) + \alpha(\gamma_{j2}|x_i \in R_{j2})$$

Do not forget that we applied this expression in Step 2(d) when $m = 1$:

$$F_1(x_i) = F_0(x_i) + \alpha(\gamma_{j1}|x_i \in R_{j1})$$

If concatenating them together, we can get this expression:

$$F_2(x_i) = F_0(x_i) + \alpha(\gamma_{j1}|x_i \in R_{j1}) + \alpha(\gamma_{j2}|x_i \in R_{j2})$$

Then, converting $F_2(x_i)$ to predicted probability by:

$$P_i = \frac{e^{log(odds_i)}}{1 + e^{log(odds_i)}} = \frac{e^{F_2(x_i)}}{1 + e^{F_2(x_i)}}$$

This will be our trained gradient boosting classification model for this simple example!

Here, $(\gamma_{j1}|x_i \in R_{j1})$ and $(\gamma_{j2}|x_i \in R_{j2})$ are the values we can find from the first and second decision trees, respectively. α is the learning rate, and we set it as 0.5 in this example.

Visually, the model is like this:

$$F_2(x) = 0.693 + 0.5 \cdot \boxed{\begin{array}{c}\text{num\_bedrooms} \le 3\\ \text{squared\_error} = 0.222\\ \text{no. of samples} = 3\end{array}} + 0.5 \cdot \boxed{\begin{array}{c}\text{num\_bedrooms} \le 4.5\\ \text{squared\_error} = 0.183\\ \text{no. of samples} = 3\end{array}}$$

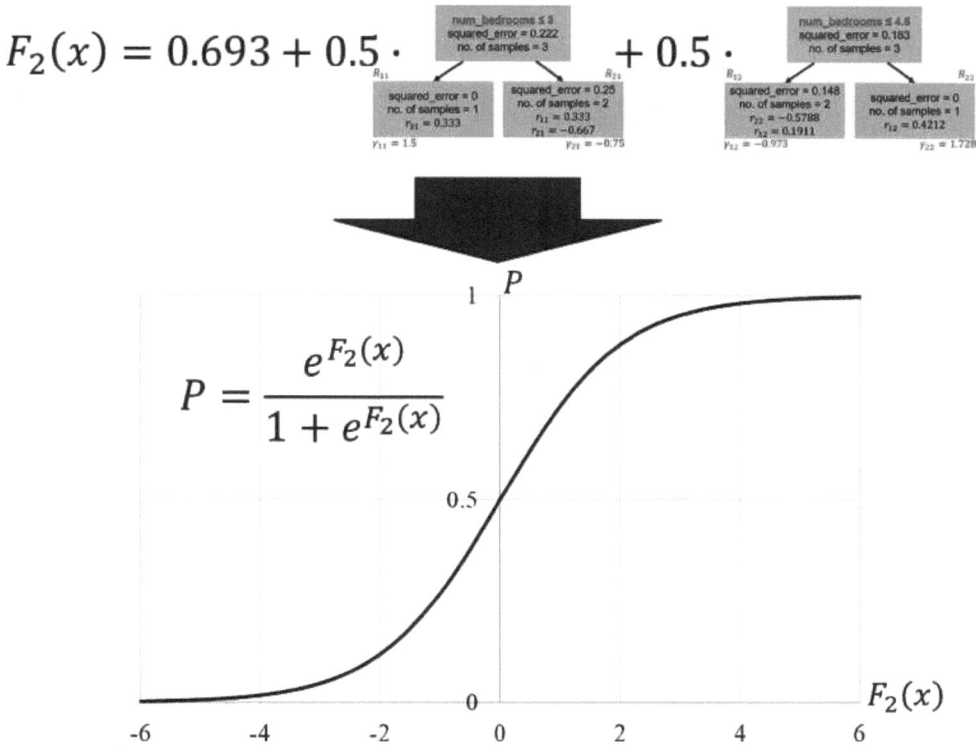

$$P = \frac{e^{F_2(x)}}{1 + e^{F_2(x)}}$$

Step 3. Output $F_m(x)$

Finally, we come to the 3rd and last step of the algorithm, making predictions for previously unseen data (*i.e.*, new data) using the trained gradient boosting classification model. For instance, if there is a house with 3 bedrooms, the predicted class by the model will be:

$$0.693 + 0.5 \cdot 1.5 + 0.5 \cdot (-0.973) = 0.9565$$

$$P = \frac{e^{0.9565}}{1 + e^{0.9565}} = 0.7224$$

Since $P \ge 0.5$, the predicted class will be 1, which means it is easy to sell this house with 3 bedrooms.

Now let us compare the results obtained above with that from the off-the-shelf gradient boosting classifier offered by the scikit-learn library.

The complete code file can be downloaded from our shared folder in Google Drive:

https://drive.google.com/drive/folders/1FqJvo4ZPazNbEH_GlHFoodqvegnQmHc n?usp=share_link

```python
import pandas as pd
import numpy as np
from sklearn.ensemble import GradientBoostingClassifier
from sklearn import tree

# The small dataset
data = np.array([[5,1],
                 [4,0],
                 [2,1]])
col_names = ['num_bedrooms', 'is_easy_sell']
print(pd.DataFrame(data, columns=col_names), "\n")

X = data[:, 0].reshape(-1, 1) # all rows, 1st column
y = data[:, 1] # all rows, 2nd column
```

```
   num_bedrooms   is_easy_sell
0             5              1
1             4              0
2             2              1
```

```python
gbc = GradientBoostingClassifier(n_estimators=2,
                                 criterion="squared_error",
                                 learning_rate=0.5,
                                 max_depth=1)
# n_estimators: The number of boosting stages (i.e., trees)
# criterion: The function to measure the quality of a split
# learning_rate: The alpha value
# max_depth: the maximum depth of each tree

gbc.fit(X, y)
```

```
print("training dataset, probabilities of belonging to class
1:\n",
      np.round(gbc.predict_proba(X)[:,1].reshape(-1,1), 4))
# same as our manually calculated probabilities
```

training dataset, probabilities of belonging to class 1:
 [[0.7653]
 [0.4579]
 [0.7224]]

```
print("training dataset, predicted class:\n",
      gbc.predict(X).reshape(-1,1))
# same as our manually calculated classes
```

training dataset, predicted class:
 [[1]
 [0]
 [1]]

```
_ = tree.plot_tree(gbc.estimators_[0][0],
                   feature_names=['num_bedrooms'],
                   filled=True)
print("First Decision Tree:")
```

First Decision Tree:

```
num_bedrooms <= 3.0
squared_error = 0.222
samples = 3
value = 0.0
```

```
squared_error = 0.0
samples = 1
value = 1.5
```

```
squared_error = 0.25
samples = 2
value = -0.75
```

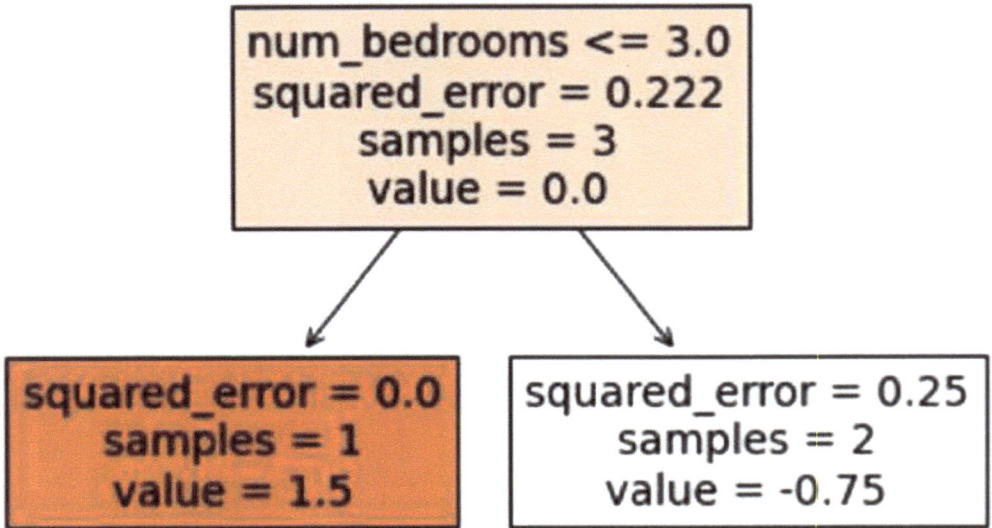

```
_ = tree.plot_tree(gbc.estimators_[1][0],
                   feature_names=['num_bedrooms'],
                   filled=True)
print("Second Decision Tree:")
```

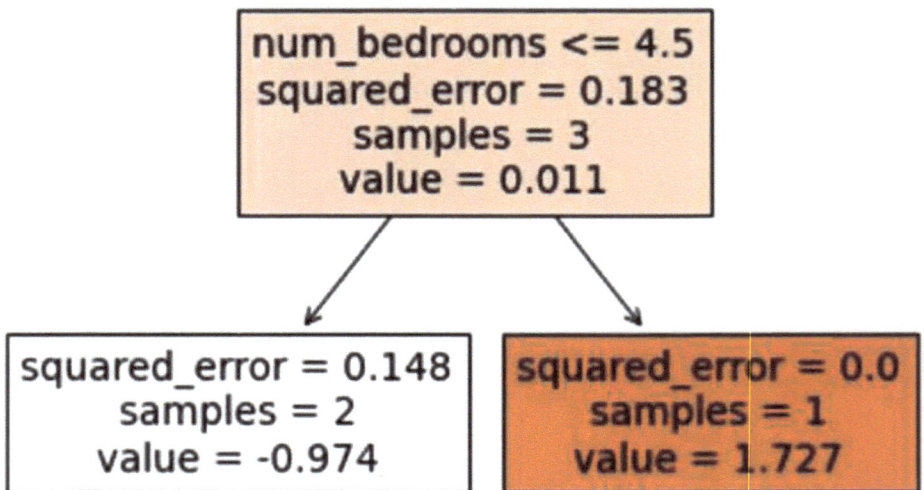

Second Decision Tree:

```
num_bedrooms <= 4.5
squared_error = 0.183
samples = 3
value = 0.011
```

```
squared_error = 0.148
samples = 2
value = -0.974
```

```
squared_error = 0.0
samples = 1
value = 1.727
```

```
# New house with 3 bedrooms, the predicted probability
# of belonging to class 1 by the model will be:
np.round( gbc.predict_proba(np.array([[3]]))[:,1], 4 )
```

array([0.7224])

```
# New house with 3 bedrooms, the predicted class
# by the model will be:
gbc.predict(np.array([[3]]))
```

array([1])

As can be seen from the results of scikit-learn gradient boosting classifier and compared with our manually calculated results, the same decision trees are generated, with the same squared_error for all the nodes of the decision trees, and the same gamma values for all the leaf nodes of the decision trees (note that scikit-learn simply uses "value" in the plots of decision trees to represent "gamma value"). Besides, the same predicted probabilities for the 3 training samples are obtained (*i.e.*, the probability of belonging to class 1 for the 3 samples, $P_1 = 0.7653$ for x_1, $P_2 = 0.4579$ for x_2, and $P_3 = 0.7224$ for x_3). Then, correspondingly, the same predicted classes are obtained (*i.e.*, x_1 predicted as class 1, x_2 predicted as class 0, and x_3 predicted as class 1). Finally, the same predicted probability and class for the previously unseen house with 3 bedrooms are obtained (*i.e.*, the probability it belongs to class 1 is 0.7224, and the predicted class is 1).

CONCLUSION

In this chapter, we discussed the concept of gradient boosting for both regression and classification. To make the material more accessible, we kept abstract mathematical theories to a minimum. Instead, we focused on two concrete numerical examples with small datasets to predict the sale price of houses and whether it is easy to sell houses in the property market, walking through them step by step. We also provided sample codes and comparisons with the gradient boosting regression and classification models from the off-the-shelf library, scikit-learn. By the end of the chapter, readers should have a well-rounded understanding of how gradient boosting machine learning works behind the scenes, how the mathematics relates to the implementation and performance of the algorithm, and be better equipped to apply it in their projects.

REFERENCES

[1] J.H. Friedman, "Greedy function approximation: A gradient boosting machine", *Ann. Stat.,* vol. 29, no. 5, pp. 1189-1232, 2001.
http://dx.doi.org/10.1214/aos/1013203451

[2] C. Wade, *Hands-On Gradient Boosting with XGBoost and scikit-learn: Perform accessible machine learning and extreme gradient boosting with Python.* Packt Publishing: Birmingham, England, 2020.

[3] Z. Wang, J. Li, G.P. Rangaiah, and Z. Wu, "Machine learning aided multi-objective optimization and multi-criteria decision making: Framework and two applications in chemical engineering", *Comput. Chem. Eng.,* vol. 165, no. 107945, p. 107945, 2022.
http://dx.doi.org/10.1016/j.compchemeng.2022.107945

[4] T. Hastie, R. Tibshirani, and J. Friedman, *The elements of statistical learning: Data mining, inference, and prediction.,* 2nd ed Springer: New York, NY, 2009.
http://dx.doi.org/10.1007/978-0-387-84858-7

CHAPTER 7

Support Vector Machine

Abstract: In this chapter, we investigate Support Vector Machines (SVM) for both linearly separable and linearly non-separable cases, emphasizing accessibility by minimizing abstract mathematical theories. We present concrete numerical examples with small datasets and provide a step-by-step walkthrough, illustrating the inner workings of SVM. Additionally, we offer sample codes and comparisons with the SVM model available in the scikit-learn library. Upon completing this chapter, readers will gain a comprehensive understanding of SVM's mechanics, and its connection to the implementation and performance of the algorithm, and be well-prepared to apply it in their practical applications.

Keywords: Support Vector Machine, Linearly Separable, Linearly Non-Separable, Polynomial Kernel, Radial Basis Function Kernel, Numerical Example, Small Dataset, Scikit-Learn

7.1. INTRODUCTION TO SUPPORT VECTOR MACHINE

Support vector machine (abbreviated as SVM) is a powerful and widely applicable machine learning algorithm that has been successfully employed across various domains, such as image and speech recognition, natural language processing, bioinformatics, and finance, to name a few. The goal of the SVM algorithm is to determine, in the space of N dimensions (where N is the number of features), a hyperplane that classifies the data points in a clearly distinguishable manner. It is defined in such a way that the margin distance between data points from different classes is maximized in the N-dimensional space [1, 2]. If the margin distance is maximized, then subsequent new data points (previously unseen) will be classified with greater confidence. For the linearly non-separable dataset, SVM primarily employs a kernel function to map the original data to a high-dimensional Hilbert Space to achieve linear separability and thereby resolve the linear non-separable problem [3]. Besides, it is worth mentioning that support vectors are just the training data points that are closer to the hyperplane. These data points are more relevant and critical to constructing an SVM model, as they help determine the equation of the separating hyperplane [4]. Fig. (**7.1**) illustrates a hyperplane, support vectors, and margin using a dataset with 10 samples from 2 classes, namely, positive (+) and negative (−) classes.

Zhiyuan Wang, Sayed Ameenuddin Irfan, Christopher Teoh & Priyanka Hriday Bhoyar

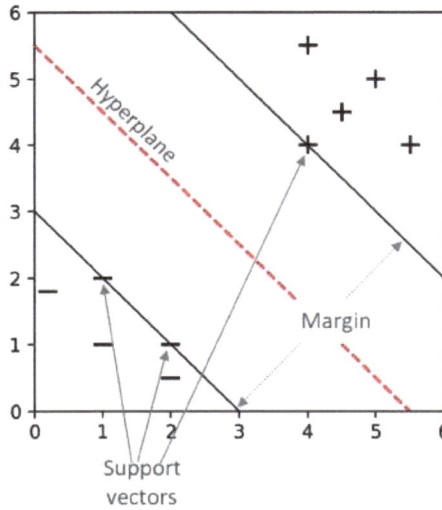

Fig. (7.1). Illustration of SVM hyperplane, support vectors, and margin.

7.2. MATHEMATICS OF SUPPORT VECTOR MACHINE: LINEARLY SEPARABLE CASE

The dataset utilized in Fig. **(7.1)** has been simplified in an effort to reduce complexity. As such, there are now only 2 data points belonging to the positive class (+), and 2 data points belonging to the negative class (−), as shown in Fig. **(7.2)**. The objective is to find the hyperplane that is tied to the maximum margin. Next, we draw a vector $\vec{w}$ (any length) that starts from the origin and is perpendicular to the hypothetical hyperplane. In addition, suppose we also have previously unseen data $\vec{u}$, and we would like to predict the class of $\vec{u}$, whether it is in the + or − class.

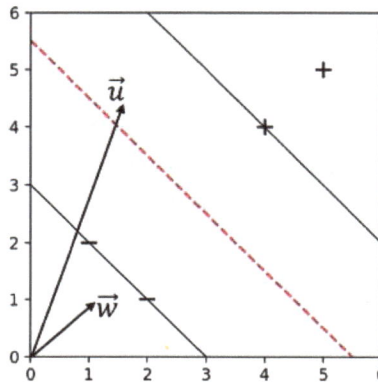

Fig. (7.2). Illustration of 2 data points of + class, 2 data points of − class, $\vec{w}$ perpendicular to the hypothetical margin, and a previously unseen $\vec{u}$.

Project $\vec{u}$ down to the vector perpendicular to the margin *(i.e., $\vec{w}$)*, if that projection is greater than or equal to ($\geq$) certain constant c, which crosses the median line, then it must be a positive (+) data point. This can be expressed mathematically as:

$$\vec{w} \cdot \vec{u} \geq c, \text{ then } \vec{u} \text{ is labeled } +$$

Simple transformations are performed:

$$\vec{w} \cdot \vec{u} - c \geq 0$$

$$\vec{w} \cdot \vec{u} + b_t \geq 0, \text{ where } b_t = -c$$

The median line of the margin:

$$\vec{w} \cdot \vec{u} + b_t = 0$$

The edge line (near +) of the margin:

$$\vec{w} \cdot \vec{u} + b_t = \delta$$

Here, δ is a positive constant

Divide both sides by δ:

$$\frac{\vec{w}}{\delta} \cdot \vec{u} + \frac{b_t}{\delta} = 1$$

Let $\vec{W} = \frac{\vec{w}}{\delta}$ and $b = \frac{b_t}{\delta}$,

The edge line (near +) of the margin is updated to:

$$\vec{W} \cdot \vec{u} + b = 1$$

The median line of the margin is updated to:

$$\vec{W} \cdot \vec{u} + b = 0$$

Symmetrically, as shown in Fig. (**7.3**), the edge line (near −) of the margin is updated to:

$$\vec{W} \cdot \vec{u} + b = -1$$

So now, it can be expressed as:

$$\overrightarrow{W} \cdot \vec{u} + b \geq 1 \text{ for } + \text{ data points}$$

$$\overrightarrow{W} \cdot \vec{u} + b \leq -1 \text{ for } - \text{ data points}$$

For the target output y_i, use $+1$ to denote the data point in the positive $(+)$ class, and -1 to denote the data point in the negative $(-)$ class:

$$y_i = +1 \text{ for } + \text{ data points}$$

$$y_i = -1 \text{ for } - \text{ data points}$$

Therefore, with these, we can get:

$$y_i(\overrightarrow{W} \cdot \vec{u} + b) \geq 1 \text{ for all data points.}$$

$y_i(\overrightarrow{W} \cdot \vec{u} + b) = 1$ for data points on the edge lines *(i.e.,* the support vectors).

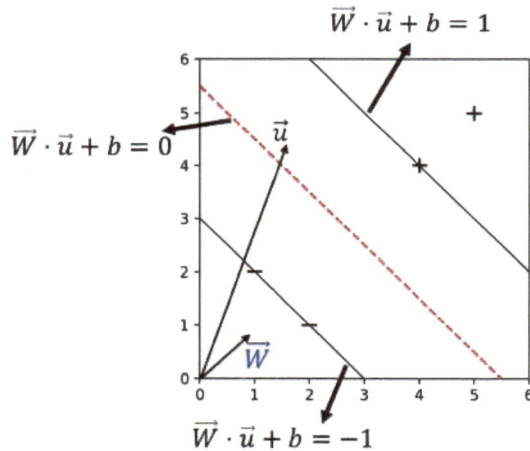

Fig. (7.3). Illustration of general equations for the hyperplane, edge line (near $+$), and edge line (near $-$), respectively.

Next, to express the margin, take 2 support vectors $\overrightarrow{x_+}$ from the $+$ class and $\overrightarrow{x_-}$ from the $-$ class, and the difference of these 2 vectors will be $\overrightarrow{x_+} - \overrightarrow{x_-}$, as shown in Fig. **(7.4)**. Recall that we have a normal vector $\overrightarrow{W}$ that is perpendicular to the margin.

The corresponding unit normal vector is $\frac{\vec{w}}{\|\vec{w}\|}$, where the denominator $\|\vec{W}\|$ is the magnitude of $\vec{W}$. Thus, the margin can be expressed as:

$$\text{margin} = (\vec{x_+} - \vec{x_-}) \frac{\vec{w}}{\|\vec{w}\|}$$

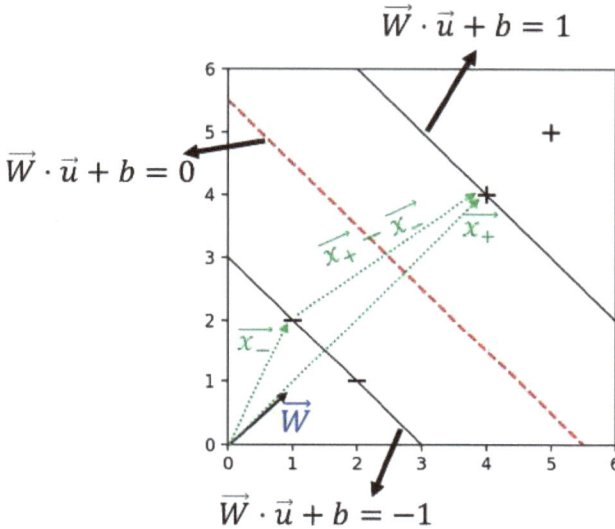

Fig. (7.4). Illustration of support vectors $\vec{x_+}$ from positive class and $\vec{x_-}$ from negative class, and their difference $\vec{x_+} - \vec{x_-}$.

Do not forget the constraint derived for all support vectors previo usly:

$$y_i(\vec{W} \cdot \vec{u} + b) = 1$$

Hence, for $\vec{x_+}$, it will be:

$$1(\vec{W} \cdot \vec{x_+} + b) = 1$$

$$\vec{W} \cdot \vec{x_+} = 1 - b$$

For $\vec{x_-}$, it will be:

$$-1(\vec{W} \cdot \vec{x_-} + b) = 1$$

$$-\vec{W} \cdot \vec{x_-} = 1 + b$$

The expression for margin is updated:

$$\text{margin} = (\overrightarrow{x_+} - \overrightarrow{x_-})\frac{\overrightarrow{W}}{\|\overrightarrow{W}\|} = \frac{\overrightarrow{W}\cdot\overrightarrow{x_+} - \overrightarrow{W}\cdot\overrightarrow{x_-}}{\|\overrightarrow{W}\|} = \frac{(1-b)+(1+b)}{\|\overrightarrow{W}\|} = \frac{2}{\|\overrightarrow{W}\|}$$

Bear in mind that the objective is to find a hyperplane that is tied to the maximum margin.

$$\text{margin} = \frac{2}{\|\overrightarrow{W}\|}, \text{ for maximization}$$

$$\rightarrow \text{equivalent to minimize the denominator } \|\overrightarrow{W}\|$$

$$\rightarrow \text{equivalent to minimize } \frac{1}{2}\|\overrightarrow{W}\|^2$$

The reason for this transformation is purely for mathematical convenience in the following derivations.

Therefore, a single objective optimization (SOO) problem has been formulated, as follows:

$$\begin{cases} minimize\ \ f = \frac{1}{2}\|\overrightarrow{W}\|^2 \\ \text{subject to the following constraint:} \\ g_i = y_i(\overrightarrow{W}\cdot\overrightarrow{x_i} + b) - 1 = 0 \ \ for\ all\ \textbf{support vectors } \overrightarrow{x_i} \end{cases}$$

This SOO problem with equality constraint can be easily solved by the method of Lagrange Multipliers, which is defined as:

$$L = f - \sum_i \alpha_i g_i$$

L is Lagrangian

f is optimization function

α is Lagrange multiplier

g is equality constraint

So, for our SOO problem, using the method of Lagrange Multipliers:

$$L = \frac{1}{2}\|\vec{W}\|^2 - \sum_i \alpha_i[y_i(\vec{W} \cdot \vec{x_i} + b) - 1]$$

$$\frac{\partial L}{\partial \vec{W}} = \vec{W} - \sum_i \alpha_i y_i \vec{x_i} = 0$$

$$\therefore \vec{W} = \sum_i \alpha_i y_i \vec{x_i}$$

$$\frac{\partial L}{\partial b} = -\sum_i \alpha_i y_i = 0$$

$$\therefore \sum_i \alpha_i y_i = 0$$

Then, substitute the latest expression found for $\vec{W} = \sum_i \alpha_i y_i \vec{x_i}$ back to the median line of the margin ($\vec{W} \cdot \vec{u} + b = 0$):

$$\sum_i \alpha_i y_i \vec{x_i} \cdot \vec{u} + b = 0$$

Similarly, the 2 edge lines ($\vec{W} \cdot \vec{u} + b = 1; \vec{W} \cdot \vec{u} + b = -1$) of the margin can also be updated as:

$$\sum_i \alpha_i y_i \vec{x_i} \cdot \vec{u} + b = 1 \quad if \ \vec{u} \ is + ve \ support \ vector$$

$$\sum_i \alpha_i y_i \vec{x_i} \cdot \vec{u} + b = -1 \quad if \ \vec{u} \ is - ve \ support \ vector$$

All the essential mathematical equations for SVM have now been derived.

7.3. NUMERICAL EXAMPLE AND CODE COMPARISON OF SUPPORT VECTOR MACHINE: LINEARLY SEPARABLE CASE

As presented in Table **7.1** and Fig. (**7.5**), suppose we have a small training dataset with only 4 samples (data points). The first 2 samples belong to the negative ($-$) class and the last 2 samples belong to the positive ($+$) class. Our task is to build an SVM classifier that can clearly distinguish the 2 classes.

Table 7.1. The small linearly separable dataset for support vector machine.

X	y
$(1, 2)$	-1
$(2, 1)$	-1
$(4, 4)$	1
$(5, 5)$	1

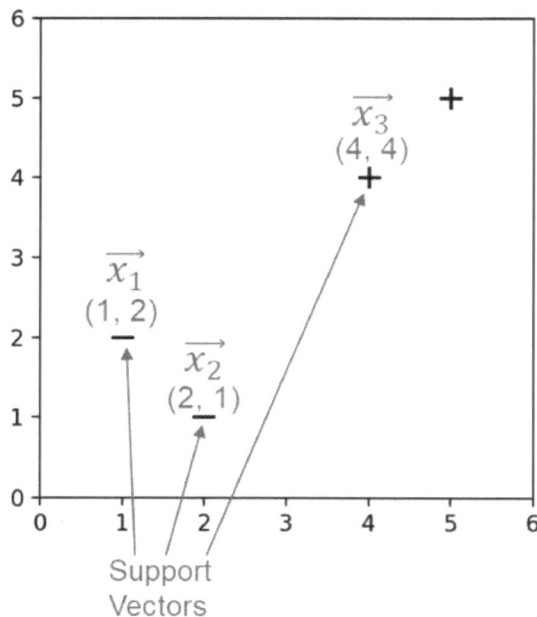

Fig. (7.5). Illustration of the 4 samples from the small training dataset and the support vectors.

We have derived the following 3 equations from the previous section:

$$\sum_i \alpha_i y_i \, \overrightarrow{x_i} \cdot \vec{u} + b = 1 \qquad \textit{if } \vec{u} \textit{ is } + \textit{ ve support vector}$$

$$\sum_i \alpha_i y_i \, \overrightarrow{x_i} \cdot \vec{u} + b = -1 \quad \textit{if } \vec{u} \textit{ is } - \textit{ ve support vector}$$

$$\sum_i \alpha_i y_i = 0$$

Now, let $\beta_i = \alpha_i y_i$, and then expand the equations:

$$\begin{cases} \beta_1 \overrightarrow{x_1} \cdot \overrightarrow{x_1} + \beta_2 \overrightarrow{x_2} \cdot \overrightarrow{x_1} + \beta_3 \overrightarrow{x_3} \cdot \overrightarrow{x_1} + b = -1 & \text{when } \vec{u} = \overrightarrow{x_1} \\[2mm] \beta_1 \overrightarrow{x_1} \cdot \overrightarrow{x_2} + \beta_2 \overrightarrow{x_2} \cdot \overrightarrow{x_2} + \beta_3 \overrightarrow{x_3} \cdot \overrightarrow{x_2} + b = -1 & \text{when } \vec{u} = \overrightarrow{x_2} \\[2mm] \beta_1 \overrightarrow{x_1} \cdot \overrightarrow{x_3} + \beta_2 \overrightarrow{x_2} \cdot \overrightarrow{x_3} + \beta_3 \overrightarrow{x_3} \cdot \overrightarrow{x_3} + b = 1 & \text{when } \vec{u} = \overrightarrow{x_3} \\[2mm] \beta_1 + \beta_2 + \beta_3 = 0 \end{cases}$$

As can be seen, the solution depends only on the dot product of pairs of support vectors. Then, calculate all the dot products of pairs of the support vectors:

$$\overrightarrow{x_1} \cdot \overrightarrow{x_1} = (1,2) \cdot (1,2) = 1 \cdot 1 + 2 \cdot 2 = 5$$

$$\overrightarrow{x_2} \cdot \overrightarrow{x_1} = (2,1) \cdot (1,2) = 2 \cdot 1 + 1 \cdot 2 = 4$$

$$\overrightarrow{x_3} \cdot \overrightarrow{x_1} = (4,4) \cdot (1,2) = 4 \cdot 1 + 4 \cdot 2 = 12$$

$$\overrightarrow{x_1} \cdot \overrightarrow{x_2} = (1,2) \cdot (2,1) = 1 \cdot 2 + 2 \cdot 1 = 4$$

$$\overrightarrow{x_2} \cdot \overrightarrow{x_2} = (2,1) \cdot (2,1) = 2 \cdot 2 + 1 \cdot 1 = 5$$

$$\overrightarrow{x_3} \cdot \overrightarrow{x_2} = (4,4) \cdot (2,1) = 4 \cdot 2 + 4 \cdot 1 = 12$$

$$\overrightarrow{x_1} \cdot \overrightarrow{x_3} = (1,2) \cdot (4,4) = 1 \cdot 4 + 2 \cdot 4 = 12$$

$$\overrightarrow{x_2} \cdot \overrightarrow{x_3} = (2,1) \cdot (4,4) = 2 \cdot 4 + 1 \cdot 4 = 12$$

$$\vec{x_3} \cdot \vec{x_3} = (4,4) \cdot (4,4) = 4 \cdot 4 + 4 \cdot 4 = 32$$

Then, plug the values into the equations:

$$\begin{cases} 5\beta_1 + 4\beta_2 + 12\beta_3 + b = -1 \\[2mm] 4\beta_1 + 5\beta_2 + 12\beta_3 + b = -1 \\[2mm] 12\beta_1 + 12\beta_2 + 32\beta_3 + b = 1 \\[2mm] \beta_1 + \beta_2 + \beta_3 = 0 \end{cases}$$

After solving the system of linear equations, β_1, β_2, β_3, and b are found to be:

$$\beta_1 = -0.08, \beta_2 = -0.08, \beta_3 = 0.16, b = -2.2$$

Utilize the solved β_1, β_2, β_3 values to find $\vec{W}$:

$$\vec{W} = \sum_i \alpha_i y_i \vec{x_i} = \sum_i \beta_i \vec{x_i} = -0.08 \begin{pmatrix} 1 \\ 2 \end{pmatrix} - 0.08 \begin{pmatrix} 2 \\ 1 \end{pmatrix} + 0.16 \begin{pmatrix} 4 \\ 4 \end{pmatrix} = \begin{pmatrix} 0.4 \\ 0.4 \end{pmatrix}$$

Update the median line of the margin *(i.e., hyperplane, $\vec{W} \cdot \vec{u} + b = 0$)*:

$$\begin{pmatrix} 0.4 \\ 0.4 \end{pmatrix} \cdot \vec{u} - 2.2 = 0$$

So, a hyperplane is essentially those $\vec{u}$ vectors that satisfy the equation above. Let us represent the vector $\vec{u}$ as coordinate $\begin{pmatrix} u_1 \\ u_2 \end{pmatrix}$ in the two-dimensional space, where u_1 is the scalar/magnitude in the horizontal axis and u_2 is the scalar/magnitude in the vertical axis, as shown in Fig. (**7.6**).

$$\begin{pmatrix} 0.4 \\ 0.4 \end{pmatrix} \cdot \begin{pmatrix} u_1 \\ u_2 \end{pmatrix} - 2.2 = 0$$

$$0.4 \cdot u_1 + 0.4 \cdot u_2 = 2.2$$

$$u_1 + u_2 = 5.5$$

Similarly, for the edge line (near +) of the margin ($\vec{W} \cdot \vec{u} + b = 1$):

$$\begin{pmatrix} 0.4 \\ 0.4 \end{pmatrix} \cdot \begin{pmatrix} u_1 \\ u_2 \end{pmatrix} - 2.2 = 1$$

$$u_1 + u_2 = 8$$

For the edge line (near $-$) of the margin ($\overrightarrow{W} \cdot \vec{u} + b = -1$):

$$\begin{pmatrix} 0.4 \\ 0.4 \end{pmatrix} \cdot \begin{pmatrix} u_1 \\ u_2 \end{pmatrix} - 2.2 = -1$$

$$u_1 + u_2 = 3$$

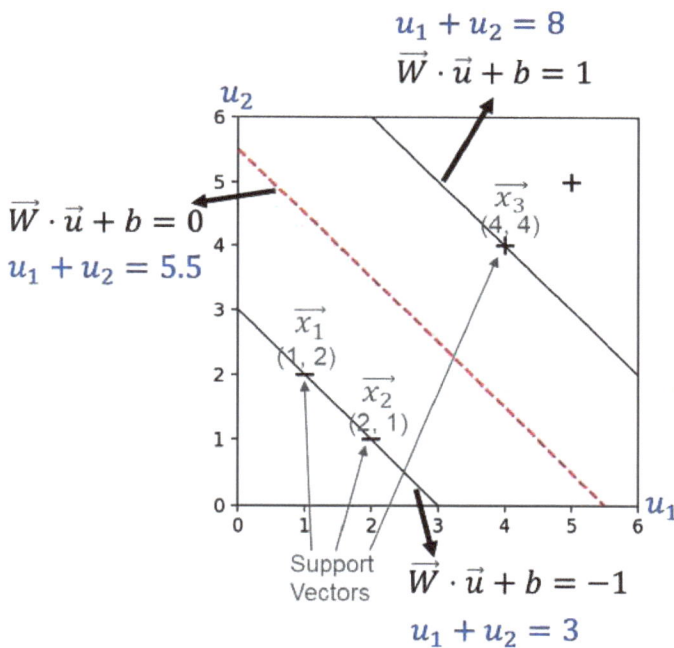

Fig. (7.6). Illustration of calculated equations for the optimal hyperplane, edge line (near $+$), and edge line (near $-$), respectively.

Now let us compare the results obtained above with that from the off-the-shelf SVM classifier offered by the scikit-learn library.

The complete code file can be downloaded from our shared folder in Google Drive:

https://drive.google.com/drive/folders/1FqJvo4ZPazNbEH_GlHFoodqvegnQmHcn?usp=share_link

```python
import numpy as np
X = np.array([[1,2],
              [2,1],
              [4,4],
              [5,5]])

y = np.array([-1,-1,1,1])

print(np.concatenate((X, y.reshape(-1,1)), axis=1))
```

```
[[ 1  2 -1]
 [ 2  1 -1]
 [ 4  4  1]
 [ 5  5  1]]
```

```python
from sklearn.svm import SVC
svcModel = SVC(kernel='linear', tol=1e-10)

svcModel.fit(X, y)

print("Desired Output: \n" + str(y))
print("Scikit-learn Predicted Output: \n" + str(svcModel.pre-
dict(X)))
# svcModel.score(X, y)
```

```
Desired Output:
[-1 -1  1  1]
Scikit-learn Predicted Output:
[-1 -1  1  1]
```

```python
svcModel.support_vectors_
```

```
array([[1., 2.],
       [2., 1.],
       [4., 4.]])
```

```python
# Weights assigned to the features when kernel="linear"
svcModel.coef_
```

```
array([[0.4, 0.4]])
```

```python
import matplotlib.pyplot as plt

def create_meshgrid(x, y, h=.02):
    x_min, x_max = x.min() - 1, x.max() + 1
    y_min, y_max = y.min() - 1, y.max() + 1
    xx, yy = np.meshgrid(np.arange(x_min, x_max, h),
np.arange(y_min, y_max, h))
    return xx, yy

def draw_contours(ax, model, xx, yy, **params):
    Z = model.predict(np.c_[xx.ravel(), yy.ravel()]) # predict
for each grid point
    Z = Z.reshape(xx.shape)
    out = ax.contourf(xx, yy, Z, **params) # filled contours
    return out

fig, ax = plt.subplots(dpi=100)
X0,X1 = X[:, 0], X[:, 1]
xx, yy = create_meshgrid(X0, X1) #create meshgrid, 6/0.02 =
300 points in x-axis and y-axis.
draw_contours(ax, svcModel, xx, yy, cmap=plt.cm.coolwarm, al-
pha=0.8)

X0_neg, X1_neg = X[:2, 0], X[:2, 1]
X0_pos, X1_pos = X[2:, 0], X[2:, 1]
ax.scatter(X0_neg, X1_neg, c='k', marker='_',
cmap=plt.cm.coolwarm, s=100)
ax.scatter(X0_pos, X1_pos, c='k', marker='+',
cmap=plt.cm.coolwarm, s=100)

ax.set_ylim([0,6])
ax.set_xlim([0,6])
ax.set_title('Decision surface when using linear Kernel')
ax.set_aspect('equal', adjustable='box')
plt.savefig("Decision_surface_when_using_linear_Kernel.png",
dpi=200)
plt.show()
```

```
# Dual coefficients of the support vector in the decision
function, multiplied by their targets
# beta_i = alpha_i * y_i
svcModel.dual_coef_
```

array([[-0.08, -0.08, 0.16]])

```
# b value
svcModel.intercept_
```

array([-2.2])

Decision surface when using linear Kernel

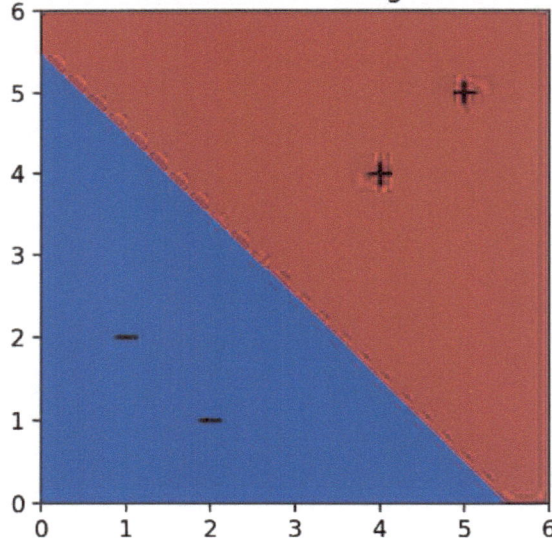

As can be seen from the results of the scikit-learn SVM classifier and compared with our manually calculated results, same weights *(i.e.,* $\overrightarrow{W} = (0.4, 0.4)$), same dual coefficients of support vector *(i.e.,* $\beta_1 = -0.08$, $\beta_2 = -0.08$, $\beta_3 = 0.16$), same intercept value *(i.e.,* $b = -2.2$), and same decision surface *(i.e.,* the hyperplane $u_1 + u_2 = 5.5$) are obtained.

7.4. MATHEMATICS OF SUPPORT VECTOR MACHINE: LINEARLY NON-SEPARABLE CASE

In the previous 2 sections, the discussion is all about the SVM for linearly separable cases. What if the problem is not linearly separable? *e.g.,* as shown in Fig. (**7.7**), where 2 samples belong to the positive (+) class and 2 samples belong to the negative (−) class in one-dimensional space. It is clear we cannot draw a single linear line to separate the 2 classes in this case.

Fig. (7.7). Illustration of 2 data points of + class and 2 data points of − class in one-dimensional space.

This is where the very powerful idea, kernel, comes into play. A kernel takes a low-dimensional input space and transforms it into a higher-dimensional space, as shown in Fig. (**7.8**). In other words, we can say that it converts non-separable problems to separable problems by adding more dimension(s) to it.

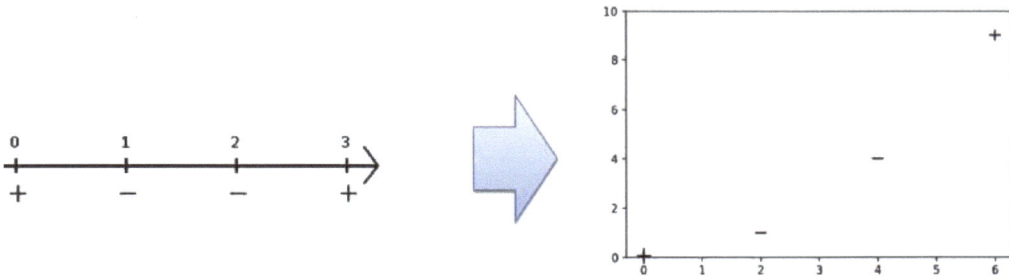

Fig. (7.8). Illustration of transforming low-dimensional input space into higher-dimensional space.

From the previous 2 sections, we have understood that the solution for SVM depends only on the dot product of pairs of the support vectors. However, now with the support vectors in original form, it is not linearly separable. We need to transform these support vectors accordingly.

Mathematically, use $\Phi(\vec{x_i})$ to denote the transformed $\vec{x_i}$, where $\vec{x_i}$ is a support vector. So now, instead of computing $\vec{x_i} \cdot \vec{x_j}$, we compute $\Phi(\vec{x_i}) \cdot \Phi(\vec{x_j})$ and it can be represented using a symbol K as a function of $\vec{x_i}$ and $\vec{x_j}$ *(i.e.,* kernel function).

$$K(\vec{x_i}, \vec{x_j}) = \Phi(\vec{x_i}) \cdot \Phi(\vec{x_j})$$

First, let us talk about the Polynomial Kernel:

$$K(\vec{x_i}, \vec{x_j}) = [\gamma(\vec{x_i} \cdot \vec{x_j}) + r]^d$$

Here,

$\vec{x_i}$ and $\vec{x_j}$ are the support vectors

d is the degree of the polynomial kernel function

γ is the kernel coefficient and r is an independent term

Use the example mentioned above in Fig. (**7.7**) to understand how Polynomial Kernel works,

Since it is one-dimensional, the vector can just be denoted as scalar, i.e., $\vec{x_i} = x_i$ (*A scalar set is, by definition, a one-dimensional vector space*).

For Polynomial Kernel:

$$K(\vec{x_i}, \vec{x_j}) = [\gamma(\vec{x_i} \cdot \vec{x_j}) + r]^d$$

Set $\gamma = 1, r = 2, d = 2$, then:

$$K(\vec{x_i}, \vec{x_j}) = [(\vec{x_i} \cdot \vec{x_j}) + 2]^2 = (x_i x_j + 2)^2 = 4x_i x_j + x_i^2 x_j^2 + 4$$
$$= (2x_i, x_i^2, 2) \cdot (2x_j, x_j^2, 2)$$

Note that $(2x_i, x_i^2, 2)$ is just the transformed $\vec{x_i}$ (*i.e.*, $\Phi(\vec{x_i})$) and $(2x_j, x_j^2, 2)$ is just the transformed $\vec{x_j}$ (*i.e.*, $(\vec{x_j})$), as shown in Table **7.2**.

Table 7.2. Original $(\overrightarrow{x_i})$ and transformed $(\Phi(\overrightarrow{x_i}))$ support vectors.

	$\overrightarrow{x_i}$	$\Phi(\overrightarrow{x_i}) = (2x_i, x_i^2, 2)$
$i = 1$	1	$(2, 1, 2)$
$i = 2$	2	$(4, 4, 2)$
$i = 3$	0	$(0, 0, 2)$
$i = 4$	3	$(6, 9, 2)$

If omitting the 3rd coordinate of $\Phi(\overrightarrow{x_i})$ as they have the same value of 2, then we can make the plot in two-dimensional space, as shown in Fig. (**7.9**).

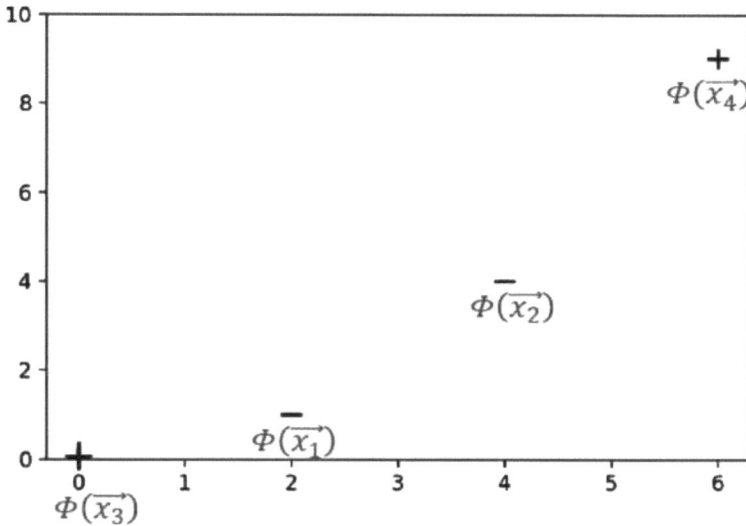

Fig. (7.9). Illustration of transformed support vectors $(\Phi(\overrightarrow{x_i}))$ in two-dimensional space.

Now, as observed, you can roughly draw a linear line to separate the positive and negative samples, which means that the linearly non-separable problem in one-dimensional space has become linearly separable in two-dimensional space!

Look back to the Polynomial kernel expression:

$$K(\vec{x_i}, \vec{x_j}) = [(\vec{x_i} \cdot \vec{x_j}) + 2]^2 = (x_i x_j + 2)^2 = 4x_i x_j + x_i^2 x_j^2 + 4$$
$$= (2x_i, x_i^2, 2) \cdot (2x_j, x_j^2, 2)$$

The amazing thing about using the kernel to calculate the dot products of transformed support vectors is that we actually do not need to transform each individual support vector (*e.g.,* from x_i to $(2x_i, x_i^2, 2)$) and then calculate their dot products. We can just plug the original support vectors into the kernel function (*e.g.,* $(\vec{x_i}, \vec{x_j}) = [(\vec{x_i} \cdot \vec{x_j}) + 2]^2$), as this effectively equals the dot products of the transformed support vectors (*e.g.,* $\Phi(\vec{x_i}) \cdot \Phi(\vec{x_j}) = (2x_i, x_i^2, 2) \cdot (2x_j, x_j^2, 2)$).

Recall that in the previous section on linearly separable cases, we have derived the following equations:

$$\sum_i \alpha_i y_i \, \vec{x_i} \cdot \vec{u} + b = 1 \quad \text{if } \vec{u} \text{ is } + \text{ ve support vector}$$

$$\sum_i \alpha_i y_i \, \vec{x_i} \cdot \vec{u} + b = -1 \quad \text{if } \vec{u} \text{ is } - \text{ ve support vector}$$

$$Hyperplane: \sum_i \alpha_i y_i \, \vec{x_i} \cdot \vec{u} + b = 0$$

$$\sum_i \alpha_i y_i = 0$$

As aforementioned, in linearly inseparable cases, instead of computing $\vec{x_i} \cdot \vec{u}$ based on original support vectors, we compute $\Phi(\vec{x_i}) \cdot \Phi(\vec{u})$ based on transformed support vectors, which can be represented using a kernel function $K(\vec{x_i}, \vec{u})$.

So, all the 4 equations above need to be updated accordingly:

$$\sum_i \alpha_i y_i \, K(\vec{x_i}, \vec{u}) + b = 1 \quad \text{if } \vec{u} \text{ is } + \text{ ve support vector}$$

$$\sum_i \alpha_i y_i \, K(\vec{x_i}, \vec{u}) + b = -1 \quad \text{if } \vec{u} \text{ is } - \text{ ve support vector}$$

$$Hyperplane: \sum_i \alpha_i y_i K(\vec{x_i}, \vec{u}) + b = 0$$

$$\sum_i \alpha_i y_i = 0$$

7.5. NUMERICAL EXAMPLE AND CODE COMPARISON OF SUPPORT VECTOR MACHINE: LINEARLY NON-SEPARABLE CASE USING POLYNOMIAL KERNEL

In this section, we will use the updated equations shown at the end of the previous section with the polynomial kernel to solve the abovementioned linearly non-separable dataset. The data points are presented in Fig. (**7.10**) and Table **7.3**.

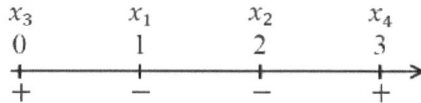

Fig. (7.10). Plot of the linearly non-separable dataset in one-dimensional space for SVM with polynomial kernel.

Table 7.3. The linearly non-separable dataset for SVM with polynomial kernel.

X	y
1	−1
2	−1
0	1
3	1

$$\sum_i \alpha_i y_i K(\vec{x_i}, \vec{u}) + b = 1 \quad \text{if } \vec{u} \text{ is } + \text{ve support vector}$$

$$\sum_i \alpha_i y_i K(\vec{x_i}, \vec{u}) + b = -1 \quad \text{if } \vec{u} \text{ is } - \text{ve support vector}$$

$$\sum_i \alpha_i y_i = 0$$

Now, let $\beta_i = \alpha_i y_i$, and then expand the equations:

$$\begin{cases} \beta_1 K(\vec{x_1}, \vec{x_1}) + \beta_2 K(\vec{x_2}, \vec{x_1}) + \beta_3 K(\vec{x_3}, \vec{x_1}) + \beta_4 K(\vec{x_4}, \vec{x_1}) + b = -1 & \text{when } \vec{u} = \vec{x_1} \\ \beta_1 K(\vec{x_1}, \vec{x_2}) + \beta_2 K(\vec{x_2}, \vec{x_2}) + \beta_3 K(\vec{x_3}, \vec{x_2}) + \beta_4 K(\vec{x_4}, \vec{x_2}) + b = -1 & \text{when } \vec{u} = \vec{x_2} \\ \beta_1 K(\vec{x_1}, \vec{x_3}) + \beta_2 K(\vec{x_2}, \vec{x_3}) + \beta_3 K(\vec{x_3}, \vec{x_3}) + \beta_4 K(\vec{x_4}, \vec{x_3}) + b = 1 & \text{when } \vec{u} = \vec{x_3} \\ \beta_1 K(\vec{x_1}, \vec{x_4}) + \beta_2 K(\vec{x_2}, \vec{x_4}) + \beta_3 K(\vec{x_3}, \vec{x_4}) + \beta_4 K(\vec{x_4}, \vec{x_4}) + b = 1 & \text{when } \vec{u} = \vec{x_4} \\ \beta_1 + \beta_2 + \beta_3 + \beta_4 = 0 & \end{cases}$$

Note that since it's one-dimensional, $\vec{x_i} = x_i$; x_1 and x_2 are the 2 negative samples; x_3 and x_4 are the 2 positive samples.

Polynomial Kernel function:

$$K(\vec{x_i}, \vec{x_j}) = [\gamma(\vec{x_i} \cdot \vec{x_j}) + r]^d$$

Set $\gamma = 1, r = 2, \ d = 2$, then:

$$K(\vec{x_i}, \vec{x_j}) = [(\vec{x_i} \cdot \vec{x_j}) + 2]^2$$

So,

$$K(\vec{x_1}, \vec{x_1}) = [(1 \cdot 1) + 2]^2 = 9; \qquad K(\vec{x_2}, \vec{x_1}) = [(2 \cdot 1) + 2]^2 = 16$$

$$K(\vec{x_3}, \vec{x_1}) = [(0 \cdot 1) + 2]^2 = 4; \qquad K(\vec{x_4}, \vec{x_1}) = [(3 \cdot 1) + 2]^2 = 25$$

$$K(\vec{x_1}, \vec{x_2}) = [(1 \cdot 2) + 2]^2 = 16; \qquad K(\vec{x_2}, \vec{x_2}) = [(2 \cdot 2) + 2]^2 = 36$$

$$K(\vec{x_3}, \vec{x_2}) = [(0 \cdot 2) + 2]^2 = 4; \qquad K(\vec{x_4}, \vec{x_2}) = [(3 \cdot 2) + 2]^2 = 64$$

$$K(\vec{x_1}, \vec{x_3}) = [(1 \cdot 0) + 2]^2 = 4; \qquad K(\vec{x_2}, \vec{x_3}) = [(2 \cdot 0) + 2]^2 = 4$$

$$K(\vec{x_3}, \vec{x_3}) = [(0 \cdot 0) + 2]^2 = 4; \qquad K(\vec{x_4}, \vec{x_3}) = [(3 \cdot 0) + 2]^2 = 4$$

$$K(\vec{x_1}, \vec{x_4}) = [(1 \cdot 3) + 2]^2 = 25; \qquad K(\vec{x_2}, \vec{x_4}) = [(2 \cdot 3) + 2]^2 = 64$$

$$K(\overrightarrow{x_3}, \overrightarrow{x_4}) = [(0 \cdot 3) + 2]^2 = 4; \qquad K(\overrightarrow{x_4}, \overrightarrow{x_4}) = [(3 \cdot 3) + 2]^2 = 121$$

Then, plug the values into the equations:

$$\begin{cases} 9\beta_1 + 16\beta_2 + 4\beta_3 + 25\beta_4 + b = -1 \\ 16\beta_1 + 36\beta_2 + 4\beta_3 + 64\beta_4 + b = -1 \\ 4\beta_1 + 4\beta_2 + 4\beta_3 + 4\beta_4 + b = 1 \\ 25\beta_1 + 64\beta_2 + 4\beta_3 + 121\beta_4 + b = 1 \\ \beta_1 + \beta_2 + \beta_3 + \beta_4 = 0 \end{cases}$$

Solving this system of linear equations gives many solutions as follows:

$$\begin{cases} \beta_1 = 2.375 - 3\beta_3 \\ \beta_2 = -4 + 3\beta_3 \\ \beta_3 \text{ is a free variable} \\ \beta_4 = 1.625 - \beta_3 \\ b = 1 \end{cases}$$

When taking $\beta_3 = 1$:

$$\beta_1 = -0.625$$

$$\beta_2 = -1$$

$$\beta_3 = 1$$

$$\beta_4 = 0.625$$

$$b = 1$$

$$Hyperplane: \sum_i \alpha_i y_i \, K(\overrightarrow{x_i}, \vec{u}) + b = 0$$

$$\therefore \beta_1 K(\overrightarrow{x_1}, \vec{u}) + \beta_2 K(\overrightarrow{x_2}, \vec{u}) + \beta_3 K(\overrightarrow{x_3}, \vec{u}) + \beta_4 K(\overrightarrow{x_4}, \vec{u}) + b = 0$$

We have found $\beta_1, \beta_2, \beta_3, \beta_4, b$, and $\overrightarrow{x_1}, \overrightarrow{x_2}, \overrightarrow{x_3}, \overrightarrow{x_4}$ are given.

Kernel function $K(\overrightarrow{x_i}, \overrightarrow{x_j}) = [(\overrightarrow{x_i} \cdot \overrightarrow{x_j}) + 2]^2$ is also known.

Also, since one-dimensional, $\vec{u} = u$.

So, a hyperplane is essentially those $\vec{u}$ that satisfy the following equation (an easily solvable quadratic equation):

$$-0.625(u + 2)^2 - 1(2u + 2)^2 + 4 + 0.625(3u + 2)^2 + 1 = 0$$

$$-0.625u^2 + -2.5u + -2.5 + -4u^2 + -8u + -4 + 4 + 5.625u^2 + 7.5u + 2.5 + 1 = 0$$

$$(-0.625u^2 + -4u^2 + 5.625u^2) + (-2.5u + -8u + 7.5u) + (-2.5 + -4 + 4 + 2.5 + 1) = 0$$

$$u^2 - 3u + 1 = 0$$

$$u = 0.382 \; or \; 2.618$$

With these, the positive and negative classes are clearly distinguishable, as shown in Fig. (**7.11**).

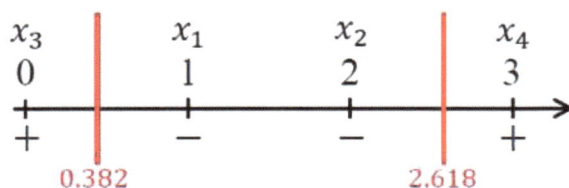

Fig. (7.11) Illustration of the determined hyperplane ($u = 0.382 \; or \; 2.618$) by SVM with polynomial kernel on one-dimensional space.

Now let us compare the results obtained above with that from the off-the-shelf SVM classifier using the polynomial kernel offered by the scikit-learn library.

The complete code file can be downloaded from our shared folder in Google Drive:

https://drive.google.com/drive/folders/1FqJvo4ZPazNbEH_GlHFoodqvegnQmHcn?usp=share_link

```python
import numpy as np
X = np.array([[1,0],
              [2,0],
              [0,0],
              [3,0]])

y = np.array([-1,-1,1,1])

print(np.concatenate((X, y.reshape(-1,1)), axis=1), "\n")

from sklearn.svm import SVC
svcModel = SVC(kernel='poly', gamma=1, degree=2, coef0=2,
tol=1e-10) # degree is d, coef0 is r

svcModel.fit(X, y)

print("Desired Output: \n" + str(y))
print("Scikit-learn Predicted Output: \n" + str(svcModel.pre-
dict(X)))
#svcModel.score(X_test, y_test)
```

```
[[ 1  0 -1]
 [ 2  0 -1]
 [ 0  0  1]
 [ 3  0  1]]


Desired Output:
[-1 -1  1  1]
Scikit-learn Predicted Output:
[-1 -1  1  1]
```

```python
import matplotlib.pyplot as plt

def create_meshgrid(x, y, h=.01):
    x_min, x_max = x.min() - 1, x.max() + 1
    y_min, y_max = y.min() - 1, y.max() + 1
    xx, yy = np.meshgrid(np.arange(x_min, x_max, h),
np.arange(y_min, y_max, h))
    return xx, yy

def draw_contours(ax, model, xx, yy, **params):
    Z = model.predict(np.c_[xx.ravel(), yy.ravel()]) # predict
for each grid point
    Z = Z.reshape(xx.shape)
    out = ax.contourf(xx, yy, Z, **params) # filled contours
    return out

fig, ax = plt.subplots(dpi=100)
X0,X1 = X[:, 0], X[:, 1]
xx, yy = create_meshgrid(X0, X1)
draw_contours(ax, svcModel, xx, yy, cmap=plt.cm.coolwarm, al-
pha=0.8)

X0_neg, X1_neg = np.append(X[0,0], X[1,0]), np.append(X[0,1],
X[1,1])
X0_pos, X1_pos = np.append(X[2,0], X[3,0]), np.append(X[2,1],
X[3,1])

ax.scatter(X0_neg, X1_neg, c='k', marker='_',
cmap=plt.cm.coolwarm, s=100)
ax.scatter(X0_pos, X1_pos, c='k', marker='+',
cmap=plt.cm.coolwarm, s=100)

x_ticks = np.append(ax.get_xticks(), [0.38,2.62])
ax.set_xticks(x_ticks)
ax.set_yticks(np.arange(-1, 1, 0.5))

ax.set_title('Decision surface when using poly Kernel, \nfor
linearly inseparable data')
plt.savefig("Decision surface when using poly Kernel for line-
arly inseparable data.png", dpi=200)
plt.show()
```

```
svcModel.support_vectors_
```
```
array([[1., 0.],
       [2., 0.],
       [0., 0.],
       [3., 0.]])
```

```
# Dual coefficients of the support vector in the decision
function, multiplied by their targets
# beta_i = alpha_i * y_i
svcModel.dual_coef_
```
```
array([[-0.625, -1.   ,  1.   ,  0.625]])
```

```
# b value
svcModel.intercept_
```
```
array([1.])
```

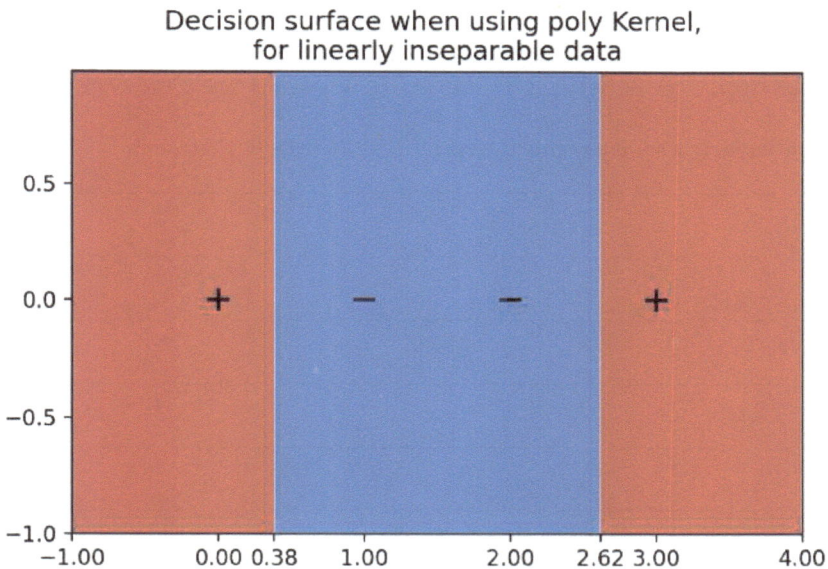

Decision surface when using poly Kernel,
for linearly inseparable data

As can be seen from the results of the scikit-learn SVM classifier using polynomial kernel and compared with our manually calculated results, the same dual coefficients of support vector *(i.e., $\beta_1 = -0.625$, $\beta_2 = -1$, $\beta_3 = 1$, and $\beta_4 = 0.625$)*, the same intercept value *(i.e., $b = 1$)*, and the same decision surface *(i.e., the hyperplane $u = 0.382$ or 2.618)* are obtained.

7.6. NUMERICAL EXAMPLE AND CODE COMPARISON OF SUPPORT VECTOR MACHINE: LINEARLY NON-SEPARABLE CASE USING RADIAL BASIS FUNCTION KERNEL

The concept of using the Radial Basis Function (RBF) kernel is the same as that of the Polynomial kernel, except for the different functions employed for transforming low-dimensional input space into higher-dimensional space.

For Polynomial kernel, it uses this function:

$$K\left(\vec{x_i}, \vec{x_j}\right) = [\gamma\left(\vec{x_i} \cdot \vec{x_j}\right) + r]^d$$

However, for RBF kernel, the function will be:

$$K\left(\vec{x_i}, \vec{x_j}\right) = e^{-\gamma\|\vec{x_i}-\vec{x_j}\|^2}$$

Here, γ is the kernel coefficient; $\vec{x_i}$ and $\vec{x_j}$ are the support vectors.

The following Table **7.4** and Fig. (**7.12**) present another linearly non-separable dataset; let us apply SVM with RBF kernel to separate the 2 classes.

Table 7.4. The linearly non-separable dataset for SVM with RBF kernel.

X	y
(1, 2)	−1
(5, 5)	−1
(2, 1)	1
(4, 4)	1

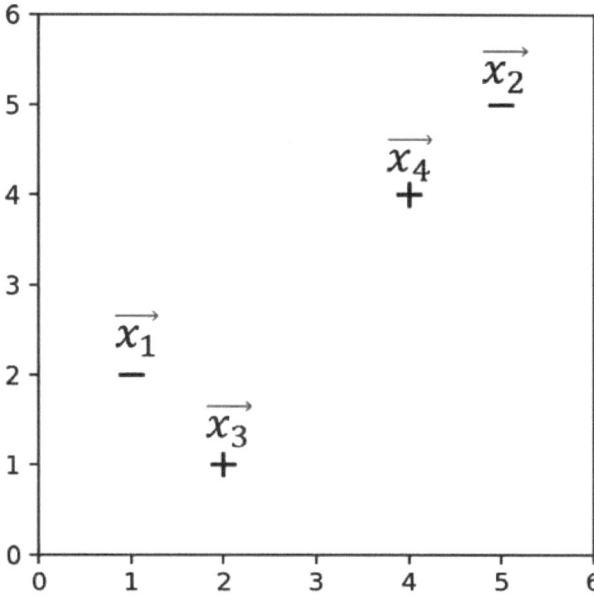

Fig. (7.12). Plot of the linearly non-separable dataset for SVM with RBF kernel.

Note that $\overrightarrow{x_1}$ and $\overrightarrow{x_2}$ are the 2 negative samples; $\overrightarrow{x_3}$ and $\overrightarrow{x_4}$ are the 2 positive samples.

$$\sum_i \alpha_i y_i \, K(\overrightarrow{x_i}, \vec{u}) + b = 1 \qquad if \; \vec{u} \; is + ve \; support \; vector$$

$$\sum_i \alpha_i y_i \, K(\overrightarrow{x_i}, \vec{u}) + b = -1 \quad if \; \vec{u} \; is - ve \; support \; vector$$

$$\sum_i \alpha_i y_i = 0$$

Now, let $\beta_i = \alpha_i y_i$, and then expanding:

$$\begin{cases} \beta_1 K(\overrightarrow{x_1}, \overrightarrow{x_1}) + \beta_2 K(\overrightarrow{x_2}, \overrightarrow{x_1}) + \beta_3 K(\overrightarrow{x_3}, \overrightarrow{x_1}) + \beta_4 K(\overrightarrow{x_4}, \overrightarrow{x_1}) + b = -1 & when \; \vec{u} = \overrightarrow{x_1} \\ \beta_1 K(\overrightarrow{x_1}, \overrightarrow{x_2}) + \beta_2 K(\overrightarrow{x_2}, \overrightarrow{x_2}) + \beta_3 K(\overrightarrow{x_3}, \overrightarrow{x_2}) + \beta_4 K(\overrightarrow{x_4}, \overrightarrow{x_2}) + b = -1 & when \; \vec{u} = \overrightarrow{x_2} \\ \beta_1 K(\overrightarrow{x_1}, \overrightarrow{x_3}) + \beta_2 K(\overrightarrow{x_2}, \overrightarrow{x_3}) + \beta_3 K(\overrightarrow{x_3}, \overrightarrow{x_3}) + \beta_4 K(\overrightarrow{x_4}, \overrightarrow{x_3}) + b = 1 & when \; \vec{u} = \overrightarrow{x_3} \\ \beta_1 K(\overrightarrow{x_1}, \overrightarrow{x_4}) + \beta_2 K(\overrightarrow{x_2}, \overrightarrow{x_4}) + \beta_3 K(\overrightarrow{x_3}, \overrightarrow{x_4}) + \beta_4 K(\overrightarrow{x_4}, \overrightarrow{x_4}) + b = 1 & when \; \vec{u} = \overrightarrow{x_4} \\ \qquad\qquad\qquad \beta_1 + \beta_2 + \beta_3 + \beta_4 = 0 & \end{cases}$$

RBF Kernel function:

$$K\left(\vec{x_i}, \vec{x_j}\right) = e^{-\gamma\|\vec{x_i}-\vec{x_j}\|^2}$$

Let $\gamma = 0.2$, then:

$$K\left(\vec{x_i}, \vec{x_j}\right) = e^{-0.2\|\vec{x_i}-\vec{x_j}\|^2}$$

So,

$$K(\vec{x_1}, \vec{x_1}) = e^{-0.2\|\vec{x_1}-\vec{x_1}\|^2} = e^{-0.2\|(1,2)-(1,2)\|^2} = e^{-0.2\|(0,0)\|^2} = e^0 = 1$$

$$K(\vec{x_2}, \vec{x_1}) = e^{-0.2\|\vec{x_2}-\vec{x_1}\|^2} = e^{-0.2\|(5,5)-(1,2)\|^2} = e^{-0.2\|(4,3)\|^2} = e^{-5}$$

$$K(\vec{x_3}, \vec{x_1}) = e^{-0.2\|\vec{x_3}-\vec{x_1}\|^2} = e^{-0.2\|(2,1)-(1,2)\|^2} = e^{-0.2\|(1,-1)\|^2} = e^{-0.4}$$

$$K(\vec{x_4}, \vec{x_1}) = e^{-0.2\|\vec{x_4}-\vec{x_1}\|^2} = e^{-0.2\|(4,4)-(1,2)\|^2} = e^{-0.2\|(3,2)\|^2} = e^{-2.6}$$

$$K(\vec{x_1}, \vec{x_2}) = e^{-0.2\|\vec{x_1}-\vec{x_2}\|^2} = e^{-0.2\|(1,2)-(5,5)\|^2} = e^{-0.2\|(-4,-3)\|^2} = e^{-5}$$

$$K(\vec{x_2}, \vec{x_2}) = e^{-0.2\|\vec{x_2}-\vec{x_2}\|^2} = e^{-0.2\|(5,5)-(5,5)\|^2} = e^{-0.2\|(0,0)\|^2} = e^0 = 1$$

$$K(\vec{x_3}, \vec{x_2}) = e^{-0.2\|\vec{x_3}-\vec{x_2}\|^2} = e^{-0.2\|(2,1)-(5,5)\|^2} = e^{-0.2\|(-3,-4)\|^2} = e^{-5}$$

$$K(\vec{x_4}, \vec{x_2}) = e^{-0.2\|\vec{x_4}-\vec{x_2}\|^2} = e^{-0.2\|(4,4)-(5,5)\|^2} = e^{-0.2\|(-1,-1)\|^2} = e^{-0.4}$$

$$K(\vec{x_1}, \vec{x_3}) = e^{-0.2\|\vec{x_1}-\vec{x_3}\|^2} = e^{-0.2\|(1,2)-(2,1)\|^2} = e^{-0.2\|(-1,1)\|^2} = e^{-0.4}$$

$$K(\vec{x_2}, \vec{x_3}) = e^{-0.2\|\vec{x_2}-\vec{x_3}\|^2} = e^{-0.2\|(5,5)-(2,1)\|^2} = e^{-0.2\|(3,4)\|^2} = e^{-5}$$

$$K(\vec{x_3}, \vec{x_3}) = e^{-0.2\|\vec{x_3}-\vec{x_3}\|^2} = e^{-0.2\|(2,1)-(2,1)\|^2} = e^{-0.2\|(0,0)\|^2} = e^0 = 1$$

$$K(\vec{x_4}, \vec{x_3}) = e^{-0.2\|\vec{x_4}-\vec{x_3}\|^2} = e^{-0.2\|(4,4)-(2,1)\|^2} = e^{-0.2\|(2,3)\|^2} = e^{-2.6}$$

$$K(\vec{x_1}, \vec{x_4}) = e^{-0.2\|\vec{x_1}-\vec{x_4}\|^2} = e^{-0.2\|(1,2)-(4,4)\|^2} = e^{-0.2\|(-3,-2)\|^2} = e^{-2.6}$$

$$K(\vec{x_2}, \vec{x_4}) = e^{-0.2\|\vec{x_2}-\vec{x_4}\|^2} = e^{-0.2\|(5,5)-(4,4)\|^2} = e^{-0.2\|(1,1)\|^2} = e^{-0.4}$$

$$K(\vec{x_3}, \vec{x_4}) = e^{-0.2\|\vec{x_3}-\vec{x_4}\|^2} = e^{-0.2\|(2,1)-(4,4)\|^2} = e^{-0.2\|(-2,-3)\|^2} = e^{-2.6}$$

$$K(\vec{x_4}, \vec{x_4}) = e^{-0.2\|\vec{x_4}-\vec{x_4}\|^2} = e^{-0.2\|(4,4)-(4,4)\|^2} = e^{-0.2\|(0,0)\|^2} = e^0 = 1$$

Then, plug the values into the equations:

$$\begin{cases} \beta_1 + e^{-5}\beta_2 + e^{-0.4}\beta_3 + e^{-2.6}\beta_4 + b = -1 \\ e^{-5}\beta_1 + \beta_2 + e^{-5}\beta_3 + e^{-0.4}\beta_4 + b = -1 \\ e^{-0.4}\beta_1 + e^{-5}\beta_2 + \beta_3 + e^{-2.6}\beta_4 + b = 1 \\ e^{-2.6}\beta_1 + e^{-0.4}\beta_2 + e^{-2.6}\beta_3 + \beta_4 + b = 1 \\ \beta_1 + \beta_2 + \beta_3 + \beta_4 = 0 \end{cases}$$

Solving this system of linear equations gives a unique solution as follows:

$$\beta_1 = -3, \beta_2 = -3, \beta_3 = 3, \beta_4 = 3, b = -0.1$$

$$Hyperplane: \sum_i \alpha_i y_i K(\vec{x_i}, \vec{u}) + b = 0$$

$$\therefore \beta_1 K(\vec{x_1}, \vec{u}) + \beta_2 K(\vec{x_2}, \vec{u}) + \beta_3 K(\vec{x_3}, \vec{u}) + \beta_4 K(\vec{x_4}, \vec{u}) + b = 0$$

We have found $\beta_1, \beta_2, \beta_3, \beta_4, b$, and $\vec{x_1}, \vec{x_2}, \vec{x_3}, \vec{x_4}$ are given.

RBF kernel function $K(\vec{x_i}, \vec{x_j}) = e^{-0.2\|\vec{x_i}-\vec{x_j}\|^2}$ is also known.

So, hyperplane is essentially those $\vec{u}$ that satisfy the following equation:

$$-3K(\vec{x_1}, \vec{u}) - 3K(\vec{x_2}, \vec{u}) + 3K(\vec{x_3}, \vec{u}) + 3K(\vec{x_4}, \vec{u}) - 0.1 = 0$$

Divide both sides by 3:

$$-K(\vec{x_1}, \vec{u}) - K(\vec{x_2}, \vec{u}) + K(\vec{x_3}, \vec{u}) + K(\vec{x_4}, \vec{u}) - 0.033 = 0$$

So, β_i and b values in the simplest form that can represent the hyperplane are:

$$\begin{cases} \beta_1 = -1 \\ \beta_2 = -1 \\ \beta_3 = 1 \\ \beta_4 = 1 \\ b = -0.033 \end{cases}$$

Let us represent the vector $\vec{u}$ as $\begin{pmatrix} u_1 \\ u_2 \end{pmatrix}$ in the two-dimensional space, where u_1 is the scalar/magnitude in the horizontal axis and u_2 is the scalar/magnitude in the vertical axis.

$$K(\vec{x_1}, \vec{u}) = e^{-0.2\|\vec{x_1}-\vec{u}\|^2} = e^{-0.2\|(1,2)-(u_1,u_2)\|^2} = e^{-0.2[(1-u_1)^2+(2-u_2)^2]}$$

$$K(\vec{x_2}, \vec{u}) = e^{-0.2\|\vec{x_2}-\vec{u}\|^2} = e^{-0.2\|(5,5)-(u_1,u_2)\|^2} = e^{-0.2[(5-u_1)^2+(5-u_2)^2]}$$

$$K(\vec{x_3}, \vec{u}) = e^{-0.2\|\vec{x_3}-\vec{u}\|^2} = e^{-0.2\|(2,1)-(u_1,u_2)\|^2} = e^{-0.2[(2-u_1)^2+(1-u_2)^2]}$$

$$K(\vec{x_4}, \vec{u}) = e^{-0.2\|\vec{x_4}-\vec{u}\|^2} = e^{-0.2\|(4,4)-(u_1,u_2)\|^2} = e^{-0.2[(4-u_1)^2+(4-u_2)^2]}$$

Then,

$$-e^{-0.2[(1-u_1)^2+(2-u_2)^2]} - e^{-0.2[(5-u_1)^2+(5-u_2)^2]} + e^{-0.2[(2-u_1)^2+(1-u_2)^2]}$$
$$+ e^{-0.2[(4-u_1)^2+(4-u_2)^2]} - 0.033 = 0$$

The plot of this equation is shown in the Fig. (**7.13**) as the curved line for separating the positive and negative classes.

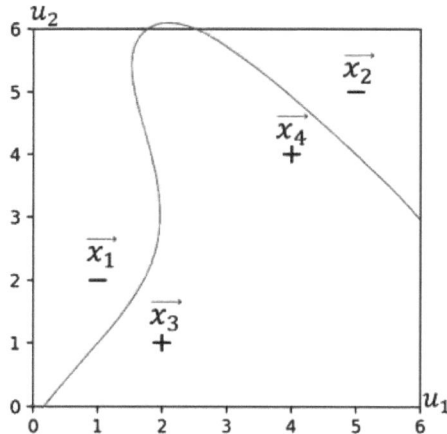

Fig. (7.13). Illustration of the determined hyperplane (curved line) by SVM with RBF kernel on two-dimensional space.

Now let us compare the results obtained above with that from the off-the-shelf SVM classifier using RBF kernel offered by scikit-learn library.

The complete code file can be downloaded from our shared folder in Google Drive:

https://drive.google.com/drive/folders/1FqJvo4ZPazNbEH_GlHFoodqvegnQmHc
n?usp=share_link

```python
import numpy as np
X = np.array([[1,2],
              [5,5],
              [2,1],
              [4,4]])

y = np.array([-1,-1,1,1])

print(np.concatenate((X, y.reshape(-1,1)), axis=1), "\n")

from sklearn.svm import SVC
svcModel = SVC(kernel='rbf', gamma=0.2, tol=1e-10)

svcModel.fit(X, y)

print("Desired Output: \n" + str(y))
print("Scikit-learn Predicted Output: \n" + str(svcModel.pre-
dict(X)))
#svcModel.score(X_test, y_test)
```

```
[[ 1  2 -1]
 [ 5  5 -1]
 [ 2  1  1]
 [ 4  4  1]]

Desired Output:
[-1 -1  1  1]
Scikit-learn Predicted Output:
[-1 -1  1  1]
```

```
svcModel.support_vectors_
```
```
array([[1., 2.],
       [5., 5.],
       [2., 1.],
       [4., 4.]])
```

```
# Dual coefficients of the support vector in the decision
function, multiplied by their targets
# beta_i = alpha_i * y_i
svcModel.dual_coef_
```
```
array([[-1., -1., 1., 1.]])
```

```
# b value
svcModel.intercept_
```
```
array([-0.03376782])
```

```python
import matplotlib.pyplot as plt

def create_meshgrid(x, y, h=.02):
    x_min, x_max = x.min() - 1, x.max() + 1
    y_min, y_max = y.min() - 1, y.max() + 1
    xx, yy = np.meshgrid(np.arange(x_min, x_max, h),
np.arange(y_min, y_max, h))
    return xx, yy

def draw_contours(ax, model, xx, yy, **params):
    Z = model.predict(np.c_[xx.ravel(), yy.ravel()]) # predict
for each grid point
    Z = Z.reshape(xx.shape)
    out = ax.contourf(xx, yy, Z, **params) # filled contours
    return out

fig, ax = plt.subplots(dpi=100)
X0,X1 = X[:, 0], X[:, 1]
xx, yy = create_meshgrid(X0, X1)
draw_contours(ax, svcModel, xx, yy, cmap=plt.cm.coolwarm, al-
pha=0.8)


X0_neg, X1_neg = np.append(X[0,0], X[1,0]), np.append(X[0,1],
X[1,1])
X0_pos, X1_pos = np.append(X[3,0], X[2,0]), np.append(X[3,1],
X[2,1])
ax.scatter(X0_neg, X1_neg, c='k', marker='_',
cmap=plt.cm.coolwarm, s=100)
ax.scatter(X0_pos, X1_pos, c='k', marker='+',
cmap=plt.cm.coolwarm, s=100)
ax.set_ylim([0,6])
ax.set_xlim([0,6])
ax.set_aspect('equal', adjustable='box')

ax.set_title('Decision surface when using RBF Kernel, \nfor
linearly inseparable data')
plt.savefig("Decision surface when using RBF Kernel for line-
arly inseparable data.png", dpi=200)
plt.show()
```

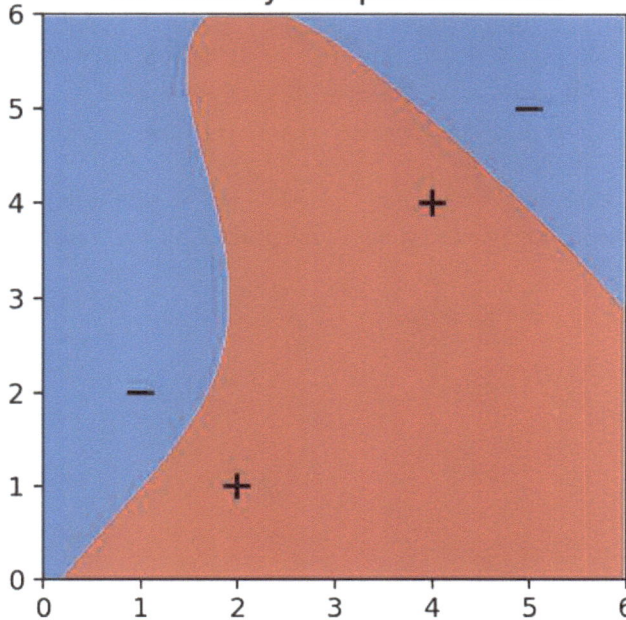

Decision surface when using RBF Kernel for linearly inseparable data

As can be seen from the results of scikit-learn SVM classifier using RBF kernel and compared with our manually calculated results, the same dual coefficients of support vector *(i.e., $\beta_1 = -1$, $\beta_2 = -1$, $\beta_3 = 1$, $\beta_4 = 1$)*, the same intercept value *(i.e., $b = -0.033$)*, and the same decision surface *(i.e., hyperplane)* are obtained.

CONCLUSION

In this chapter, we discussed the concept of SVM for both linearly separable and linearly non-separable cases. To make the material more accessible, we kept abstract mathematical theories to a minimum. Instead, we focused on concrete numerical examples with small datasets, walking through them step by step. We also provided sample codes and comparisons with the SVM model from the off-the-shelf library, scikit-learn. By the end of the chapter, readers should have a well-rounded understanding of how SVM machine learning works behind the scenes, how the mathematics relates to the implementation and performance of the algorithm, and be better equipped to apply it in their projects.

REFERENCES

[1]   Z. Wang, J. Li, G. P. Rangaiah, and Z. Wu, "Machine learning aided multi-objective optimization and multi-criteria decision making: Framework and two applications in chemical engineering," *Comput. Chem. Eng.*, vol. 165, no. 107945, p. 107945, 2022.

   http://dx.doi.org/10.1016/j.compchemeng.2022.107945

[2]   A. Geron, *Hands-on machine learning with scikit-learn, keras, and tensorflow*, 3rd ed. O'Reilly Media, 2022.

[3]   V. N. Vapnik, *Statistical learning theory*. Nashville, TN: John Wiley & Sons, 1998.

[4]   S. Raschka, *Python Machine Learning*. Birmingham, England: Packt Publishing, 2015.

## CHAPTER 8

K-means Clustering

Abstract: In this chapter, we explore the K-means clustering algorithm, emphasizing an accessible approach by minimizing abstract mathematical theories. We present a concrete numerical example with a small dataset to illustrate how clusters can be formed using the K-means clustering algorithm. Additionally, we provide sample codes and comparisons with the K-means model available in the scikit-learn library. Upon completing this chapter, readers will gain a comprehensive understanding of the mechanics behind K-means clustering, and its connection to the implementation and performance of the algorithm, and be well-prepared to apply it in practical use.

Keywords: K-Means Clustering, Distance Metrics, Numerical Example, Small Dataset, Scikit-Learn

8.1. INTRODUCTION TO CLUSTERING AND DISTANCE METRICS

In unsupervised learning, the algorithm is not provided with labeled training data. Instead, it is only given a set of input examples, and the primary objective of unsupervised learning is to uncover the inherent structure or patterns within the data, enabling the algorithm to make predictions, decisions, or recommendations based on these discovered patterns [1]. This contrasts with supervised learning, where the algorithm is given both input examples and corresponding labeled outputs and can learn by making predictions and comparing them to the true labels. The ability of unsupervised learning algorithms to discover hidden structures and relationships in the data without relying on labeled examples makes them particularly valuable in situations where obtaining labeled data is challenging, time-consuming, or expensive.

Unsupervised learning has a variety of applications, such as anomaly detection, clustering, and dimensionality reduction. For example, an unsupervised learning algorithm might be used to cluster customers based on their usage of electronic devices, with the goal of identifying potential users of blue light filter lenses. One cluster may consist of customers who spend a significant amount of time on screens and use multiple devices frequently, indicating that they may be potential users of blue light filter lenses. Another cluster may consist of customers who use electronic devices infrequently, indicating that they may not be interested in purchasing blue light filter lenses. The clustering information can provide valuable insights for marketing efforts and enable precise targeting of potential customers.

Zhiyuan Wang, Sayed Ameenuddin Irfan, Christopher Teoh & Priyanka Hriday Bhoyar

There are numerous unsupervised machine learning algorithms available, including K-means clustering, principal component analysis, and hierarchical clustering. In this chapter, we will delve into the details of K-means clustering. Before using the K-means clustering algorithm, it is important to note that distance metrics are crucial for accurately measuring the distance between data points in two to n-dimensional space and forming appropriate clusters. There are four popular distance metrics, namely, Euclidean distance, Manhattan distance, Cosine similarity, and Chebyshev distance.

8.1.1. Euclidean Distance

Euclidean distance is a commonly used distance metric that calculates the distance between two points by determining the shortest path between them. The formula for calculating Euclidean distance is the square root of the sum of the squared differences in the coordinates of the two points. This measure is useful for understanding the relationship between data points in a multi-dimensional space.

Euclidean distance between points A and B is defined as:

$$D_{AB} = \sqrt{(x_2 - x_1)^2 + (y_2 - y_1)^2 + \cdots + (z_2 - z_1)^2} \qquad (8.1)$$

Here, the coordinate of point A is $(x_1, y_1, \ldots, z_1)$ and point B is $(x_2, y_2, \ldots, z_2)$.

8.1.2. Manhattan Distance

Manhattan distance, also known as the taxicab distance, is a distance metric that calculates the distance between two points by adding up the absolute differences in their coordinates. It is called the taxicab distance because it represents the distance that a taxicab would have to travel to get from one location to another if it could only move horizontally or vertically.

Manhattan distance between points A and B is defined as:

$$D_{AB} = |x_2 - x_1| + |y_2 - y_1| + \cdots + |z_2 - z_1| \qquad (8.2)$$

Here, the coordinate of point A is $(x_1, y_1, \ldots, z_1)$ and point B is $(x_2, y_2, \ldots, z_2)$

8.1.3. Cosine Similarity

The cosine similarity is a distance metric that determines how similar two vectors are to one another by computing the cosine of the angle that separates them.

Cosine similarity between A and B is defined as:

$$\cos(\theta) = \frac{A \cdot B}{\|A\| \, \|B\|} \tag{8.3}$$

Here, θ is the angle between the vectors A and B.

$A \cdot B$ is the dot product of vectors A and B

$\|A\|$ and $\|B\|$ are L2 norm of the vectors A and B, respectively.

8.1.4. Chebyshev Distance

Chebyshev distance, also known as the chessboard distance, is another metric that measures the distance between two vectors in a vector space. It is calculated by determining the greatest difference between the two vectors along any coordinate dimension.

Chebyshev distance between points A and B is defined as:

$$D_{AB} = Max(|x_2 - x_1|, |y_2 - y_1|, \dots, |z_2 - z_1|) \tag{8.4}$$

Here, the coordinate of point A is $(x_1, y_1, \dots, z_1)$ and point B is $(x_2, y_2, \dots, z_2)$.

8.2. ALGORITHM OF K-MEANS CLUSTERING

K-means clustering was first developed by Stuart Lloyd at Bell Labs in 1957 for pulse-code modulation. The idea was not publicly published outside of the company until 1982. The K-means clustering algorithm is also known as the Lloyd-Forgy algorithm due to the development of a nearly identical method by Edward W. Forgy in 1965 [2]. It has since become a widely used algorithm in the field of unsupervised machine learning for clustering data into groups with similar characteristics.

Let us understand the working of the K-means algorithm and how it forms clusters. If we were given the centroids for an unlabeled dataset, it would be easy to label all the samples by assigning each of them to the cluster with the closest centroid. On the other hand, if we were provided with the labels for all the samples, we could easily find all the centroids by calculating the mean of the samples for each cluster. However, since neither the labels nor the centroids are given to us, it is unclear how to proceed. To get started, we can simply place the centroids randomly (*e.g.,* by selecting k samples at random and using their positions as the initial centroids). The next step is to label the samples, then update the centroids, label the samples again, update the centroids again, and so on, until the centroids stop shifting. The method will not continue to oscillate indefinitely as it is designed to converge after a certain number of steps [3].

In a nutshell, the K-means clustering algorithm can be divided into the following 6 steps [4]:

1. Randomly initialize k centroids for k clusters (*i.e.,* selecting k samples at random and using their positions as the initial centroids).
2. Compute the Euclidean distance of each sample to these k centroids.
3. Assign each sample in the dataset to the closest centroid.
4. Calculate the mean of the samples in each cluster.
5. Reassign the centroids to the mean of the samples in each cluster.
6. Repeat step 2 to 5 till there is convergence (*i.e.,* the k centroids no longer move or until a predetermined number of iterations is reached). The final clusters and centroids represent the output of the K-means algorithm.

A key challenge in applying the K-means clustering algorithm is selecting an appropriate value for the number of centroids, k. The elbow method can be used to determine the optimal value of k. It does this by fitting the model for a range of values for k and selecting the k that results in the lowest Within-Cluster Sum of Squares (WCSS). WCSS measures the sum of the squared distance between each sample in a cluster and the centroid of that cluster. A lower WCSS indicates a better fit, as it means that the samples are closer to their centroids. As shown in Fig. (**8.1**) for a sample plot, the elbow point corresponds to the value of k at which the WCSS begins to level off, indicating that adding additional clusters is not significantly improving the fit; and this point is then selected as the optimal value of k. For the numerical example in Section 8.3, we will use $k = 3$ to demonstrate the 6 steps of the K-means clustering algorithm. In Section 8.4, we will explain why $k = 3$ was chosen for this dataset.

8.3. NUMERICAL EXAMPLE OF K-MEANS CLUSTERING

As shown in Table **8.1**, a small dataset contains the marks of 6 students, S1 to S6, for two subjects, namely, Math and Science. Our task is to cluster these students based on their marks into different groups using the K-means clustering algorithm.

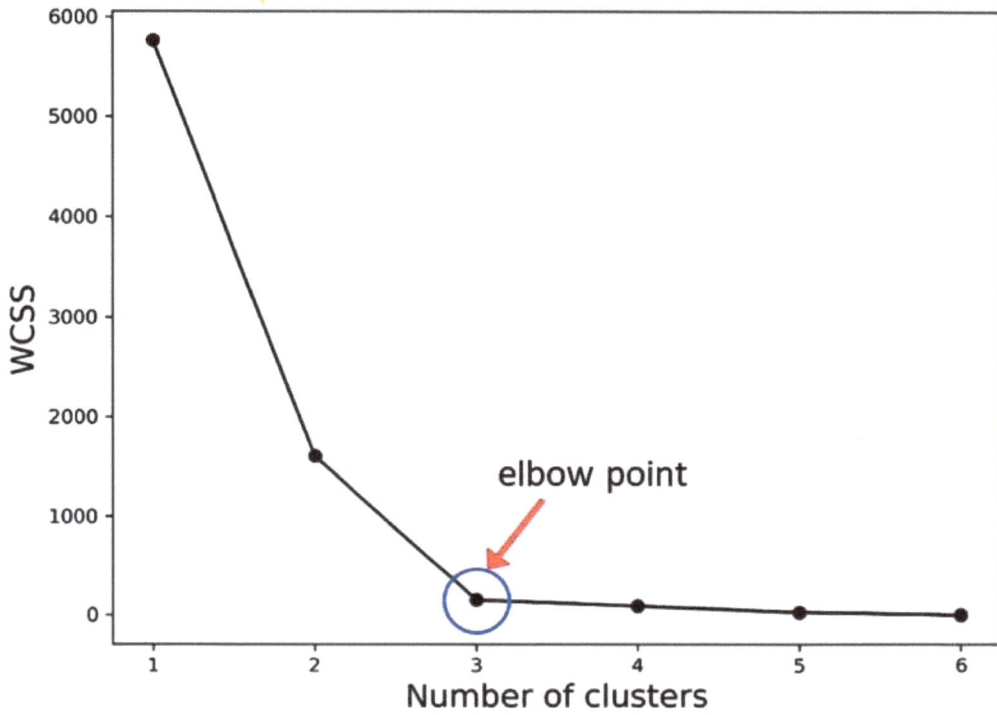

Fig. (8.1). Sample plot of Within-Cluster Sum of Squares (WCSS) *vs.* Number of clusters.

Table 8.1. **The small dataset for K-means Clustering.**

Student No.	Math Marks	Science Marks
S1	40	45
S2	60	75
S3	65	70
S4	90	90
S5	100	95
S6	45	35

In the first iteration, randomly take the marks of students S6, S2, and S3 as the centroids of the initial 3 clusters (*i.e., k* =3). Denote the 3 centroids as C1 (45, 35), C2 (60, 75), and C3 (65, 70), respectively. We will then calculate the Euclidean distance from each of the samples to the centroids.

Calculate the distance from C1 to all the 6 samples:

$$\text{Distance from C1 to S1} = \sqrt{(45-40)^2 + (35-45)^2} = 11.18$$

$$\text{Distance from C1 to S2} = \sqrt{(45-60)^2 + (35-75)^2} = 42.72$$

$$\text{Distance from C1 to S3} = \sqrt{(45-65)^2 + (35-70)^2} = 40.31$$

$$\text{Distance from C1 to S4} = \sqrt{(45-90)^2 + (35-90)^2} = 71.06$$

$$\text{Distance from C1 to S5} = \sqrt{(45-100)^2 + (35-95)^2} = 81.39$$

$$\text{Distance from C1 to S6} = \sqrt{(45-45)^2 + (35-35)^2} = 0$$

Calculate the distance from C2 to all the 6 samples:

$$\text{Distance from C2 to S1} = \sqrt{(60-40)^2 + (75-45)^2} = 36.06$$

$$\text{Distance from C2 to S2} = \sqrt{(60-60)^2 + (75-75)^2} = 0$$

$$\text{Distance from C2 to S3} = \sqrt{(60-65)^2 + (75-70)^2} = 7.07$$

$$\text{Distance from C2 to S4} = \sqrt{(60-90)^2 + (75-90)^2} = 33.54$$

$$\text{Distance from C2 to S5} = \sqrt{(60-100)^2 + (75-95)^2} = 44.72$$

$$\text{Distance from C2 to S6} = \sqrt{(60-45)^2 + (75-35)^2} = 42.72$$

Calculate the distance from C3 to all the 6 samples:

$$\text{Distance from C3 to S1} = \sqrt{(65-40)^2 + (70-45)^2} = 35.36$$

$$\text{Distance from C3 to S2} = \sqrt{(65-60)^2 + (70-75)^2} = 7.07$$

$$\text{Distance from C3 to S3} = \sqrt{(65 - 65)^2 + (70 - 70)^2} = 0$$

$$\text{Distance from C3 to S4} = \sqrt{(65 - 90)^2 + (70 - 90)^2} = 32.02$$

$$\text{Distance from C3 to S5} = \sqrt{(65 - 100)^2 + (70 - 95)^2} = 43.01$$

$$\text{Distance from C3 to S6} = \sqrt{(65 - 45)^2 + (70 - 35)^2} = 40.31$$

All the calculated Euclidean distances in the first iteration of the K-means algorithm are presented in Table **8.2**.

Table 8.2. The calculated Euclidean distances from each sample to the 3 centroids in the first iteration of K-means clustering.

-	C1	C2	C3
S1	11.18	36.06	35.36
S2	42.72	0	7.07
S3	40.31	7.07	0
S4	71.06	33.54	32.02
S5	81.39	44.72	43.01
S6	0	42.72	40.31

Using the data in Table **8.2**, we can determine which sample is assigned to which cluster in the first iteration of the K-means algorithm based on its distance to the 3 centroids. As shown in Table **8.3**, the samples are assigned to the closest centroids. For instance, S1 is closer to C1 than to C2 and C3, so it is assigned to C1; S2 is closer to C2 than to C1 and C3, so it is assigned to C2; S3 is closer to C3 than to C1 and C2, so it is assigned to C3.

The visual representation for the clustering as of now is as follows:

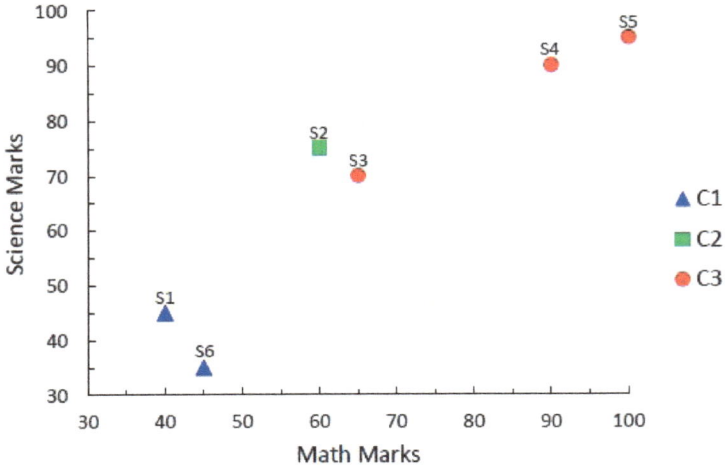

After clustering the samples, we need to recalculate the new centroid for each cluster by taking the mean of samples assigned to that cluster.

Table 8.3. The assigned centroid for each sample in the first iteration of K-means clustering.

-	C1	C2	C3	Assigned Centroid
S1	11.18	36.06	35.36	C1
S2	42.72	0	7.07	C2
S3	40.31	7.07	0	C3
S4	71.06	33.54	32.02	C3
S5	81.39	44.72	43.01	C3
S6	0	42.72	40.31	C1

New centroid C1 is the mean of S1 and S6:

$$C1= \left(\frac{40+45}{2},\ \frac{45+35}{2}\right) = (42.5, 40)$$

New centroid C2 is the mean of S2:

$$C2 = \left(\frac{60}{1}, \frac{75}{1}\right) = (60, 75)$$

New centroid C3 is the mean of S3, S4, and S5:

$$C3 = \left(\frac{65+90+100}{3}, \frac{70+90+95}{3}\right) = (85, 85)$$

Now, we can proceed with the second iteration of the K-means clustering algorithm with the newly updated C1, C2, and C3.

Calculate the distance from C1 to all the 6 samples:

$$\text{Distance from C1 to S1} = \sqrt{(42.5 - 40)^2 + (40 - 45)^2} = 5.59$$

$$\text{Distance from C1 to S2} = \sqrt{(42.5 - 60)^2 + (40 - 75)^2} = 39.13$$

$$\text{Distance from C1 to S3} = \sqrt{(42.5 - 65)^2 + (40 - 70)^2} = 37.5$$

$$\text{Distance from C1 to S4} = \sqrt{(42.5 - 90)^2 + (40 - 90)^2} = 68.97$$

$$\text{Distance from C1 to S5} = \sqrt{(42.5 - 100)^2 + (40 - 95)^2} = 79.57$$

$$\text{Distance from C1 to S6} = \sqrt{(42.5 - 45)^2 + (40 - 35)^2} = 5.59$$

Calculate the distance from C2 to all the 6 samples:

$$\text{Distance from C2 to S1} = \sqrt{(60 - 40)^2 + (75 - 45)^2} = 36.06$$

$$\text{Distance from C2 to S2} = \sqrt{(60 - 60)^2 + (75 - 75)^2} = 0$$

$$\text{Distance from C2 to S3} = \sqrt{(60 - 65)^2 + (75 - 70)^2} = 7.07$$

$$\text{Distance from C2 to S4} = \sqrt{(60 - 90)^2 + (75 - 90)^2} = 33.54$$

$$\text{Distance from C2 to S5} = \sqrt{(60 - 100)^2 + (75 - 95)^2} = 44.72$$

$$\text{Distance from C2 to S6} = \sqrt{(60 - 45)^2 + (75 - 35)^2} = 42.72$$

Calculate the distance from C3 to all the 6 samples:

$$\text{Distance from C3 to S1} = \sqrt{(85-40)^2 + (85-45)^2} = 60.21$$

$$\text{Distance from C3 to S2} = \sqrt{(85-60)^2 + (85-75)^2} = 26.93$$

$$\text{Distance from C3 to S3} = \sqrt{(85-65)^2 + (85-70)^2} = 25.0$$

$$\text{Distance from C3 to S4} = \sqrt{(85-90)^2 + (85-90)^2} = 7.07$$

$$\text{Distance from C3 to S5} = \sqrt{(85-100)^2 + (85-95)^2} = 18.03$$

$$\text{Distance from C3 to S6} = \sqrt{(85-45)^2 + (85-35)^2} = 64.03$$

All the calculated Euclidean distances in the second iteration of the K-means algorithm are presented in Table **8.4**.

Table 8.4. The calculated Euclidean distances from each sample to the 3 centroids in the second iteration of K-means clustering.

-	C1	C2	C3
S1	5.59	36.06	60.21
S2	39.13	0	26.93
S3	37.5	7.07	25
S4	68.97	33.54	7.07
S5	79.57	44.72	18.03
S6	5.59	42.72	64.03

Using the data in Table **8.4**, we can update which sample is assigned to which cluster in the second iteration of the K-means algorithm based on its distance to the 3 centroids. For instance, as shown in Table **8.5**, S3 is closest to C2, and it is now assigned to C2 (note that S3 was assigned to C3 in the first iteration).

Table 8.5. The assigned centroid for each sample in the second iteration of K-means clustering.

-	C1	C2	C3	Assigned Centroid
S1	5.59	36.06	60.21	C1
S2	39.13	0	26.93	C2
S3	37.5	7.07	25	C2
S4	68.97	33.54	7.07	C3
S5	79.57	44.72	18.03	C3
S6	5.59	42.72	64.03	C1

The visual representation for the clustering as of now is as follows:

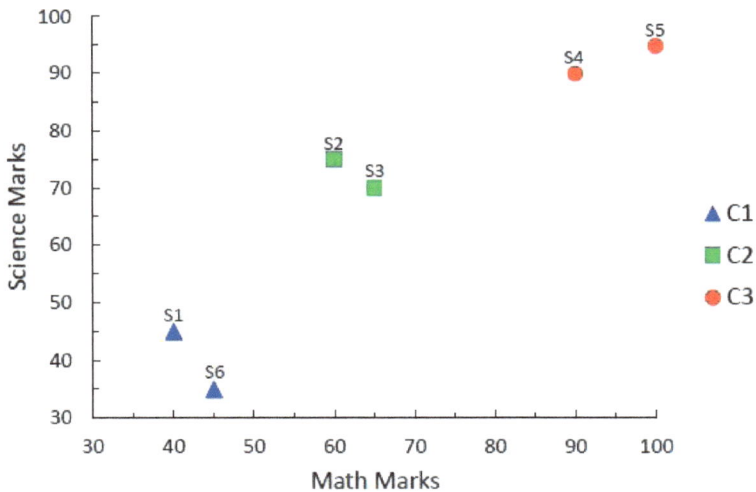

After clustering the samples, we need to recalculate the new centroid for each cluster by taking the mean of samples assigned to that cluster.

New centroid C1 is the mean of S1 and S6:

$$C1 = \left(\frac{40+45}{2}, \frac{45+35}{2}\right) = (42.5, 40)$$

New centroid C2 is the mean of S2 and S3:

$$C2 = \left(\frac{60+65}{2}, \frac{75+70}{2}\right) = (62.5, 72.5)$$

New centroid C3 is the mean of S4 and S5:

$$C3 = \left(\frac{90+100}{2}, \frac{90+95}{2}\right) = (95, 92.5)$$

Now, we can proceed with the third iteration of the K-means clustering algorithm with the newly updated C1, C2, and C3.

Calculate the distance from C1 to all the 6 samples:

$$\text{Distance from C1 to S1} = \sqrt{(42.5 - 40)^2 + (40 - 45)^2} = 5.59$$

$$\text{Distance from C1 to S2} = \sqrt{(42.5 - 60)^2 + (40 - 75)^2} = 39.13$$

$$\text{Distance from C1 to S3} = \sqrt{(42.5 - 65)^2 + (40 - 70)^2} = 37.5$$

$$\text{Distance from C1 to S4} = \sqrt{(42.5 - 90)^2 + (40 - 90)^2} = 68.97$$

$$\text{Distance from C1 to S5} = \sqrt{(42.5 - 100)^2 + (40 - 95)^2} = 79.57$$

$$\text{Distance from C1 to S6} = \sqrt{(42.5 - 45)^2 + (40 - 35)^2} = 5.59$$

Calculate the distance from C2 to all the 6 samples:

$$\text{Distance from C2 to S1} = \sqrt{(62.5 - 40)^2 + (72.5 - 45)^2} = 35.53$$

$$\text{Distance from C2 to S2} = \sqrt{(62.5 - 60)^2 + (72.5 - 75)^2} = 3.54$$

$$\text{Distance from C2 to S3} = \sqrt{(62.5 - 65)^2 + (72.5 - 70)^2} = 3.54$$

$$\text{Distance from C2 to S4} = \sqrt{(62.5 - 90)^2 + (72.5 - 90)^2} = 32.6$$

$$\text{Distance from C2 to S5} = \sqrt{(62.5 - 100)^2 + (72.5 - 95)^2} = 43.73$$

$$\text{Distance from C2 to S6} = \sqrt{(62.5 - 45)^2 + (72.5 - 35)^2} = 41.38$$

Calculate the distance from C3 to all the 6 samples:

$$\text{Distance from C3 to S1} = \sqrt{(95 - 40)^2 + (92.5 - 45)^2} = 72.67$$

$$\text{Distance from C3 to S2} = \sqrt{(95 - 60)^2 + (92.5 - 75)^2} = 39.13$$

$$\text{Distance from C3 to S3} = \sqrt{(95 - 65)^2 + (92.5 - 70)^2} = 37.5$$

$$\text{Distance from C3 to S4} = \sqrt{(95 - 90)^2 + (92.5 - 90)^2} = 5.59$$

$$\text{Distance from C3 to S5} = \sqrt{(95 - 100)^2 + (92.5 - 95)^2} = 5.59$$

$$\text{Distance from C3 to S6} = \sqrt{(95 - 45)^2 + (92.5 - 35)^2} = 76.2$$

All the calculated Euclidean distances in the third iteration of the K-means algorithm are presented in Table **8.6**.

Table 8.6. The calculated Euclidean distances from each sample to the 3 centroids in the third iteration of K-means clustering.

-	C1	C2	C3
S1	5.59	35.53	72.67
S2	39.13	3.54	39.13
S3	37.5	3.54	37.5
S4	68.97	32.6	5.59
S5	79.57	43.73	5.59
S6	5.59	41.38	76.2

Using the data in Table **8.6**, we can update which sample is assigned to which cluster in the third iteration of the K-means algorithm based on its distance to the 3 centroids.

Table 8.7. The assigned centroid for each sample in the third iteration of K-means clustering.

-	C1	C2	C3	Assigned Centroid
S1	5.59	35.53	72.67	C1
S2	39.13	3.54	39.13	C2
S3	37.5	3.54	37.5	C2
S4	68.97	32.6	5.59	C3
S5	79.57	43.73	5.59	C3
S6	5.59	41.38	76.2	C1

The visual representation for the clustering as of now is as follows:

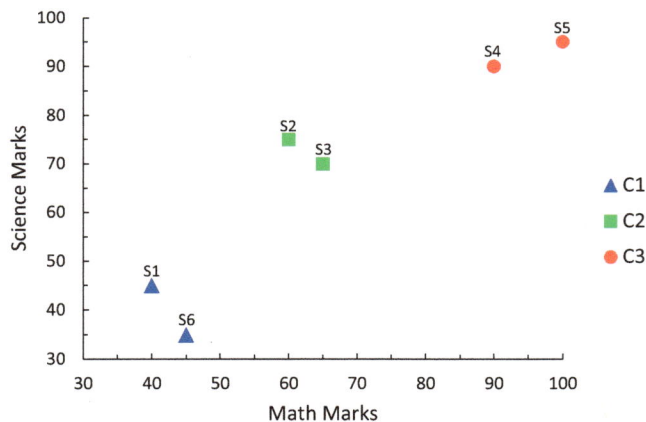

From Table **8.7** and the visual representation above, we can see that the cluster assignments for all samples remain unchanged in the third iteration compared to the second iteration. As a result, the K-means clustering algorithm converges and stops here. The final centroids are C1 (42.5, 40), C2 (62.5, 72.5), and C3 (95, 92.5).

8.4. SAMPLE CODES AND COMPARISON

Now, let us compare the results obtained above with that from the off-the-shelf K-means model offered by the scikit-learn library.

The complete code file can be downloaded from our shared folder in Google Drive:

https://drive.google.com/drive/folders/1FqJvo4ZPazNbEH_GlHFoodqvegnQmHcn?usp=share_link

```python
import os

# optional: to avoid memory leak on
# Windows with MKL when using KMeans
os.environ["OMP_NUM_THREADS"] = '1'

from sklearn.cluster import KMeans
import pandas as pd
import matplotlib
import matplotlib.pyplot as plt
import numpy as np
import pandas as pd
```

```python
data = np.array([[40,45],
                 [60,75],
                 [65,70],
                 [90,90],
                 [100,95],
                 [45,35]])

col_names = ["Math", "Science"]
data = pd.DataFrame(data, columns=col_names)
print(data, "\n")
```

```
   Math  Science
0    40       45
1    60       75
2    65       70
3    90       90
4   100       95
5    45       35
```

```python
kmeans = KMeans(n_clusters=3, random_state=0)
kmeans.fit(data)

kmeans.cluster_centers_
```

```
array([[95. , 92.5],
       [62.5, 72.5],
       [42.5, 40. ]])
```

```python
plt.figure(figsize=(8, 6))
labels = kmeans.labels_
colors = ['red','green','blue']
plt.scatter(data['Math'], data['Science'], c=labels,
            cmap=matplotlib.colors.ListedColormap(colors))
plt.xlabel('Math Marks', fontsize=16)
plt.ylabel('Science Marks', fontsize=16)
#plt.savefig("kmeans_small_dataset.jpg")
plt.show()
```

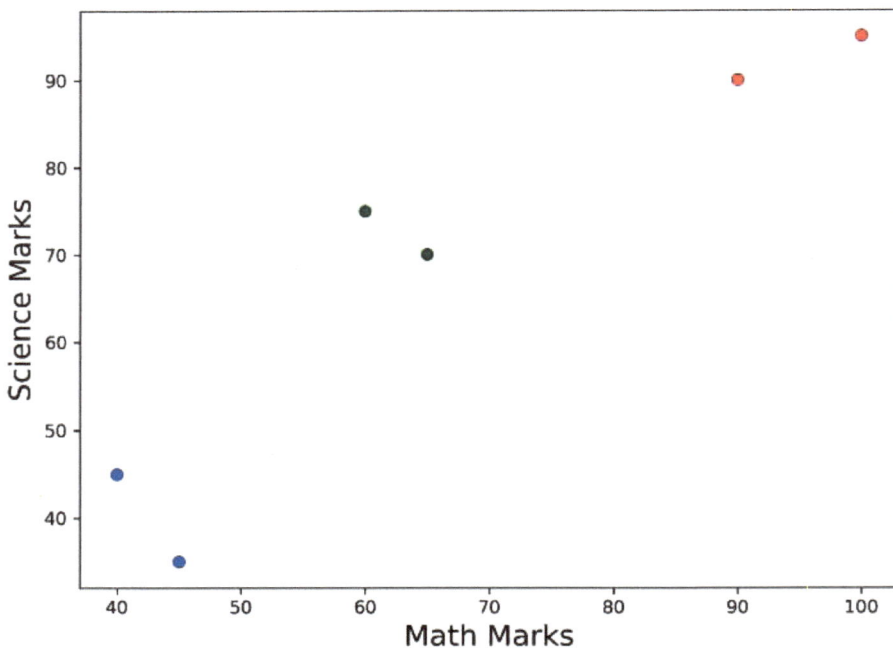

```
# within-cluster sum of squares (WCSS)
# to help decide optimal no. of clusters
wcss=[]
for i in range(1,7):
    kmeans = KMeans(n_clusters=i, random_state=0)
    kmeans.fit(data)
    wcss.append(kmeans.inertia_)

plt.figure(figsize=(8, 6))
plt.plot(range(1,7), wcss, marker='o', c='black')
plt.xlabel('Number of clusters', fontsize=16)
plt.ylabel('WCSS', fontsize=16)
#plt.savefig("elbow_kmeans.jpg")
plt.show()
```

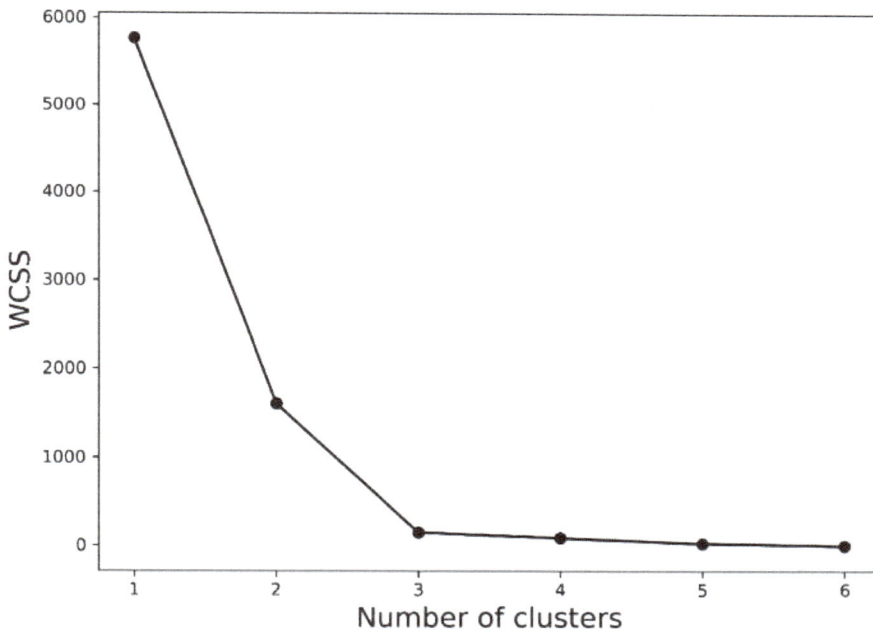

As can be seen from the results of the scikit-learn K-means model and compared with our manually calculated results, the same clusters and final centroids are obtained, *i.e.,* (42.5, 40), (62.5, 72.5), and (95, 92.5). Additionally, the within-cluster sum of squares (WCSS) is used to determine the optimal number of clusters.

Here, we chose 3 clusters because WCSS does not significantly decrease beyond this point.

CONCLUSION

In this chapter, we discussed the concept of the K-means clustering algorithm. To make the material more accessible, we kept abstract mathematical theories to a minimum. Instead, we focused on a concrete numerical example with a small dataset to show how the clusters can be formed using the K-means clustering algorithm. We also provided sample codes and comparisons with the K-means model from the off-the-shelf library, scikit-learn. By the end of the chapter, readers should have a well-rounded understanding of how K-means clustering works behind the scenes, how the mathematics relates to the implementation and performance of the algorithm, and be better equipped to apply it in their projects.

REFERENCES

[1]   K.P. Murphy, *Machine Learning: A Probabilistic Perspective..* MIT Press: London, England, 2012.
[2]   S. Lloyd, "Least squares quantization in PCM", *IEEE Trans. Inf. Theory,* vol. 28, no. 2, pp. 129-137, 1982.
      http://dx.doi.org/10.1109/TIT.1982.1056489
[3]   A. Geron, *Hands-on machine learning with scikit-learn, keras, and tensorflow.,* 3rd ed O'Reilly Media, 2022.
[4]   E. Alpaydin, *Introduction to Machine Learning.,* 4th ed MIT Press: London, England, 2020.

SUBJECT INDEX

A

Algorithm 1, 3, 4, 5, 6, 96, 97, 98, 99, 105, 115, 116, 117, 159, 160, 192, 194
  complex 6
  decision tree building 105
  nearest neighbor 1
Applications 1, 2, 3, 4, 5, 6, 71, 116, 160, 194
  real-world 6, 71
Artificial 1
  intelligence 1
  neural network 1

C

Complex decision-making processes 97
Computer vision 1, 116
Cosine similarity 195
Credit risk assessment 71
Cross-entropy loss function 74, 136, 137
Customer churn prediction 71

D

Dataset 4, 23, 46, 64, 92, 99, 100, 107, 160, 161, 196, 197
  small categorical 100
  unlabeled 196
Decision tree(s) 97, 99, 100, 101, 109, 115, 117, 118, 121, 122, 125, 126, 134, 149, 158
  algorithms 97, 99
  learning 99, 100
  machine learning 97
De facto feature 1, 2
Differentiable loss function 118, 119, 136, 139
Distance 160, 195, 196, 197, 199, 200, 202, 203, 205, 206, 207
  chessboard 196
  margin 160

squared 197

E

Electric vehicle industry 3
Electronic devices 194
Encoded data 111
Encoding 101
Ensemble Learning 116
Entropy 87, 88, 90, 99, 100, 101, 102, 103, 104, 107, 108, 109, 114, 115
  def 107
  value, calculated 107

F

Feature(s) 8, 11, 12, 30, 34, 35, 41, 50, 53, 74, 77, 78, 103, 104, 105, 107, 109, 118
  less important 41
  num 12, 35, 53, 78
  outlook 103, 104, 105
  returned 109
  selection 41
  size 12, 35, 53, 78
  values 8, 11, 30, 34, 50, 53, 74, 77, 107, 118

G

Google drive 19, 43, 61, 87, 106, 132, 155, 170, 181, 190, 208
Gradient boosting 116, 118, 119, 125, 131, 132, 138, 149
  algorithm 132, 138
  model 116, 118, 125, 131, 149
  regression model 119, 131
Gradient descent 9, 20, 31, 33, 43, 52, 62, 75, 89
  of updating weights 33
  optimization algorithm 9, 20, 31, 43, 52, 62, 75, 89
Graphics processing units (GPU) 1

www.ingramcontent.com/pod-product-compliance
Lightning Source LLC
Chambersburg PA
CBHW050839220326
41598CB00006B/399